Swedish C

Swedish Chicago

THE SHAPING OF AN IMMIGRANT COMMUNITY, 1880–1920

Anita Olson Gustafson

NIU Press / DeKalb, IL

© 2018 by Northern Illinois University Press
Northern Illinois University Press, DeKalb, Illinois 60115
All rights reserved
Printed in the United States of America

27 26 25 24 23 22 21 20 19 18   1 2 3 4 5

978-0-87580-791-1 (paper)
978-1-60909-246-7 (e-book)

Book and cover design by Yuni Dorr

Library of Congress Cataloging-in-Publication Data
is available online at http://catalog.loc.gov

CONTENTS

GUSTAFSON LIST OF ILLUSTRATIONS

INTRODUCTION

This book examines the history of the Swedish community in Chicago between the years 1880 and 1920, a time when immigration from Sweden soared and the city itself grew remarkably. During these years, the Swedish population in the city moved from three centrally located ethnic enclaves to neighborhoods widely scattered throughout the city, and this study traces that outward progression and the impact it had upon Swedish ethnic identity. My central argument is that, rather than ethnicity disappearing as Swedes moved to new neighborhoods, the early enclave-based culture successfully survived and adapted to a progressively dispersed pattern of Swedish settlement in Chicago and its suburbs. Swedish community life in the new neighborhoods flourished as immigrants built a variety of ethnic churches, created meaningful and diverse social affiliations, and in the process, forged a complex Swedish American identity that combined their Swedish heritage with their new urban realities.

For the tens of thousands of emigrants who left Sweden for Chicago, the move to Chicago and subsequent moves within the city were not random acts. Many of these individuals viewed their decision to leave Sweden with little regret as they hoped for a more prosperous future; others longed for the life they had left behind in Sweden and never quite adjusted to the urban bustle surrounding them.[1] Overall, these immigrants were dreamers; they had high expectations of improving their lives and economic circumstances. They made decisions about their future in an increasingly global economy and labor market in an era when, due to improvements in communication and transportation, Chicago was a well-known destination for Swedish emigration. The Sweden they left behind was becoming overpopulated while at the same time remaining economically underdeveloped. So they followed the trail of men and women who had migrated before them and who often provided connections that helped them find work and housing. Most of them left behind a rural past for the economic and social opportunities provided by a burgeoning American city. Hence, they faced a dual adjustment process—from Sweden to America and from a rural past to an urban future.

Without a doubt, Chicago shaped these Swedes' lives in profound ways, determining the types of jobs they would find, the variety of people they would encounter, and the locations of neighborhoods where they would live. But these immigrants were also a creative group of people. They brought with them a strong sense of their ethnicity that they continued to express in Chicago, settling in Swedish neighborhoods and continuing to correspond with those whom they left behind in Sweden. They also built Swedish institutions and they spoke the Swedish language in their homes, churches, and clubs. Swedes arriving in Chicago after 1880 benefited from the strong community already created by their predecessors, but they did not hesitate to reshape that community and build new ethnic institutions as necessary to make their own urban experience more meaningful and relevant. Ultimately, their decisions—whether to emigrate, to make Chicago their permanent home, or to move to a new home in the city—were made in the context of the evolving Swedish community in Chicago, their strong family connections, and the changing nature of the urban landscape and economic environment in Chicago. They did not leave Chicago untouched, but rather, they shaped the expanding Swedish community in the city—in effect, making significant portions of Chicago Swedish.

In other words, Swedish ethnicity in America was continuously developing. An important purpose of this study is to gain an understanding of what it meant to be an ethnic American at the turn of the twentieth century, and how notions of ethnicity changed over time, even within particular ethnic communities. Most historians now agree that immigrants did not lose their past upon arrival in America, nor were they able to completely retain their traditions unchanged. Adaptation to America was not linear, but involved a process of change that combined a person's past experiences with his or her present conditions. For example, Josef J. Barton examines changes in traditional behavior among Slovaks, Italians, and Rumanians in Cleveland and argues for a model of assimilation "that accounts for persistence of the relation between ethnicity and social status while it allows for the strength of assimilative forces."[2] The key to this process is to distinguish between acculturation, a change in habits and beliefs, and structural assimilation, the entrance into close personal relationships with members of the charter society. Kathleen Neils Conzen, in her study of the German community in Milwaukee, points out that the complex, highly stratified German ethnic community retarded structural assimilation in American society but it did not preclude it.[3] Writing about Italian immigrants in San Francisco, Dino Cinel argues that continuity and change should not be viewed as mutually exclusive categories: "The drive for material success put a premium on change; the attachment to tradition made Italians resist it."[4] The Italian attitudes toward assimilation were often ambivalent and contradictory.

Hence, models of assimilation that stress America as a melting pot on one hand, or a "salad bowl" of cultural pluralism on the other, need to be modified. Jon Gjerde, studying rural Norwegians in Wisconsin, suggests understanding adaptation as a dialectic process. Adaptations were often the outcome of familiar types of behavior functioning under new conditions rather than entirely new behavioral concepts.[5] John Bodnar furthers this point by portraying the immigrant as an intelligent individual who was able to selectively choose the most meaningful aspects of the new culture while retaining remnants of the old, creating a synthesis of the two.[6] Peter Kivisto refers to this phenomenon as "variable ethnicity" in which immigrants "play an important role in the construction, destruction, and reconstruction of ethnic attachments and loyalties."[7] Werner Sollors calls it the "invention of ethnicity," in which new immigrant groups "constantly change and redefine themselves."[8] Kathleen Neils Conzen and others refine this point further by arguing that ethnicity is "a process of construction or invention which incorporates, adapts, and amplifies preexisting communal solidarities, cultural attributes, and historical memories. That is, it is grounded in real life context and social experience."[9]

This study focuses on how the Swedish community created new ways of ethnic interaction that synthesized their past with their present—in the process creating a middle ground that was both Swedish and American.[10] It builds on the most comprehensive work about the Swedish community in Chicago, Ulf Beijbom's 1971 study *Swedes in Chicago: A Demographic and Social Study of the 1846–1880 Immigration*, but offers a very different interpretive framework. Beijbom focuses on the early Swedish community, documenting the squalid conditions of the initial Swedish settlements and the subsequent development of three tightly knit enclaves. His demographic approach utilizes census material through 1880 to track Swedes in Chicago, and after that date, he predicts a linear pattern of assimilation in which suburbanization led directly to Americanization. The logical conclusion of this perspective is that the qualitative aspect of Swedish community life related directly to the tight settlement patterns of Swedes in the city and eroded after they left those enclaves. My book challenges that assumption: I argue that Swedish ethnicity remained strong in Chicago after 1880, even if it was transformed into more scattered and complex residential patterns.[11]

My research has benefited from and overlapped with the work of other historians who deal more directly with the qualitative components of the Swedish community. In 1992 Philip J. Anderson and Dag Blanck compiled and edited *Swedish-American Life in Chicago: Cultural and Urban Aspects of an Immigrant People, 1850–1930*. These articles cover a range of issues contributing to community life, such as religion, socialism, trade unionism, Swedish literary and educational trends, and the role of women. The authors follow up on many of the issues raised by Beijbom and fill in the gaps in the post-1880 period.[12] Another important study is Per Nordahl's 1994 book *Weaving the Ethnic Fabric: Social Networks Among Swedish-American Radicals in Chicago 1890–1940*. Nordahl focuses on the labor movement, and examines how "the community that met the Swedes when they came to Chicago was characterized by competition and fragmentation."[13] All of these historians paint a picture of an ethnic community that continued to thrive well into the twentieth century as older immigrants matured and others continued to arrive directly from Sweden, creating a complex interaction of people, ideas, and institutions in Swedish Chicago.

In challenging Beijbom's contention that Swedish ethnic identity disappeared as settlement became more dispersed, I show that urban settings can be rich in complex communal relationships. Scholars once portrayed a strict dichotomy between rural and urban societies, the former being rich in expressions of community and the latter fostering a social order that alienates and isolates its people.[14] According to this argument, relationships that occurred in a community were based on common place and common experience. By extension, immigration from rural areas in Europe to urban America was also considered, in the words of Oscar Handlin, an uprooting experience. Community expressions were lost as immigrants in America faced an alienating and uncertain future.[15] This study argues against declining notions of community in the modernizing urban context of Chicago.

My interpretation builds on the work of scholars who have discounted a conceptualization of community based on rural sentimentalities, arguing that it romanticized the past and infused rural society with communal meanings that it did not in reality possess.[16] Thomas Bender further points out that the theory of territorially based community is not relevant in modern society. To define community in such static and sharply demarcated terms denies the process of historical development and confuses a particular manifestation of community with its essential character. Bender suggests that after about 1870, American communities became less territorially based and relied more upon extended social networks "marked by mutuality and emotional bonds."[17] This was exactly the type of community Swedes in Chicago created after 1880—one based upon diverse affiliations that connected them to others with similar values and cultural understandings. And their presence in the city helped further reshape that community.

One important means of measuring and examining the creation of an immigrant community is to look at the network of Swedish voluntary associations created in Chicago between 1880 and 1920. These networks are a major emphasis of this book. Although not all Swedes in Chicago joined an ethnic organization, those who did so were people who wanted to shape their social and cultural environment; these "joiners" were part of a self-articulated Swedish community. According to Dag Blanck, these people made up the heart of the Swedish community. They understood that being part of the Swedish community meant more than originating from the same country, it meant actively involving themselves in institutions of their choosing.[18] Raymond Breton further argues that an ethnic community should be understood as a "cultural-symbolic entity," a system of "ideas, images, and symbols" in which individuals "construct a meaningful experience within its boundaries."[19] Community is, therefore, a negotiated order and Swedish organizational "joiners" can be viewed as community creators.

Swedish immigrants continued to create and re-create their community life in Chicago, combining their previous experiences in Sweden with their new life in an American city. This process of community renewal was not a simple one, as immigrant arrivals continued to bring new ideas and experiences with them from Sweden. In other words, not only was the Swedish community in Chicago evolving, so too was the Sweden from which the immigrants came. Swedish economic, social, religious, and cultural trends changed significantly between 1880 and 1920. Hence, as the Swedish community in Chicago grew in size, visibility, and complexity after 1880, newcomers infused it with energy and influences very different from those of earlier immigrants. Dag Blanck remarks that this Swedish American identity "exhibit[s] a duality . . ." that draws on "cultural elements from both Sweden and the United States while at the same time maintaining a distance from both."[20]

As Swedes in Chicago created their internally complex community, they also operated within an increasingly racially and ethnically diverse city. German and Irish settlers significantly outnumbered Swedes from the 1880s through the 1910s. By the 1920 census, the surge in immigration from Eastern Europe moved Polish and Italian settlers in Chicago numerically ahead of the Swedes. When World War One broke out and many white male workers were pulled into the war, black migration from the South grew to fill the void. As more African Americans arrived in Chicago as part of the Great Migration, racial tensions in the city exploded into open racial hostility when white workers returning from the war attempted to regain their jobs in a tightening economy.[21] Chicago was a contested space where racial and ethnic dynamics provided the context for the formation of a Swedish American identity.

By the early twentieth century, Swedish immigrants in America identified with notions of whiteness that allowed them entry into mainstream American culture. As they forged a Swedish American identity in the evolving and expansive cityscape of Chicago, Swedes were careful to promote their proud Nordic heritage in order to distinguish themselves from groups many Americans perceived as less desirable. As David R. Roediger points out, the contested nature of whiteness was not new. He argues that in the nineteenth century, "working class formation and the systematic development of a sense of whiteness went hand in hand for the white working class."[22] He points out that Irish immigrants embraced notions of white supremacy as they sought to win acceptance as "white" among a native population that often saw them as "other," mitigating the development of a wider class consciousness. Matthew Frye Jacobson further suggests that a line between who was white and who was not was contested well into the twentieth century. Native-born white Americans often saw immigrants from various parts of Europe as belonging to separate and distinct races and questioned their ability to assimilate into American social and political culture. In such a context it was crucial for a group to embrace its identity as white. As Jacobson argues, "*Becoming* Caucasian . . . had been crucial to the politico-cultural saga of European migration and settlement, and the process by which this came about touches the histories of every other racially coded group on the American scene."[23]

The existence of nonwhite groups in America helped further define many Europeans as "white" by the early twentieth century, and this was certainly the case for the Swedes. As Dag Blanck points out, Swedish immigrants were well aware of these dynamics and "sought to position themselves favorably in the U.S. ethno-racial hierarchy."[24] For example, Blanck notes that Swedes living in antebellum Texas embraced slavery. Swedish immigrants in the Midwest identified with the Republican Party in the mid-to-late nineteenth and early twentieth centuries. Swedish settlers in Worcester, Massachusetts emphasized their Protestantism and internalized anti-Irish stereotypes. For a group of people leaving behind the rigid social structures of Sweden, it was more important than ever to assure that the Swedish working class in America would be afforded privileges of inclusion that went along with conceptions of race. By 1900, through the efforts of Swedish American leaders and reinforced by settlement patterns where they most frequently lived beside other northern European immigrant groups, Swedish immigrants had firmly established themselves as white Americans.

This book creates a link between Swedish residential patterns, their dispersal throughout the city of Chicago, and the community affiliations created by the immigrants themselves. Chapter 1 provides background on the Swedish migration to Chicago. It also charts the movement of Chicago's Swedes away from the centralized enclaves of the pre-1880 era to a number of regions on the outskirts of the city. Chapter 2, using immigrant letters and journals, examines the immigrants' perceptions of the transitions they experienced. Chapter 3 focuses on the Swedish churches that provided a framework for the elaboration of Swedish religious dialogue and expression in a setting very different from Sweden. As immigrants moved from Sweden to Chicago, and as they moved within Chicago, their religious affiliations provided important sources of stability in their lives even while those affiliations reflected at times divisive theological disputes. In America, however, religious nonconformity and voluntarism made the churches very different kinds of associations than they had been in Sweden.

Secular associations, particularly the large fraternal orders, provided another kind of membership and, like the churches, created webs of affiliation, primarily for Swedish men in Chicago. In doing so, they added to the organizational diversity in Swedish Chicago and reflected deep divisions between religious and secular Swedes. Chapter 4 discusses secular organizations, showing how their internal operations created mechanisms for mutual support among their members through social relationships and economic safeguards. Chapter 5 looks at the more elite organizations in the Swedish community: those that attempted to unite the various Swedish associations in Chicago in order to promote the idea that Swedes fit well within the white American mainstream, and others that tried to provide a clearinghouse for Swedish ideas and debates. The end result was a very dynamic, diverse, divided, and dispersed Swedish community, rooted solidly in the proliferating and changing neighborhoods in which the Swedish immigrants lived.

Overall, the move from Sweden to America did not result in a linear process of adaptation, nor did assimilation directly correlate with residential dispersal. Swedish immigrants held on to meaningful traditions and behaviors—as evidenced by the nature of their participation in Swedish churches and secular organizations—while taking hold of other American institutions and habits. In some respects, their behavior in Chicago was fairly typical among many white American urban dwellers in the late nineteenth and early twentieth centuries: as conditions in the inner city deteriorated and new immigrants and African Americans arrived in the city, Swedes moved to new, more isolated neighborhoods and commuted to work. In doing so, they did not sacrifice their Swedish ethnic identity. Their adaptation to life in Chicago was a synthetic development that combined the old with the new, creating a new Swedish American culture—a middle ground between their Swedish past and the American present. The immigrant generation began the process of acculturation, leaving it to their children and grandchildren to achieve complete structural assimilation.

This project has been a lengthy work in progress, and I am grateful to the many people who have assisted me over the years. Many thanks to Henry C. Binford and Josef J. Barton, who helped me develop my ideas as a graduate student at Northwestern University. Philip J. Anderson, Dag Blanck, Timothy J. Johnson, Per Nordahl, and the late Erik Lund helped me refine key aspects of my argument. My good friend and colleague Melissa Walker offered valuable feedback as my manuscript neared completion. My husband, Charles, my son, Karl, and my mother, Lorraine, gave valuable moral support. Financial assistance was provided at various stages by the Thord-Gray Memorial Fund, the American Scandinavian Foundation, the Alumnae of Northwestern University and, in the form of a sabbatical leave, Presbyterian College. More recent assistance has come from Amy Farranto and Nathan Holmes at Northern Illinois University Press, archivists Anna-Kajsa Echague and Stephen Spencer at the F. M. Johnson Archives and Special Collection at North Park University, and Joel Thoreson at the Archives of the Evangelical Lutheran Church in America. Finally, this manuscript would not have reached completion without the mentorship of the late H. Arnold Barton. I am grateful for the time he took to read and reread my manuscript and to offer valuable advice for further revision and improvement. His outstanding scholarship in Swedish American history provides a foundation for all of us who work in this field and he is sorely missed.[25]

CHAPTER 1

SWEDISH IMMIGRATION TO CHICAGO

"If you come [to America], don't travel without safe companionship."

—Hanna Carlson to her sister, Hilma, still in Sweden

The movement of Swedish people to Chicago was part of a larger pattern of migration from Scandinavia to the United States. Sweden was one of the many European regions sending its sons and daughters to North America in search of work and a more secure future. Overpopulation and the comparatively late industrialization of the Swedish economy, coupled with the attraction of an expanding American labor market, convinced 1,250,000 Swedes to leave their homeland between 1845 and 1930. The majority of these people settled in the United States, and one million never returned to Sweden. In 1910, one-fifth of all people who were born in Sweden lived in America. Only Ireland and Norway lost a higher proportion of their population in the migration to America.[1] As these Swedes transitioned to their new homes, they brought significant portions of their Swedish culture with them and forged Swedish American communities throughout the United States. From 1880 to 1920, Chicago grew to become the largest Swedish urban community in America; hence it played an important role in the larger Swedish migration.

One typical Swede who moved to Chicago was Carl Olson, whose arrival in Chicago coincided with a surge in the growth of the Swedish community in that city. Although Carl was only one single man who immigrated to America, his story represented that of many of Chicago's Swedish immigrants. Born in 1883 in the rural parish of Regna in Östergötland, Sweden—a province southwest of Stockholm—Carl grew up in modest circumstances. He lived on a small farm named Borstorp, of which his father Per Gustaf Olsson was part owner, and where his family had lived for several generations. Borstorp was beautifully situated on a winding country road. In one direction lay the parish church, where his grandparents were buried and where his parents would also one day be laid to rest; in the other direction lay a farm named Ralstorp where Hanna Carlson lived, the woman who would follow him to America and whom he would one day marry. At age twenty, Carl moved to America to find employment. He worked in a lumberyard in Benton Harbor, Michigan and a coal mine in West Virginia, and he poured cement in St. Louis, Missouri before moving to Chicago. Carl returned to Sweden in 1906 and then permanently moved to Chicago in 1909 where, after a series of odd jobs, he became a building contractor. Hanna followed Carl to Chicago in 1910, traveling in the company of his younger brother, Eric Albin Olson, and finding employment in Chicago as a domestic servant in a wealthy American family until she and Carl were married in the city in 1918.[2] Settling in Chicago, Carl and Hanna took part in a vibrant ethnic community that helped ease their transition to their new home.

What compelled Carl, Hanna, and Eric—and thousands of others of their generation—to follow the lead of earlier immigrants and leave their ancestral home for an uncertain future in urban America? How could they reconcile their rural, agricultural upbringing in a beautiful region of gently rolling hills to living in a city of more than a million people who spoke a countless variety of languages and who lived in houses built on small city lots? And why would they willingly choose such an undertaking? More than any other factor, Carl Olson moved to America to pursue economic opportunities unavailable to him in Regna. He was the seventh child and the third son in his family. He held out little hope of inheriting a substantial portion of his parents' rather meager property, since laws of inheritance in Sweden dictated that property be divided equally among all sons and daughters of a family. Furthermore, his betrothed, Hanna Carlson, lived on a larger and more prosperous farm, and by emigrating Carl believed that he had a greater chance of achieving economic success and proving himself worthy of Hanna's hand in marriage. If he stayed in Regna, his only option would be to work as a farmhand and hope to save enough money to one day buy his own farm—a scenario as unappealing as it was unlikely.[3] To an ambitious young man like Carl Olson, the move to America represented his best chance for social and economic advancement. He and hundreds of thousands of other Swedish men and women became part of a transatlantic labor market fueled by the uneven pace of industrial growth that left few opportunities for economic advancement in Sweden.

Although economic dislocations encouraged Swedes to leave, emigration was not an act of sheer desperation for most Swedish migrants. Swedes were better educated than most people in the Western world. Estimates put the basic literacy

FIGURE 1. Carl and Hanna (Carlson) Olson wedding picture. The Olsons were married in Chicago in 1918, several years after immigrating to Chicago. In many ways they were typical Swedish immigrants. He worked in construction and she was a domestic worker until their marriage. Author's personal collection.

rate in 1850 at 90 percent, slightly higher than figures for the white American population, and second in Europe only to Iceland.[4] Advances in agriculture and medicine actually contributed to the need for so many to emigrate: cultivation of the potato and development of a compulsory smallpox vaccine led to a decline in mortality rates in the early nineteenth century, and birthrates remained high throughout the period of mass emigration. Farmland in southern and central Sweden—the regions that ranked highest in rates of emigration—was already pushed to its limit and could not accommodate the expanding population.

The exact causes of the mass migration from Sweden to the United States varied over time. Sten Carlsson divides the era into five time periods in order to explain with greater precision the origins of this population movement. His analysis reflects the sensitivity of emigration trends to variations in the labor needs of the United States. The 14,500 Swedes who left for America between 1845 and 1854 (Stage One) consisted of fairly secure artisans and farmers, as well as some religious dissenters such as the Janssonists who found their way to Bishop Hill, Illinois.[5] These people settled in America because it offered greater economic opportunities and social and religious freedom than they experienced in Sweden. Swedish crop failures in 1867 and 1868 produced emigrants who were perhaps the most desperate of all the Swedish emigrants. From 1868 to 1873, 103,261 people emigrated from Sweden (Stage Two), and even after the period of famine subsided, the flow of traffic continued as many people left to settle with their relatives in the United States or were lured by the open farmland in the American West. From 1873 to 1878, conditions in Sweden improved and emigration figures diminished.

The largest number of Swedish immigrants arrived after 1879. Migration surged from 1879 to 1893 (Stage Three) when nearly half a million Swedes arrived in the United States, an average of over 32,500 per year. A number of economic conditions created this mass exodus. In 1879, crises in the timber and iron industries led many sawmill workers and metalworkers to emigrate. The greatest number of emigrants during the decade of the 1880s came from Sweden's agricultural sector, which was devastated when an influx of grain from Russia and the United States caused the bottom to fall out of the Swedish grain market. These problems induced younger children from farm families, farmhands and maidservants to migrate. While the rural exodus continued in the early 1890s, emigration broadened to also include more Swedes with industrial, urban backgrounds as more people left Stockholm and industrial areas in northern Sweden.

Economic depression in the United States diminished the flow of people to America between 1893 and 1900. Then, from 1900 until the beginning of World War I (Stage Four), nearly 290,000 people left Sweden, and authorities there began to worry about the adverse effects of this population depletion upon the country's labor supply. During this period increasing labor conflicts in Sweden led many workers to emigrate, especially those blacklisted for their labor activity. The 1920s represented the last phase of Swedish emigration to America, when over 100,000 people left (Stage Five). Depression in the United States in the 1930s effectively ended the attractions the labor market once held, and Sweden's modernizing economy and social welfare system opened up new opportunities and security to Swedish workers, bringing the era of Swedish mass migration to a close.[6]

After 1860, migration shifted from a family movement to one dominated by unmarried individuals, due in large part to the growth of labor opportunities in urban areas. Carlsson characterizes the average Swedish emigrant during the late nineteenth and early twentieth centuries as someone much like Carl Olson: a young, unmarried man or woman, who neither owned property nor possessed secure, permanent employment.[7] To these people, a move across the Atlantic represented a viable option in their search for work. In many cases, family and friends who preceded them to America created networks of communication and settlement that eased their transition into living quarters and workplaces. Swedish immigrants in America also helped their family and friends migrate in a more direct way, by purchasing a prepaid ticket for them to travel from Sweden. Furthermore, a significant number of Swedes realized that their migration need not be permanent. Lars-Göran Tedebrand estimates that 18 percent of Swedes who arrived in America from 1875 to 1930 returned to their homeland.[8] The growing ease of transatlantic travel, expanded trade between Europe and the United States, and improved communication that brought news of American events to remote Swedish villages, all served to broaden the Swedish worldview and allowed Swedes to assess employment options with a global perspective.

THE JOURNEY FROM SWEDEN

By 1880, few Swedes encountered great hardships on the journey from Sweden to America, even if the trip at times became tedious and uncomfortable. Before the mid-1860s, sailing vessels carried Swedish immigrants directly from Sweden to America, a difficult passage that lasted on average between six and eight weeks. Lars Ljungmark points out that beginning in the 1850s through the 1860s, English and American steamship lines gained control of the Atlantic overseas passenger traffic, reducing the length of the journey significantly. After the 1860s, Swedish travel patterns changed and immigrants usually traveled from Göteborg by ship over the North Sea to the English port city of Hull, by railroad from Hull to Liverpool, and then over the Atlantic from Liverpool to New York, Boston, or Quebec.[9] Immigrants usually traveled in steerage, where they slept in rooms with a dozen or more other passengers and had no privacy. By the late 1880s steam travel had completely replaced sailing vessels, and the crossing generally took between ten and twelve days. The entire journey was longer, however, since many immigrants who took trains to Göteborg from their home villages waited there several days for a ship to sail to Hull, and again waited in Liverpool for a vessel to depart for America. Despite these delays, the entire journey was much less arduous than what faced earlier immigrants from Sweden.

Immigration from Sweden to America, as well as from other European countries, was big business by the late nineteenth century, and a number of shipping lines competed for passengers. Cunard, Inman, Allan, and Guion Lines dominated the industry and hired subagents to lure immigrants to purchase tickets on their vessels. Ljungmark notes that subagents earned commissions of $1.35 to $2.70 per emigrant and "gradually acquired the role of salesmen for the glowing opportunities on the other side of the Atlantic—land, jobs, and the American way of life."[10] Despite the activity of these agents, Ljungmark concludes that the overall trends of migration had more to do with the lure of American land and labor opportunities and the difficulty of conditions in Sweden than with the work of the subagents. By 1915, the Swedish American Line joined the competition for passengers and offered direct service from Göteborg to New York, but immigrant traffic from Sweden was soon disrupted by war, and soon thereafter by economic depression. By the 1930s, the heyday of immigrants traveling from Sweden to America was long past.

Many Swedish immigrants found ways to personalize the journey from Sweden to America. Emigrants' families and friends often accompanied them to the nearest train station to bid farewell. Hilma Svensson, for example, listed twenty relatives and close friends who saw her off at the train station in Sweden, some of whom brought flowers and reading material for the journey.[11] Others may not have had such a large farewell party, but eventually they all set out on their own or with others traveling to the same destination. For Hilda Svensson (no apparent relation to Hilma noted above), after bidding farewell to her father and brother at the train station in Sävsjö, she took a train to Göteborg, where she had to wait for five days until boarding a ship headed across the North Sea to Hull, England. There she boarded another train to Liverpool where again she waited for four days until boarding her ship to cross the Atlantic, a vessel that carried 1,400 passengers to America. The voyage started smoothly, but about halfway into the trip the ship encountered a storm at sea in which water ran down the stairways and passengers were forced to stay below deck. After eleven days, however, they arrived in Boston, much to Hilda's relief. She soon found herself on yet another train and arrived two days later in Chicago. From start to finish, her journey lasted three weeks and three days and followed a pattern of travel typical for most immigrants.[12]

Despite the rough weather, many people had pleasant memories of the transatlantic crossing. E. E. F. Frost wrote to his parents that "We got food on the boat, so much we could not eat more, and good food too. The worst part of the journey was the train, because you had to sit really cramped, and you could hardly think about sleeping."[13] Hilma Svensson noted in her journal that "The [ship's] crew was so polite to us. We had good food and service the entire time, from 8 in the morning until 12 at night. . . . We slept well every night, with 16 to 20 in each cabin."[14] Pleasant traveling companions also made the journey much more enjoyable. Hilma Svensson wrote that "During the entire trip, we were four girls who kept each other company," all coming from the Jönköping area of southern Sweden. Svensson recalled that "We cooked coffee in our coffee pot two times each day. When it was ready, we got good cakes from the bakery on the boat.[15] Two of the women separated from the group in Boston to head for Brockton, Massachusetts. Svensson and another friend journeyed together as far as Chicago, where the latter continued on to Portland. While not all immigrants agreed that they liked the food served on the ships, few faced intolerable conditions typical of journeys earlier in the nineteenth century.[16]

Finding safe companions with whom to travel was of paramount concern to young, single immigrants, particularly women. In 1912, Hanna Carlson admonished her younger sister, Hildur, not to travel alone should she decide to come to Chicago. "I know what people say, that it is not hard to travel alone and that you can find companionship along the way. . . . But if you should come here, don't travel without safe companionship."[17] Anders Gustafsson wrote to his brother-in-law Johannes Jansson: "I wrote earlier about your daughter—she could have had pleasant traveling companions [with whom to come to America], but it was too late to send her a ticket by the time I heard that she might want to come. If you want to send her here, she could go with Holm's mother, or with Clas Jansson from Hagen."[18] When so many were leaving the Swedish countryside for America, it was usually not too difficult to find traveling companions for the journey. Furthermore, many poor immigrants who followed family and friends to America traveled there on prepaid tickets purchased by those same earlier immigrants they hoped to join. Not only did this make the experience more agreeable and safe to all involved, it reflected the complex webs of relationships evident among Swedish immigrants and those left behind. As Swedes settled in Chicago, it was easier for others to follow.[19]

CHAIN MIGRATION

The increasing ease of transatlantic travel allowed for immigrants to make rational choices to migrate that often followed preexisting patterns. Jon Gjerde documented the chain migration of a group of rural Norwegian immigrants who left the village of Balestrand, Norway and settled on farmland in the upper middle western United States.[20] In a similar fashion, many Swedes who moved to Chicago followed people from their village or other relatives who traveled before them. With more children surviving into adulthood in late nineteenth-century Sweden, few families could afford to care for all of their children. Often, as young people came of age, they faced the choice of working on a neighboring farm or moving to an American city. If an older sibling or neighbor had already made the trek to America, it was reassuring to those who followed. The possibility of land ownership and economic advancement in the crowded countryside of Sweden was remote, and thus the move to a city such as Chicago offered the real possibility of improvement and security.

Providing a comprehensive analysis of chain migration to Chicago such as the one conducted by Gjerde is no easy task. However, gleaning smaller snippets from church records in Chicago is possible and provides evidence of family migrations carried out over a period of years. For example, a sample of members of the Austin Covenant Church on Chicago's West Side, traced back to their home parishes in Sweden, clearly illustrates the tradition of emigration established within many of the families who worshiped at the church.[21] Although such an approach does not provide overarching statistics regarding how common chain migration was among all of Chicago's Swedes, it does bring to life personal stories of immigrants who moved to the city and gives evidence of the family context in which they made their decisions. It also synthesizes records from Chicago and Sweden to provide a more complete picture of the immigrants' lives.

The story of Gustaf Johnson is but one example of a family's migration pattern gleaned from church records. Born to Peter Andersson and Maria Petersdotter in 1869, he was the third child in the family. Gustaf's father owned a small piece of land in the area of Rydaholm's parish in Jönköping County. Despite the fact that he was the oldest son in this farming family, Gustaf emigrated when he was eighteen years old. Not only were the family's landholdings small, but six more children were born after him, making their situation very difficult. He had a good reason to emigrate: Gustaf's oldest sister moved to America when she was only seventeen years old, seven years prior to his own departure. The second sister moved to work at another farm in the parish when she was eighteen, then moved to the United States two years after Gustaf. A history of emigration had been established within the family, perhaps making the decision to leave less traumatic. Furthermore, the woman whom Gustaf Johnson married in Chicago in 1914 was herself a link in a chain of family migration. Ada Lundgren came to America in 1903 and joined the Austin Covenant Church. A younger sister and two younger brothers immigrated later, each at a separate time, and all eventually joined the church in Austin. After Gustaf and Ada married, they moved to Kingsburg, California, and within seven years, Ada's siblings had followed them there from Chicago. To Gustaf and Ada, the move to America was a viable option in order to pursue their search for work in a time of economic uncertainty, and took place within a context of family migration.[22]

Many other immigrants faced similar situations and made decisions to migrate within a clear pattern of chain migration. Ernst Carlstrom was born in Jönköping County in 1881, the ninth of twelve children. When Ernst was ten years old, his father died, forcing the children to find employment as soon as they were old enough to do so. By the time Ernst left for America when he was twenty years old, an older brother and a sister had already emigrated, setting a precedent for Ernst's decision to leave home for the United States.[23] For other Swedish families, migration absorbed the entire group. Johan August Lind and Klara Sussana Petersdotter moved to Chicago with their six children in 1887 when the youngest was two years old.[24] The move for Lars Andersson and Kajsa Andersdotter's family was much more haphazard, as they moved back and forth across the ocean on a number of occasions. Lars moved to America first in 1881, and the next year two of his daughters, Emma Christina and Brita Lena, followed him there. After two years, both daughters returned to Sweden. In 1885, Lars died in America and economic conditions deteriorated for the family. Emma Christina and Brita Lena returned to America and settled permanently in Chicago, followed by their mother, the now-widowed Kajsa, and their youngest sister. They all joined the Austin Covenant Church, and the three sisters all married men in the church and retained their membership for many years.[25]

Even if an immigrant was the first or the only member of a family to move to America, regional family migration patterns within Sweden often provided a context of mobility.[26] Such was the case of Charlotta Anderson, the first in her family to move across the Atlantic, whose decision to leave resulted from her family's economic instability. Born in 1864 to tenant farmers, Charlotta was the fourth of seven children. Her older brother and one older sister moved out of the parish to find work when they were eighteen and nineteen years old respectively. Charlotta moved to a nearby parish for work when she was sixteen, and then moved to America nine years later.[27] Another young immigrant, Hulda Rosell, was born in 1879, the second of six children. When Hulda was nine years old, her father committed suicide, leaving the family to fend for itself. Most of the children moved away from home by the time they were seventeen, and Hulda moved to a nearby farm when she was sixteen. Four years later she returned home and worked as a maid at her neighbor's farm, and then, when she was twenty-two years old, she emigrated to Chicago.[28]

Although not quantifiable, these scenarios paint fairly typical pictures of the pressures leading to an individual's emigration from Sweden. These immigrants all made rational decisions to leave Sweden and find work in Chicago. Difficult circumstances pushed many to leave their childhood homes when they were old enough to do so, but family and friends often created a context for move-ment that would ease the transition to their new destination. Once in Chicago, the immigrants in this sample joined the Austin Covenant Church, while many others joined one or more of the dozens of other Swedish institutions in Chicago. These organizations—whether secular or religious—assisted these Swedes as they adjusted to their new lives and provided a context for the evolution of the Swedish community in Chicago.

THE GROWTH OF ETHNIC CHICAGO

From its establishment, Chicago was a city of immigrants, so it was not unusual that so many Swedes settled there. Countless early Swedish immigrants passed through Chicago on their way to the rich farmland in the Midwest, but an increasing number began to realize the opportunities that Chicago offered, and they remained in the city. Still other Swedes found their way to Chicago from other places in America, including from rural farming regions. Chicago attracted Swedish immigrants because of its very newness—industrial development pro-vided jobs, railroads converged on the city and eased transportation, and the sur-rounding countryside offered plenty of space for expansion. And it was in this new creative space that Swedes found jobs, built homes, established churches and secular associations, and assisted later arrivals as they adjusted to city life.

The most numerous of the earliest immigrant groups in Chicago were the Irish and German settlers who originally came to work on the Illinois and Michigan Canal in 1836. Swedes were not far behind, however. The first significant Swedish settlement in Chicago began in 1846, more than a generation before the immi-grants who are the focus of this book arrived. That year, a number of disillusioned followers of the self-appointed Swedish prophet, Erik Jansson, stopped in Chicago instead of following the religious leader to his colony in Bishop Hill, Illinois. A handful of Swedes had arrived before that date, but never in large numbers. Even by 1848, only forty Swedes permanently resided in Chicago.[29] That number steadily grew in subsequent years, as the Swedish population reached approxi-mately eight hundred in 1860, six thousand in 1870, and then more than doubled to nearly thirteen thousand by 1880.[30]

These early Swedish settlers faced many challenges as they lived and worked in Chicago. According to Ulf Beijbom, early settlement patterns of Swedes in Chicago can be divided into three distinct periods: the squatter period, from 1846 to 1860; the formation of three main enclaves, between 1860 and 1880; and finally, the era of the suburb after 1880.[31] During the early squatter period, squalid conditions predominated and life was marred by poverty and cholera epidemics. Beijbom notes that early Swedish observers described these fellow immigrants as being in "needy circumstances," living in "miserable shanties or in small and narrow rented rooms," surrounded "almost everywhere [by] desolation."[32]

By 1860, as Swedes became a bit more economically secure, they moved to newly developing ethnic enclaves located within the city limits. The largest such enclave emerged north of the Chicago River on the Near North Side and became known as Swede Town. It was a working-class neighborhood in close proximity to factory jobs and offered low property prices and rent. Other Swedish enclaves, numerically less significant, developed on the South Side, a region of the city fast becoming Chicago's industrial center, and the West Side, where new public transportation routes linked it to the rest of the city and allowed working-class people to move there while retaining easy access to their jobs. By 1870, Chicago's Swedish residents represented the largest single cluster of Swedes in the United States. As the Swedish population in Chicago doubled during the following decade, Swedes were outnumbered only by the German, Irish, and English immigrant groups living in the city. By the end of this second phase of settlement, Swedes remained in these three centrally located ethnic clusters.

During these early decades of Chicago's history, residents transformed the city into a large, sprawling metropolis. The Chicago Fire of 1871 furthered this process by pushing residents away from central districts into newly developing areas. Fire codes established after the fire created stricter building regulations within the city limits, encouraging many people to relocate to areas where land could be purchased cheaply and wooden houses erected quickly. The city itself became regionally specialized as business construction dominated the downtown area and expensive residences relocated farther to the north and the south. Burned-out industries on the Chicago River's North Branch, such as the McCormick Reaper Plant, moved to cheaper land bordering the South Branch of the river. Expanding truck farms, located predominantly to the north, northwest, and south of Chicago, supplied produce for the city. American, German, Swedish, and Dutch farmers operated most of these farms. As Chicago's population doubled from 500,000 people in 1880 to one million in 1890, many of these regions were subdivided to provide additional housing for Chicago's burgeoning population. In 1889, Chicago annexed dozens of new neighborhoods, and the city grew by 125 square miles.[33] Swedish settlers had plenty of opportunities to take advantage of new housing options available to Chicago's residents.

The population of Chicago continued to grow at a phenomenal rate, and its ethnic composition diversified even further in subsequent decades. Between 1890 and 1910 the city's population doubled a second time to over two million people. By 1920 the population reached 2,700,000 and continued to be heavily ethnic. Poles ranked as the largest foreign-born group, followed by Germans, Russians,

Italians, and in fifth place, Swedes.[34] These trends reflected the growing importance of immigration from southern and eastern Europe, not only to Chicago but to the nation as a whole. New workers continued to find jobs in industrial sectors such as steel production, meatpacking houses, and the garment industry.[35] Swedes found work in all of these areas, in addition to developing a particular niche in the construction and painting industries. By this time Chicago had become a vibrant, well-established city—the second-largest in the United States—and contained a mosaic of ethnic communities scattered throughout its landscape.

As Chicago's population grew, its inhabitants lived in widely dispersed areas, and although many of these regions technically lay within the city limits, population hubs remained isolated from each other, interspersed with small farms, and removed from the city. This isolation diminished, however, as the gradual expansion of Chicago's transportation network linked these suburban-like regions to the city. Industrial expansion and population growth on the South Side led to the earliest development of transit facilities in that region of the city. Streetcar lines ran south to Fifty-fifth Street as early as 1878 and extended to Seventy-first Street in 1891. Two years later, the South Side's Jackson Park became the center of international fame as the Columbian Exposition drew millions of visitors to that part of the city. By the time of the fair, four railroads and Chicago's first elevated train provided suburban service to the South Side. During construction of the elevated train, workers in many areas cleared trees for the rail line, and much of the land remained undeveloped prairie. By 1908, the elevated system on the South Side included Englewood, Kenwood, Normal Park, and the Stockyard branches.[36]

The expansion of transportation networks spread to other parts of the city as well. Between 1893 and 1915, separate companies built elevated train lines stretching west, northwest, and north from downtown to beyond the city limits. Extensive streetcar service operated on the North Side and the West Side. The steam railroad and the Chicago Milwaukee Electric Railway linked Evanston with the downtown Chicago district. The elevated train system created an even more efficient and cheaper way to commute to work. In 1900, 81 million passengers used the elevated system, and within a decade, that figure doubled.[37] By 1920, most of Chicago's incorporated area was fully integrated into the metropolitan transportation system, linking dispersed neighborhoods with business and industrial districts as well as with each other.

The growth of public transportation allowed more established immigrant groups to move into newly developing regions of Chicago, creating new ethnic settlements in scattered areas of the city. These new neighborhoods were initially suburban in character—they were residential areas removed from overcrowded urban conditions. In these places, immigrants could build new houses and join the ranks of middle-class homeowners. As the Germans, Irish, Swedes, and

Norwegians moved to new neighborhoods, immigrants from Poland, Russia, and Italy, as well as African Americans migrating from the South, replaced them in the city's older and less desirable central districts. Chicago residents found themselves part of a diverse, expanding, and structurally changing city. The number of immigrants in Chicago peaked in 1930, when the foreign-born and their children accounted for more than two-thirds of the city's population.[38]

The settlement of Swedes in Chicago took place within this context of population growth and outward expansion. The 1884 Chicago school census shows that Swedes were only beginning to respond to opportunities for outward migration from the city's central Swedish enclaves. This census gives a comprehensive listing of population by ethnic group, making it possible to analyze the density of Swedes and other immigrant groups in wards and in smaller districts within those wards. According to the 1884 census, 23,755 Swedes lived in Chicago: 58 percent on the North Side, 26 percent on the West Side, and 16 percent on the South Side. On the North Side, the Swedish population continued to center around the enclave known as Swede Town, concentrating most heavily in the region bordered by Division, Superior, Franklin, and Larrabee Streets, and the North Branch of the Chicago River. Other important areas of Swedish settlement on the North Side surrounded this core; only one ward district as far north as Lincoln Park reflected any significant Swedish settlement. On the West Side, no such tight clustering of the Swedish population existed. The heaviest density of Swedes occurred in the southeast portion of North Lawndale, with other significant areas located in the Near West Side, and in German and Norwegian sections of West Town. On the South Side, no census district held over three hundred Swedes. The largest concentration of Swedish population there occurred in an east-west corridor through Armour Square, McKinley Park, Bridgeport, and Douglas. Swedes most often settled in regions of Chicago with other immigrants, usually those from Germany, Ireland, and Norway, whose pattern of migration roughly resembled their own. No Swedish neighborhood was ethnically homogeneous; hence Swedes continually interacted with other ethnic groups in the city.[39]

The 1910 Chicago school census provides indisputable evidence of Swedish suburbanization. This census also gives population figures for Chicago's wards, and although no entire ward was dominated by Swedes, the largest proportion of Swedes was found in the southwest section of the city, in an area that included the neighborhoods of Englewood and South Englewood. Another large concentration of Swedes centered in a northern ward that encompassed neighborhoods such as North Center in the western part of Lake View, Lincoln Square, and the western section of Andersonville. All of these regions also consisted of a large number of Germans, who continued to rank as Chicago's largest immigrant group. Smaller Swedish settlements arose around the perimeter of the city, encompassing

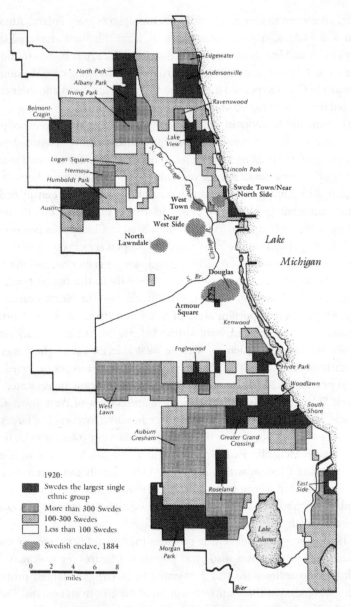

FIGURE 2. Map of census tracts of Chicago in 1920, showing areas and density of Swedish neighborhoods. Adapted from Ernest W. Burgess and Charles Newcomb, eds., *Census Data of the City of Chicago, 1920* (Chicago" University of Chicago Press, 1931), 134. From Anita R. Olson, "The Community Created: Chicago Swedes 1880–1920," in *Swedish American-Life in Chicago: Cultural and Urban Aspects of an Immigrant People, 1850–1930*, ed. Philip A. Anderson and Dag Blanck (Urbana and Chicago: University of Illinois Press, 1992), 52.

Roseland, Pullman, and West Pullman on the South Side; Austin, Belmont Cragin, Hermosa, and Humboldt Park on the West Side; and parts of Lake View, Uptown, and Edgewater on the North Side. Further clusters of Swedish residents were found in the northwestern part of the city, including Jefferson Park, Forest Glen, North Park, and Albany Park. The Old Swede Town had diminished as the heart of Swedish Chicago: by 1910 only 4 percent of the Swedes in the city lived there, a figure that declined further in subsequent years.[40]

The 1920 United States Census confirms this process of outward migration and population dispersal. By then, the majority of Swedes lived in a ring outside the city's core away from the industrial areas along the North and South branches of the Chicago River. Primary areas, defined in this study as districts where Swedes were the largest single ethnic group per census tract, occurred in the North Side neighborhoods of Lake View near Belmont Avenue and Clark Street, Andersonville at Clark Street and Foster Avenue, and North Park located farther west on Foster Avenue. In western Chicago, Swedes dominated the Austin and Belmont Cragin communities. In the southern part of Chicago, primary areas included one census tract in Armour Square—an old Swedish neighborhood—and several areas on the Far South Side of Chicago: Hyde Park, Woodlawn, Englewood, West Englewood, South Shore, Greater Grand Crossing, East Side, Morgan Park, and Roseland. Overall, 40 percent of Chicago's Swedes lived in these types of primary areas. In addition, another 14 percent of the Swedish population resided in areas with significant Swedish settlement but where Swedes were not the largest single ethnic group, regions scattered throughout the northern and southern parts of the city. Putting these two groups together, over half of the Swedes in Chicago lived in neighborhoods with a high density of Swedes and a strong Swedish presence. The balance of the Swedish population lived in smaller Swedish neighborhoods or scattered throughout the city.[41]

Swede Town and other previously important Swedish enclaves such as West Town and the area on the South Side between Twenty-first and Thirty-fourth Streets, displayed a remarkable decline in their importance to Swedish settlement in the census records. These areas came to be dominated largely by immigrants from southern and eastern Europe and by African Americans—groups who arrived more recently than had the Swedes. Despite this influx of new groups into the city—or perhaps because of it—Swedes least often settled in census districts dominated by Greeks, Czechs, Hungarians, Russians, Poles, Yugoslavians, Italians, and African Americans. Instead, they continued to live in neighborhoods with Germans, Irish, and Norwegians, groups whose timing of arrival paralleled their own and who were also ready to settle in up-and-coming neighborhoods, leaving older districts to the poorer newcomers.

THE EXTENSION OF THE SWEDISH COMMUNITY

Swedish immigrants found new ways to express and invigorate their ethnicity in this growing urban context. The argument here differs from Beijbom's, who projects that residential expansion after 1880 diminished Swedish ethnicity and represented a move toward greater assimilation. He writes that "whereas the enclaves in the river wards functioned as hard-core united Swedish cells, the new residential sectors were spread out over wide areas where the distances quickly weakened this unity." Suburban Swedes usually owned their homes, and their move there reflected greater social and economic advancement. Beijbom believes that "the tendency to assimilate was also supported among the suburbanites by their reluctance to go against the social patterns of their new environment."[42] While these generalizations hold true after 1920 when the second generation came of age and moved to incorporated towns outside the city limits, they do not accurately reflect the 1880–1920 period.

The creation of Swedish institutions throughout Chicago corresponded to the outward movement of the Swedish population, continuing and actually extending the group's presence in the city. The defining nature of community life evolved from smaller enclave-based associations to a diverse and complex array of Swedish organizations that transcended neighborhood boundaries. From 1880 to 1920, the Swedes built more than 72 churches and over 130 secular clubs in Chicago, all of which used Swedish as their primary language but differed considerably in ideological orientation. In the process of building these institutions, Swedish immigrants brought their past experiences with them to fulfill essentially new tasks. For example, religious debates and divisions, often carried to America from Sweden, manifested themselves in the variety of denominational churches built and supported by Swedes. The survival of these churches in turn depended upon continual support from their voluntary membership, a vastly different arrangement from Sweden's state-supported Lutheran Church, where membership was automatic at birth. Secular societies tended to develop in neighborhoods after the establishment of the mainline Swedish churches, at a point when the Swedish population was large enough to sustain a variety of organizational interests.[43] The function and success of social organizations was also closely tied to the needs of their members. Such membership at times had roots in the traditions brought from Sweden, but even more importantly reflected the need for a particular type of Swedish social interaction in a city with a diverse ethnic complexion. Hence, ethnic institution building in Chicago was itself an expression of a new, Swedish American identity and resulted in the creation of diverse Swedish community institutions located in widespread areas of the city.

In 1880, thirteen Swedish churches existed in Chicago, representing a variety of denominational options to Swedish settlers and providing a framework for further institutional expansion. All but one of these were located in the three original Swedish enclaves identified by Beijbom. The variety of churches established—Augustana Lutheran, Mission Covenant, Free Church, and the Swedish branches of the Methodist and Baptist churches—reflected the particularistic denominational interests of the Swedish people. Since transportation networks in the city of Chicago were not fully developed in the 1880s, members of these older churches who moved to new suburbs of Chicago could not easily reach their old congregations, so they built more than two dozen new churches closer to their homes which reflected their denominational persuasion. Once built, these churches became a magnet for first-time members.

Growth continued in the 1890s and during the first decade of the twentieth century, when the number of Swedish churches grew by forty-two as Swedes continued to move to new neighborhoods. From 1910 to 1920, the number of Swedish-speaking churches established in Chicago dropped sharply—only three new churches were founded. The era of rampant institutional expansion drew to a close as the number of Swedes in Chicago dropped and an American-born, English-speaking generation took their place.[44]

Likewise, secular organizational life, in its infancy in 1880, matured in the subsequent decades. According to Beijbom, forty Swedish organizations existed in Chicago prior to 1880, varying in purpose from general social interaction aimed at the middle class to trade societies and sports and recreation clubs. Beijbom describes the Svea Society, formed in 1857, as "the archetypal Swedish American secular organization."[45] Formally incorporated in 1862 and centered on the Near North side, its members associated together "for the encouragement of literary pursuits and for mutual assistance."[46] Even at this early date, the Svea Society began providing sickness and funeral benefits to its members, an important selling point for future organizations. Its high-society functions, however, focused Svea's appeal on upper-crust Swedes, and although the society survived into the early twentieth century, its influence never matched that of its early existence. Other significant organizations in the early Swedish community included Svithiod, a South Side club formed around 1875 that subsequently changed its name to Balder; Nordstjernan (The Northstars), founded in 1879 in southwestern Chicago, just north of the McCormick Reaper Plant where many of its members worked; and Iduna, an organization started by Northstars on the South Side.

Although these organizations began health underwriting functions, they were never generally accessible to Swedes in all areas of the city. An early observer of Swedish activities in Chicago noted that "The Northstars held their reputation for thirty years, but then it slipped. The . . . organization was always against the proposal to split into branches."[47] Members who moved to the South Side began Iduna as a separate organization because the structure of the Northstars was not flexible enough to allow for expansion. All of these organizations shared characteristics that diminished their relevance to the Swedish community over the long haul: their activities took place in older Swedish neighborhoods that were losing their importance to the Swedish population, and they refused to create branch organizations that would bring them into the new Swedish enclaves. Overall, most of the Swedish clubs formed in the early Swedish community in Chicago were loosely organized, and few survived beyond 1880. None held positions of leadership after that date.

The newer organizations differed significantly from their predecessors. Functionally, many of them served purposes of social interaction, much like earlier associations. In the case of fraternal societies, however, that social agenda was balanced with a beneficiary system that provided sick and death benefits to workers and their families unprotected in their American work environment. The social insurance program broadened the appeal of many benevolent societies beyond the middle class to include mostly working-class individuals. Unlike the churches, membership in secular clubs was often gender-based. Many fraternal organizations initially limited their membership to men, forcing women to join auxiliary groups or to form their own separate organizations.[48] Structurally, the new associations departed widely from earlier models, as groups such as the Svithiod and Viking Orders created overarching grand lodges with smaller, neighborhood lodges functioning as subordinated clubs. These societies expanded in much the same fashion as the churches, spreading from the older enclaves to the new neighborhoods as Swedish settlers moved to these areas of Chicago. The largest growth spurt of lodge building occurred in the first decade of the twentieth century. This expansion under the guise of central grand lodges created an umbrella effect that kept the structure of large organizations intact while allowing for branch lodges to follow the Swedish population into dispersed areas throughout the city. The formation of these various associations further increased the diverse nature of the Swedish community.[49]

By 1920, the era of Swedish population growth and rampant institutional expansion drew to a close as a generational shift took place.[50] Swedes who had arrived in Chicago during the migration surge of the 1880s were aging; many of them had lived in the city for nearly forty years. At the same time, the second-generation Swedish population continued to grow and vastly outnumbered their immigrant forebears. While the religious institutions established before 1920 remained a significant force in the Swedish community, the nature of those institutions changed to include more second- and third-generation Swedish Americans and non-Swedes.[51] During the 1920s, due in large part to patriotic pressures exerted during World War One and to the needs of an American-born generation, many churches moved toward using English as their primary language.[52] Similar pressures occurred in the secular clubs as members slowly embraced English in order to reach out to a new generation. Any institutional growth beyond 1920 occurred in a context in which American influences in the Swedish community rivaled and often surpassed the declining impact of new immigrant arrivals.

NEIGHBORHOODS IN TRANSITION

As Swedes abandoned their older ethnic enclaves for new neighborhoods, the neighborhoods themselves underwent a transformation from farmland, to subdivision, to ethnic enclave. Both small and large Swedish hubs began as outlying farming regions, subdivided into urban settlements on the outskirts of the city. New settlers moved to these areas to build their own homes and improve their living conditions. For example, Swedes living in the South Side enclave of Armour Square in the 1880s worried about their health. Factories continued to spring up in the area, and the stockyards polluted the air. When they had the opportunity to move farther south to new suburbs such as Englewood, many Swedes did so, and they left the old neighborhoods to the city's newer immigrants. Some economic stability was needed to afford a new home in Englewood, but as one son of Swedish immigrants remembered, "It was just as cheap in the long run to go to the newer sections and build a new home" than to upgrade an older home in Armour Square. Furthermore, the same man, himself a son of Swedish immigrants, distanced himself from the newer immigrants flooding into the city. He noted that "the people in [Armour Square] began to be nothing but foreigners who cared nothing for making the neighborhood attractive."[53] To Swedes who had any intention of staying in Chicago, conditions in Armour Square were not acceptable, and as they moved, they also distanced themselves from newer migrants to the city.

As Swedes moved away from deteriorating subdivisions, suburbs became new kinds of enclaves as Swedes transferred ethnic affiliations and divisions to their new neighborhoods. In the process, they created a rich and diverse community life that extended throughout the city. In Englewood, for example, truck farms gave way to initial subdivisions as early as 1868. After the city of Chicago annexed the region in 1889, it expanded rapidly, fueled to a large degree by South Side activity surrounding the Columbian Exposition of 1893. Swedes entered the region in significant numbers in the 1890s, but a few had lived in the area for at least fifteen years prior to that.[54] Swedes founded the first Swedish church in Englewood in

1875, and as the Swedish population there grew, eight new churches were built by 1890. From 1891 until 1916, at least eight beneficiary societies started lodges in the greater Englewood area.

As long as the influx of Swedes to Englewood continued, these institutions thrived. But the trend reversed itself in the early decades of the new century, and the creation of new Swedish organizations began to decline. Membership in the Swedish churches in Englewood peaked in 1905 in the Methodist Church, 1913 and 1915 in the Lutheran churches, and in 1917 and 1920 in the Covenant churches. Englewood, like Armour Square before it, was filling up, and new home-builders were forced to look elsewhere. Swedes maintained a strong presence in the neighborhood, but the community was no longer infused with large numbers of newcomers; thereafter Englewood's Swedish ethnic identity began a gradual, continual decline. This decline testified to the remarkable fluidity of urban America—within a single generation, the institutions created by these immigrants diminished in significance as Swedish American children moved out of these fairly new ethnic neighborhoods.

Similar patterns of movement occurred on Chicago's North Side. Swede Town continued to be the largest single hub of Swedish population during the 1880s, after which time its relative importance to Swedish settlement declined. Church membership in that region peaked during 1887 at Immanuel Lutheran Church, and in 1892 and 1893 in the Covenant Church and Methodist Church respectively.[55] A German grocer living in the district during this period noted that "It was an Irish, German and Swedish neighborhood then. The people didn't live in segregated groups but did live altogether harmoniously."[56]

The nature of Swede Town, however, soon began to change. A Jewish business leader observed that the coming of the elevated train (the "L") changed the neighborhood dramatically. "It became a poorer district and more commercialized. The 'L' was noisy and people did not like to live near it, consequently, rents decreased."[57] A Swedish woman attributed falling rents to "the factories [that] have been encroaching upon the district." Swedes were also unhappy with demographic changes as Italians and African Americans moved into the area. "Before the Italians came," claimed this same Swedish woman, "the district was much better and cleaner." She noted that "The Swedish people sold two of their churches to the Negroes very cheaply."[58] The Free Church and the Baptist Church moved to new locations on the North Side in 1910 and 1911, and Immanuel Lutheran relocated further north to Edgewater in 1920. A number of people believed that "The coming of Italians has . . . caused the Swedish and Irish to move north."[59] Hence, Swedes moved for two overarching reasons. First, the possibility of building new homes in attractive neighborhoods proved to be a powerful incentive for moving to new areas of the city. Second, by moving to new areas Swedish immigrants separated themselves from more recent newcomers to the city, thereby physically preserving their own ethno-racial understandings.

One of the destinations for Swedish settlers was Lake View, a neighborhood north of Swede Town. In the 1870s, Lake View was largely a rural community where truck farming and livestock trading dominated local affairs. Gradually, the area began to assume the characteristics of an urban neighborhood. In the next decade—known as the "Golden Years" in Lake View—building boomed and the population skyrocketed. The *Chicago Land Use Survey*, conducted in 1940 and published in 1942, estimated that 43 per cent of all homes in Lake View were built between 1880 and 1894.[60] Churches of a variety of denominations and ethnic persuasions were begun in Lake View during this time, including five Swedish churches. From 1890 to 1919, Swedes established eleven lodges in the area. Although Trinity Lutheran Church continued to grow after 1920, membership in Lake View's Methodist Church peaked in 1908 and in the Covenant Church in 1913. By this time, a University of Chicago student noted that "the Belmont Avenue–Clark Street neighborhood had definitely taken on the aspect of a temporary stopping place for immigrants. Since then the older residents have moved farther north."[61] Lake View continued to be an important Swedish enclave, but it was beginning to relinquish its prominence to Andersonville, its neighbor to the north.

The development of a Swedish enclave in the Summerdale-Andersonville area demonstrates the persistence of ethnicity in a new suburb. Before 1890, this region was mostly rural, inhabited by a handful of American, German, and Swedish settlers who operated truck farms or blacksmith shops, or earned some kind of livelihood off the traffic passing through on its way to the city. Developers subdivided the land in 1890, but the boom in settlement came after 1908, when transportation links to the city improved and made Andersonville a viable residential option to those people who commuted to work. Fred Nelson, a Swede who moved to Summerdale in 1892, observed that at the time only a few Swedish families lived there, most of them arriving after 1890: "The influx [of Swedes] was always gradual. . . . I would say the reason Swedish people came here was because lots were cheap. They came from Swedish settlements further south."[62]

The Ebenezer Lutheran Church, formed in 1892, was the first Swedish church in Andersonville. Before that time, Swedes had not migrated to the area in any significant numbers, and the Swedish population could not sustain its own ethnic institutions. Many of the early Swedish settlers, therefore, attended American churches, since no ethnic options existed. A pastor of the Summerdale Congregational Church reminisced about the time when his church was truly a community church, drawing in its neighbors no matter what their ethnic persuasion. "There were some Scandinavians in the locality when the church was started in 1890. . . . But after 1900 with the increase in the Scandinavian element in our population, the membership decreased, for the Scandinavians very naturally and properly went to their own religious organizations as they were organized. In 1914, then, when the Swedish influx assumed its largest proportions, our little church was nearly in a state of insolvency."[63] A member of another Congregational Church in the area remembered that "When the Swedish churches came and took the Swedish members away from us we couldn't make the church pay."[64] Swedes who once had no alternative but to join American churches attended their own ethnic institutions once they were built, demonstrating the strength of Swedish affiliations even after a period of interaction with non-Swedes.

Not all Swedish groups were equally represented in each new Swedish neighborhood. In some areas, the earliest Swedish settlers stamped their surroundings with their own particular organizational preferences in an effort to insulate themselves from intra-ethnic divisions. In the Ravenswood neighborhood, for example, Covenant, Methodist, and Baptist churches were established between 1887 and 1907, but no Lutheran church nor any significant secular lodges were founded. Farther west on Foster Avenue at Kedzie Avenue, the Swedish settlement of North Park was dominated by members of the Covenant Church whose ethno-religious mindset persisted as they created a new subdivision devoid of other Swedish denominations or secular organizations. The creation of the North Park community represented an effort by its founders to distinguish themselves as a group and to preserve their own particular values for future generations.

The city of Chicago officially recorded a map of the North Park area in 1855 as part of Jefferson Township. After that time, Swedish and German farmers bought most of the surrounding territory and, like their Andersonville counterparts, operated truck farms on which they raised specialized crops for transportation into Chicago to trade for much-needed provisions. At the beginning of the 1890s, the area retained its rural and isolated feel. Pehr Peterson, a Swedish settler not connected to the Covenant Church, ran a substantial agricultural operation directly north of North Park. He employed thirty-one workers on his farm, most of whom were recently arrived immigrants from Sweden. By contrast, most of the developers of North Park had lived in America for more than a decade and a half and identified closely with the newly formed Covenant denomination.

Two early settlers, brothers Peter J. Youngquist and Claes August Youngquist, followed the transition in the nature of the North Park community from rural farmland to Swedish subdivision. They moved to the area when it was a sparsely settled agricultural region and established themselves as small-scale farmers. Despite living in such a remote area, they retained their ties to the North Side Mission Covenant Church in Swede Town. By 1893, they joined with other like-minded Covenanters in Chicago to establish the Swedish University Association.

FIGURE 3. North Park University's first building, "Old Main," about 1890. The neighborhood had just been subdivided, yet the rural feel to the surroundings remained. Courtesy of Covenant Archives and Historical Library, North Park University, Chicago.

The organization, with the Youngquist brothers' help, purchased farmland in the North Park area in order to lure the Covenant's denominational college from Minneapolis to Chicago. At the same time, they attempted to build a Swedish Covenant colony around the school that would one day become North Park University. They also founded North Park Covenant Church within the new subdivision. Although the developers failed to preserve the homogeneity of the North Park vicinity over the long run, the institutions founded there maintained a strong Swedish American presence in the neighborhood throughout the next century.[65]

THE EVOLUTION OF THE SWEDISH COMMUNITY

As suggested in this study, movement to Chicago's new subdivisions and early suburbs did not necessarily reflect a decline in Swedish ethnic identity. Swedes, upon settling in these outlying regions in the 1880s and 1890s, discovered new types of ethnic relationships that relied less upon tightly knit, centralized enclaves, and more upon webs of social and institutional connections of their own creation. They transformed new neighborhoods into vibrant ethnic urban neighborhoods. Thus, while Swedes and their children resided in neighborhoods scattered throughout Chicago—places that were never completely homogeneous—the Swedish ethnic identity in the city thrived. Swedes living in Chicago between 1880 and 1920 continually remodeled Swedish ethnic affiliations, adapting them to the needs of a dynamic and evolving immigrant community in a diverse and expanding American city.

By 1920, Swedish arrivals in Chicago were greeted by a complex ethnic community fundamentally different from the community of 1880. The city of Chicago had grown and expanded, and its population had become more ethnically diverse. The Swedish enclaves, no longer as centralized as they had been in 1880, spread throughout the city. Swedes coped with this dispersion by creating and maintaining institutions that were Swedish American in character: they allowed for continuity of expression in terms of their ideological, religious, and social values, and they mitigated any possible dislocating and alienating effects of migration by creating new types of connection. Instead of the suburban environment shaping Swedish behavior by loosening ethnic ties, the newly developing regions of Chicago allowed Swedish immigrants to exert power over their social environment and re-create their community affiliations. While reflecting the diversity within the Swedish community, the existence of these institutions strengthened ethnic consciousness in neighborhoods removed from central Chicago and asserted the Swedish presence in widespread areas of the city. Even so, after 1920 the influence of first-generation Swedes in these scattered neighborhoods diminished as the immigrant population aged, fewer newcomers arrived, and the neighborhoods themselves underwent further demographic transformation.

CHAPTER 2

THE SWEDISH IMMIGRANT EXPERIENCE
IN CHICAGO

Finding a Middle Ground

"I'm sure it would have been hard for you to send [your daughter] away to a foreign country, but it wouldn't have been so dangerous for her. It is only a five-minute walk to our [Swedish] church and school . . . she [would] have just as good a home here [in Chicago with us] as she would with you [in Sweden]."

—Anders Gustaf Gustafsson to his brother-in-law,
Johannes Jansson, Feb. 29, 1880

Swedish immigrants in Chicago added to the organizational complexion of the Swedish community as they settled in new subdivisions, created new associations, and adapted old ones to reflect their own experiences. As Swedes moved into and within Chicago, they created a "middle ground" for themselves—a sense of place that helped them adjust to their new lives but not lose ties to their past.[1] While finding new jobs, moving into new subdivisions, and creating new associations, they forged a new world for themselves that was at once Swedish and American, but not distinctly either. This chapter examines the ways that the immigrants settled in their new homes throughout Chicago and the strategies they used to help them adjust to life outside of Sweden. Through the immigrants' voices themselves—their letters home, their diaries, their editorials, their activities—we can learn more about the encounter between the individual immigrant and the bustling city of Chicago. The stories they left behind show the importance that work, family, and community played in their lives and give us a personal look into their world.

ELLEN WINBLAD'S JOURNEY

The move to America was at once a story of hope and adventure on the one hand as well as uncertainty and loss on the other. Swedish immigrants welcomed the opportunity to find work, to build new homes, to join Swedish organizations, and to socialize with their peers. They also worried about the economy, their health, and the family they had left behind in Sweden, particularly their parents. The decision to leave their homeland to settle in Chicago was made out of economic necessity. For example, like thousands of other immigrants, Ellen Winblad left Sweden to find work and assist her family. She wrote home to her parents in Sweden, giving them a personal account of her immigrant experience and keeping them connected to her new life in Chicago. Her story is obviously unique to her, yet it parallels those of tens of thousands of young Swedes who found their way to Chicago.[2]

Although she was a young, single woman, Ellen Winblad's journey to America took place in a family context. She left Sweden in 1892 at the age of fifteen, in the company of her half brother and a small party from her home village of Torpa. They encountered rough waters on the North Sea on their way to England, but the voyage over the Atlantic from Liverpool passed smoothly and quickly. Three days after her arrival in New York, she made her way to the Englewood neighborhood of Chicago, where she quickly reconnected with her other brother, Emil. No doubt Ellen's parents had difficulty letting her go off to a faraway American city, but knowing that she was in the safe hands of her brothers provided them with some relief. Her letters home continued to be peppered with references to cousins and other family members and friends who had moved to Chicago before her—hence she was a link in an already-established pattern of chain migration from Torpa to Chicago.[3]

Ellen found employment as a domestic worker at the Chicago home of relatives with whom she lived. Her days were filled with polishing floors, cleaning rugs, doing laundry, and ironing clothes. She also sewed and mended the family's clothing and helped cook their food. During the economic downturn in 1893, she took in outside sewing to earn extra money, but observed that this was often difficult because during hard times people often just wore their old clothes. In spite of the heavy workload, Ellen observed that "it is a little more comfortable here than in Sweden."[4] She especially was impressed with the washing machine that would wring out the wet clothes, sparing the women from doing the wash by hand. Luckily she remained healthy, but she noted that during the hot summer months, when temperatures could soar to 104 degrees, many residents of the city were hospitalized with typhoid fever and sunstroke.[5] In such circumstances she felt blessed to be spared a similar fate.

Despite the hard work, Ellen Winblad fully engaged in Swedish community life in Chicago while she lived there. These activities provided an important context for her adjustment to a foreign city. In her first letter home Ellen bragged that her brother Emil's home was "like the finest gentleman's home in Sweden," but more importantly, it was directly across the street from a Swedish church, deeming it even more respectable.[6] She joined the church choir and enjoyed many outings with churchgoers, including Saturday night parties and summer excursions to the park. On one such occasion she was one of "twelve girls and our cavaliers" who enjoyed a moonlight picnic in a beautiful park setting.[7] Another memory she cherished was singing with some four hundred other Swedish girls in a performance at the Central Music Hall. Clad in white dresses and singing Swedish songs, these young women's music evoked strong recollections of Sweden.[8] On Ellen's nineteenth birthday, family members successfully planned a surprise party for her. Friends and family members crowded into the house where she lived and surprised her even further by presenting her with a fine gold watch. She was truly overcome by their generosity. These activities kept her busy and personalized the city in meaningful ways. As Ellen wrote her parents, "I am always out doing something."[9] The fact that much of what she did was with other Swedes created a Swedish dimension to her life in an American multiethnic city.

Ellen never forgot her connections to Sweden and sorely missed her parents. After seven years of living in Chicago she returned home to Sweden at age twenty-two. Ellen's parents were anxious to have their children take over their farm in Sweden. Ellen's relatives in Chicago were divided about whether to stay in Chicago or return to Sweden, no doubt reflecting the divided heart of the immigrants. Sweden represented a secure but somewhat stagnant past; Chicago offered a less predictable future, but one full of possibilities and opportunities. In the end, her brothers stayed in Chicago and it was Ellen who returned to Sweden. As her time of departure neared, she wrote her parents that "I have decided to never leave you in this life [again]."[10] When she left home as a young teenager, she "didn't know . . . what it would be like to be away from mamma and papa." Even so, she was grateful for the experience of living and working in Chicago, concluding that "it was such that I should go out in the world."[11]

SWEDISH CONNECTIONS IN CHICAGO

Just as did Ellen Winblad, many immigrants sought out relatives and friends already residing in Chicago as they looked for work and places to live. When Hilma

Svensson arrived in Chicago, she recalled that "my cousin Karl and my uncle met me. We then took the streetcar home, arriving before 9 in the morning."[12] When Hilda Svensson parted company with her traveling companions in Chicago, she "got off the train and looked out at all the people to see if there was anyone I could recognize, and then I saw my beloved sister and brother-in-law. I was so happy that I cannot describe it with a pen."[13] After leaving behind their childhood homes, and in many cases their parents as well, young women like Ellen and Hilma found an instant connection in Chicago through their relatives residing there who had gone before them.

The connections between relatives did not always go so smoothly. With the help of his traveling companion, E. E. F. Frost found his way to his relatives' home in 1906, but to his dismay, found that they were out of town: "When we came to Chicago at 9 in the morning, Per took me on the streetcar and found [his way] immediately, but there was no one home." His relatives returned from a visit to another town in Illinois a few days later and immediately opened their home to him.[14] Although many of these young, single Swedes came to Chicago without members of their immediate nuclear family with them, they quickly reestablished their connections to extended family and friends from their villages in Sweden. This process personalized the city and further suggests that their migration was not random but that it followed predetermined patterns.

Even so, the city of Chicago must have seemed like an exotic destination with so many people and nationalities present there. While E. E. F. Frost waited for his relatives in Chicago to return home, he found lodging with a saloon keeper: "I got dinner [at the saloon] and got to eat at the same table as [the saloon keeper] with piano music and birdsong. His daughter, about 12 or 13 years old, played the piano, and they had a couple of canaries that sang in time with the music. Then I went out in the park for a walk and saw everything I possibly could."[15]

In 1923, Herman Olson arrived to a somewhat different Chicago, one congested with automobiles and skyscrapers. He wrote his parents about riding the streetcar throughout the city and climbing onto the roof of a twenty-two-story building— something he had never seen before. He visited the zoo and observed the traffic with alarm: "Sometimes it's so packed with cars they can only move 2 to 3 feet at a time. . . . Olof picked me up at the station. It was so full of cars that I was nearly afraid to ride, which I can hardly believe."[16] Because the majority of these Swedes emigrated from small, rural villages, they faced a complex adjustment process. They needed to acclimate themselves to a large and modern city, find employment, and come to terms with a new and unfamiliar language. Personal connections carried with them from Sweden eased these transitions, but the reality was that Chicago was a very different place than the one to which they were accustomed.

ECONOMIC OPPORTUNITIES

Ever since the middle of the nineteenth century, Chicago had had a reputation as a place to do business and find work—a reputation well known in Sweden and beyond. Labor opportunities more than any other factor drew Swedes and other immigrants to Chicago. And once immigrants achieved some semblance of economic stability, they could devote time to community networking. The Swedish business districts themselves also helped further Swedish American culture by providing necessary and desirable goods and services in a common language. They created a middle ground where Swedes could do business in Swedish, meet other Swedes in the neighborhood, and purchase items needed for their new life in Chicago.

Chicago was an ideal environment for the growth of job opportunities for Swedish immigrants and for the creation of Swedish business districts, because business in the city as a whole was booming. As Peter A. Coclanis notes, Chicago's growth after mid-century was "the stuff of legends." Between 1850 and the 1920s, Chicago found itself at the center of a vast, expanding industrial web, fed by the expansion of capitalism on a global scale. The Erie Canal linked the Great Lakes to Buffalo and ultimately New York City in 1825; by 1848, the completion of the Illinois and Michigan Canal connected Chicago to the Mississippi River. Canals were soon overshadowed by railways, and by the mid-1850s, Chicago had already emerged as a significant center of railroad traffic. As many Americans moved further west to develop farms on the prairies, Chicago became a point of debarkation, and later it grew to be a processing center for the goods they produced, especially grains and meat. Heavy industry also expanded rapidly, particularly iron, steel, lumber, furniture, clothing, and tobacco manufacturing. As Coclanis further observes, "Chicago formed the core of one of the most heavily industrialized regions on earth before 1900."[17]

Over a million people poured into the city from around the world to find jobs in its booming economy. Not only was large industry growing, many small manufacturing and business facilities also provided work. The arrival of so many newcomers increased the demand for new housing, further expanding the construction industry where many Swedish immigrants found work. Beginning in the 1880s, new techniques in structural engineering not only allowed for the construction of skyscrapers, they also brought water, gas, steam heat, and indoor toilets to many new homes popping up around the city.[18] As new subdivisions developed to accommodate the growing population, many of these areas were annexed by Chicago to create an even more dynamic, complex, and sprawling city. As described in the previous chapter, Swedish immigrants took advantage of the opportunity to move into homes in these new neighborhoods, and in doing so they created pockets of Swedish ethnicity throughout the city.

Swedish business districts emerged in neighborhoods where Swedes resided. Although no systematic study of Swedish businesses in Chicago has been done, a few people who lived in these Swedish communities have recorded their memories of local businesses they frequently visited. For example, in the early 1960s Henry Bengston, a Swedish labor advocate, described the business district in the heavily Swedish neighborhood of Lake View at about the turn of the twentieth century. He remembered businesses such as the Petersen Furniture Store (which he describes as Nordic since it likely was Norwegian), Johanson Jewelry Store, and Axel Gustafson's Men's Store. A Swedish saloon, restaurant, rooming house, shoe store, and photo studio also dotted the landscape. He identified only one non-Scandinavian place of business in the area near Belmont Avenue and Clark Street. Perhaps one of the most popular attractions was a shop named "Dalkullan," a store that had relocated from an older Swedish district around Oak Street specializing in Copenhagen Snuff, Swedish newspapers, and books. Its competitor was another shop, run by Carl Youngberg, that had also moved from the old Swede Town. According to Bengston, Youngberg "listened patiently to his customers' problems and often extreme political and religious views. He let them all have their say and encouraged them to each in his own way solve the problems of the world and eternity. In the meantime he sold them newspapers, snuff and good nickel cigars."[19]

Another densely populated Swedish neighborhood was the South Side's Englewood region, and a distinctly Swedish business district developed there as well. Edward E. Osberg was born there to parents who were Swedish immigrants, and in the late twentieth century, he recorded his memories of growing up in a pervasively Swedish American community. Osberg described a Swedish dry goods store, bakery, hardware store, and drugstore as well as Swedish doctors, bankers, and funeral homes. Not only did these types of businesses take care of most of the immigrants' needs, they also personalized the city for nearby residents. For example, Mr. Peterson, who owned the local shoe store, seemed to have plenty of business but was rather unfriendly to his customers. Clarence Bergstrom sold Osberg's Uncle Oscar his first car, and Mr. Jennings, who owned a variety store, gave Osberg a candy bar every time his grandfather sent him there on an errand. Knute Malm operated the nearby delicatessen and was a great storyteller, plying the local children with tall tales about Sweden's legendary king Gustavus Adolphus. "Upside Down Johnson" was so named because he printed all of his store's advertisements upside down in the local newspaper, and real estate developer Clarence O. Rosen helped found the Englewood Business Men's Association. The city may have been a very big place, but to young children such

Figure 4. Dalkullen Publishing and Importing Company. Taken around 1900, this storefront was located at 113 Oak Street, the old "Swede Town" neighborhood, but soon relocated to Lake View. Many Swedish businesses had by this time already started relocating to the Lake View, Andersonville, and Englewood neighborhoods. Courtesy of Swedish-American Archives of Greater Chicago, North Park University, Chicago.

as Edward E. Osberg, life came down to activities and personalities that were centered on a handful of city blocks in a tightly knit Swedish community.[20]

Chicago's employment opportunities and housing developments were well known in Sweden due to two main factors: the letters immigrants wrote back to Sweden and the arrival of Swedish American newspapers detailing working conditions in American cities. The Swedish ethnic press was very active during the heyday of immigration, and Chicago proved to be a center of this activity. At one time or another, at least thirty-six Swedish-language newspapers emerged in Chicago, ranging from pietistic religious newspapers to more liberal secular ones. One of the long-standing periodicals was *Hemlandet, det Gamla och det Nya*, the mouthpiece of the Swedish Augustana Lutheran denomination. Founded in Galesburg, Illinois in 1855, its publishers relocated to Chicago in 1859. Swedish Methodists also moved their newspaper, *Sändebudet*, to Chicago from Rockford in 1862. The Swedish Mission Friends started *Missions-Vännen* in 1874, and three years later the Swedish Baptists founded *Evangelisk Tidskrift*. A secular newspaper, *Svenska Amerikanaren*, founded in 1866, displayed an antireligious bent. It united with the *Nya Verlden* in 1877, and the new enterprise was christened *Svenska Tribunen*. Another *Svenska Amerikanaren* took its place, this one published by the radical journalist Herman Roos. Taken together, these newspapers presented a vast array of political and religious opinions, and continued to do so well into the twentieth century. Although many of them targeted Swedes living throughout America, the newspapers also heavily reported on activities taking place in Swedish Chicago. Not only did their articles reflect a vibrant and diverse Swedish American community, they also focused attention on opportunities available in Chicago for employment, entertainment, worship, and ethnic connections.[21]

Oftentimes residents of rural Swedish parishes knew more about what was taking place in Chicago than in Stockholm—particularly if they had relatives or friends who had settled there. In their letters, Swedish immigrants perceptively described working conditions in Chicago to their relatives in Sweden, usually balancing accounts of opportunities for success with descriptions of the city's often precarious economy. In this manner, Swedes in Chicago assisted others still living in Sweden to make an informed decision about emigration. For example, in the 1880s, Anders Gustafsson witnessed a decade of vast expansion in Chicago's population and physical size. Despite the fact that he was himself an immigrant, he observed the large number of newcomers arriving to Chicago with some concern. Newly arrived immigrants were forced to take whatever work they could get, effectively keeping wages low and making finances difficult for those who were already established in the city.[22] Three years later, Anders still expressed some alarm about the newcomers. "We can get along quite nicely here, if we just have a little bit of money. Even here, things are more expensive than they were several years ago. There is not much work to be had either, the reason being that so many thousands of immigrants come here daily, and they all want to have work, food, and lodging. Employers pay so little for the work, and food gets more and more expensive, for the rich know how to take advantage of a situation."[23]

Women usually found positions as domestic workers or they sewed piecework for extra income. Historian Joy Lintelman argues that the move to Chicago for these young, single Swedish women represented a positive and lucrative opportunity. Swedes in Chicago viewed domestic service as a respectable occupation for women, much more so than factory work, and many were attracted to the city to find domestic positions. Swedish women also brought with them from Sweden skills in domestic work that could be put to good use by their new employers.[24] Anders Gustafsson believed that these skills put women in a strong position to find jobs. Although it is difficult to prove his perceptions, he observed that "it's easier for the girls to find work than it is for the men," mainly because Swedish maids were in such strong demand.[25] Another immigrant, Betty Johnsson, whose story is told in more detail later in this chapter, usually had no problem finding employment: "I can tell you that I am in my usual position and that they have increased my salary now for me so that I get 3 dollars per week."[26] One advantage for domestic workers was that they frequently lived with their employers, giving them a secure place to live while still allowing them to take part in activities within Chicago's Swedish community. These domestic positions were not without their drawbacks, however. The work was difficult, the hours were long, and there was little to protect a worker from abuse at the hands of an employer. Despite the fact that Hanna Carlson discouraged her sister from leaving home at the young age of twenty to seek employment in Chicago, she offered to help her find work should she decide to come. "I will find a position for you, I hope that will work; it is not the worst." Hanna revealed her own ambivalence about immigration when she advised: "you ask if it is dumb to travel here, I cannot say that [it is] for those who want to work and earn money . . . [but] you have it so well where you are."[27]

A more detailed and pessimistic account among the letters, which looked at the tenuous economic climate in Chicago during the 1890s, came from L. J. Peterson. As the decade wore on, jobs became difficult to find due to the stagnating American economy, and immigrants had to weigh carefully the potential costs and benefits of a move to America. Writing in 1891, Peterson's observations convey a sense of the uncertain job market in urban America in comparison with the slower but, in his eyes, more predictable rural economy of Sweden. He wrote that "some of the poor here are lucky and become rich. It's clear that it's easier for a poor person to get along here, even if they must (as I) remain poor for as long as they live." He advised that people who were financially secure in Sweden should remain there, even though they might have opportunities to do well in America.

He cautioned that "the matter of leaving the certain good of the homeland for an uncertain good here is worth consideration, . . ." and he himself regretted that he had left Sweden permanently. Even so, he indicated that he would help ease the transition for relatives who wished to locate to Chicago by helping them to find work and housing, and thus to "avoid much of the despair that many newcomers must go through here."[28] Peterson obviously had mixed feelings about his decision to move to Chicago: success came through hard work, but it was not guaranteed in the city's turbulent economy. And even though he believed that a comfortably established farmer was better off staying in Sweden, few there enjoyed such a position and hence had little hope of economic improvement in Sweden. As evidenced from the continually growing stream of immigrants, many Swedes chose to try their luck in Chicago. However reluctantly, Peterson would do what he could to help family and friends immigrating to Chicago find work.

Many thousands of young Swedish men found jobs in construction work, particularly in decades such as the 1880s and 1920s when new construction boomed. Herman Olson described the conditions of such work when he wrote to his parents back in Sweden. In his first letter home in 1923, he told his parents that he lived on the South Side of Chicago with an American family in order to be closer to his work. He also benefited by finding work with his relative, Arvid, a rather successful contractor. His starting wages, he wrote, were 82½ cents per hour, and he worked forty-four hours per week "when you first start, then it becomes a little better."[29] The next year, he wrote that he was working as a bricklayer. "They're building a three-story house that I am working on. They take on their buildings so that they have many of them at a time. A little ways from here, they've bricked up a two-story [building] for six families."[30] Herman continued to work for Arvid, cementing the foundations of houses and laying brick, and observed that "Arvid and his partner have made good money this year, they're building . . . small houses . . . 2 to 3 stories. One now has 27 'flats' (or places for 27 families)."[31] He also offered to help others find work, but recommended that it would be best if a person arrived in the city with a trade. The economy dictated the level of success of the immigrant in Chicago, but a safety net of friends and acquaintances usually mitigated the possibility of outright failure.

LETTERS HOME

Maintaining connections with family in Sweden was an important anchor in the immigrants' lives. They exchanged information not only about the economic climate in Chicago, but also about agricultural conditions and crop yields in Sweden, and about the health of loved ones and friends. Swedes in Chicago craved for details about life back in Sweden, and greetings and news about family and friends passed freely over the ocean. Hanna Gustafson appreciated the news she heard from her cousin in Sweden: "It was nice to hear from you, and to hear that your children are healthy and strong, and that sister Anna shall come for a visit." She longed to join expeditions to pick lingonberries in the Swedish forest, commenting that "we can buy lingonberries in the stores here, but they are so sour and awful."[32] L. J. Peterson was also concerned that the connections remained firm between him and those back in Sweden. He wrote to "please give our dearest greetings" to family in Sweden and to "others who might know us," and he sent warm regards from other family members in Chicago. Many other immigrant letters bear witness to tender feelings and a desire to stay connected. Anders Gustafsson sent news of loved ones in Chicago, offered to take in a young relative should she come to Chicago, and pleaded with his brother-in-law that he not "be forgotten by [his] relatives when [he] lives in such a faraway foreign country . . . send me a few simple lines!"[33]

Family connections only went so far in protecting immigrants from dangers that surrounded them. Although the worst cases of cholera epidemics had diminished by 1880, the city still struggled with pollution, a poor water supply, and overcrowding. These conditions contributed to outbreaks of diseases such as diphtheria, whooping cough, typhoid, and smallpox, and epidemics continued to break out until the early twentieth century.[34] The writers of most letters back to Sweden were preoccupied with health and the reality of death and aging, often infusing their language with religious sentiments that undoubtedly helped them cope with such uncertainties. And it became clear in their comments that good health was a tenuous thing in both Sweden and Chicago.

Like many families, Anders Gustafsson's worked together to survive financially. In 1885, he wrote to his relatives that "Even though we are getting older, we get on well because the girls are living with us. . . . We work together for our income, so that's OK, even though the pay for work is low, so it's quite hard for many to make ends meet."[35] Pooling resources helped Anders and his family weather Chicago's economic uncertainty. But working together could not assure good health and ongoing financial stability. In a series of letters written to his brother-in-law from 1880 to 1907, Anders discussed health issues in an almost fatalistic manner. In 1880, he wrote to Johannes Jansson, sympathizing that Johannes had become too sick to work, "but we must do what the Lord grants us." As far as his own family's health, Anders commented, "We can't complain! We are getting old and our health is beginning to fail, and are beginning to await the end, but we must thank God that we do not thus far need to lie bedridden." Anders noted that for the time being his daughters enjoyed good health and "we work together to make our living. As long as they are good to us, and stay with us, all goes well, but should they ever leave us, we would be in a desperate position."[36] If correspondence from Sweden was delayed, Anders feared the worst: "Since I have not received an answer to the letter I sent you in July, I shall now write you a few more lines in case you are still living, which we do not know. . . . I hope this letter has found all of you in possession of the good gift of health, which is the greatest treasure which we may have here in this earthly life."[37] Over the next two decades, Anders's letters continued to be filled with references to health and death. By 1907, he had reached his eighty-fourth birthday, his wife had died, but he continued to write.[38] The following year, Anders's daughter wrote to her cousin herself, after her father had passed away. "I am alone now," she wrote, "so that time passes rather slowly, but as long as I have my health, things are all right."[39]

The preoccupation with health on both sides of the Atlantic was reflected in many other immigrants' letters. Charles G. Sundell wrote to his parents that "It was much to my happiness that I read that all of you at home there have the precious gift of health, and are feeling well. This is an indescribably great goodness from God; to enjoy the treasure of health is the basis for our daily happiness, especially when we are also guarded from the many accidents and dangers in life which plague so many people."[40] In 1891, L. J. Peterson wrote to his brother-in-law, "It is a great thing as time goes by to have one's health and to feel content. Anna is now healthier than I can remember her having been in a long time, and Hanna is as healthy and happy as she was before her long fever, but is not yet in possession of her old frame of mind and strength."[41] Epidemics and poor health care created an environment of uncertainty among the immigrants and their loved ones in Sweden.

One particularly poignant story that reflects the uncertainties of life in immigrant Chicago emerges from the letters of Betty Johnsson. Betty was a fairly typical young woman who emigrated to Chicago in the early 1880s to find work as a domestic maid in an American family. Her letters reflect the mixed emotions surrounding her departure from Sweden and the risk of illness faced by all immigrants. She lived for a time with her cousin and his wife before finding work, and she attended a Swedish church and participated in parties and summer excursions. Overall, she liked her new life: "I can let you know that I'm really enjoying Chicago. This summer they planted a big green park. It is so beautiful . . . they have water . . . so that you can ride a boat. . . . There are also big, beautiful trees and even flowers that are so beautiful I cannot describe them to you."[42] But thoughts of Sweden and her family were never far away. In 1882, she wrote, "Yes, it would be so pleasant if I could get together with you in the fall one day this year, but I can't. But I hope God gives you beautiful days."[43] Three years later, these feelings remained strong. "I see in your letter that you often remember me. I am glad to hear that you have not forgotten me, although I am a long ways from you. I have wished many times to get to see you but we are so far separated that it seems quite impossible."[44] One year later, Betty Johnsson became sick and died, never making it back to see her family.

After her death in 1886 Betty Johnsson's cousin, O. H. Peterson, wrote to Betty's family about the issue of settling her small estate and taking care of her possessions. In Sweden, law dictated that when a person died, the court inventory all of his or her possessions and determine a value for the estate. The dead person's debts would be settled and law mandated that one-eighth the value of the estate be given to the poor. Possessions of the deceased were sometimes sold at the time of death in order to liquidate the estate.[45] Contrary to the custom in Sweden, it was not easy to sell Betty's belongings in Chicago, but the process her cousin followed in settling her estate resembled the procedure in Sweden: "We found that it was difficult to settle [Betty's affairs], partly because most of the clothes she left were quite worn and torn here and there; and partly because it is rather unusual in this country for people to buy old clothes."[46] Peterson and his mother, a sister to Betty Johnsson's mother, settled her debts, sold what they could, and sent the rest of her valuable belongings to her parents in Sweden. In an apparent response to a request by Betty's parents, Peterson also charged her eighteen dollars for the ten weeks she lived with his family before her death. He wrote his aunt apologetically, "Now I should not name such a small thing for one who was such a close relative to me if she had not left any money after her, and you asked me to let you know about the state of affairs. I even want to say that she wanted to pay herself after she got work [again]," but her premature death prevented her from doing so.[47]

The inventory of Betty's possessions that Peterson sent to his aunt and uncle in Sweden provides an interesting profile of the life of an immigrant maid.

> I'll send the following things which Betty left behind: A hair-chain from Betty's hair, which probably cost 5 or 6 dollars; a gold watch which cost 25 dollars; a ring; a breast-pin, another one which has the pin broken off; a man's breast pin; a little knife; a glove-buttoner; a finger-box, a collar button, and so on; two handkerchiefs; one Swedish silk shawl, one item of hand-work out of silk and velvet which she sewed herself, with others; and a name plate from Betty's coffin . . . to remember her by. The girl who took Betty's position has taken the chain which Betty has around her neck in the portrait. When my wife asked her about it she said that Betty had given it to her. All her Swedish clothes she had given away. She was buried in a light gray silk dress which was very expensive; for here it is common to dress in [one's best] clothes. Such presents which she received went back to those who gave them to her. . . . I sent a fine box to Morris, for they were not engaged . . .

A dear greeting, in closing from me and my wife. Let us hear from you at the earliest convenient chance. I will gladly communicate any further information. Written with love by your nephew and cousin, O. H. Peterson. (A lock of Betty's hair is enclosed.)[48]

He wrote again the next month, asking verification of the package's arrival and informing them that Morris, Betty's one-time boyfriend, had married someone else.[49] For Morris and for Peterson, life continued, but for Betty's parents, a box full of their daughter's belongings, punctuated by a lock of her hair, undoubtedly confirmed their worst fears—that they would never see their daughter again once she had departed for America.

Thus, letters home reflected the immigrants' conflicting emotions of pain, joy, and regret. Charles G. Sundell received financial assistance from his father in Sweden to help him through some difficult times. "When have I been deserving of such?" he lamented. He declared to his father "how *good* you have been to me, your child, and son," and he prayed for "forgiveness for all of the sorrow which I caused you when I was still at home." His lack of obedience caused him deep regret and sorrow. But then his tone changed as he shared the news of his recent marriage to Ida Maria Johansson from Princeton, Illinois. "I hope it is happy news to you," he wrote.[50]

Hanna Carlson, in expressing her concern that her sister Hildur not leave home for Chicago, also conveyed the emotional difficulties that she herself experienced after leaving her childhood home. She told Hildur, "Never have you talked about wishing to travel here before; it made me astonished and grieved, for I cannot agree that you shall go from mamma and home yet, Hildur . . . for you are not more than 20 years old." Hanna missed her mother, and in perhaps an effort to appease her own guilt, pleaded with her sister that "it would be so hard for mamma if you leave." In the days before telecommunication, departing for America meant leaving behind opportunities for conversation and spontaneous contact with loved ones in Sweden. Hanna felt this loss deeply. "You say you have no one to talk with," she wrote her sister, "but you have mamma now; if you come here maybe you shall wish more than once that you could talk to her!" Her letter closed with this final admonition: "You don't know what it is like to be without a home, but if you move from home [in Sweden], you will get to experience it."[51] Hanna Carlson, as noted in chapter 1, married Carl Olson and remained in Chicago. Her sister Hildur eventually forgot about her boyfriend, Eric, who had moved to Chicago. She married someone else and settled in Sweden close to her childhood home. Surely even those who looked forward to the opportunities offered by a city such as Chicago missed those whom they left behind.

FIGURE 5. Hanna Carlson, taken shortly before she immigrated in 1910. Like thousands of other women, Hanna Carlson left rural Sweden to become a domestic worker in Chicago. Author's personal collection.

CELEBRATING COMMUNITY

Connections to family and friends back in Sweden and in Chicago could not always alleviate the challenges of adjustment to life in a new land. Many Swedes in Chicago found comfort in their faith as a counterpoint to the risks faced in a modernizing city. Individual attitudes toward religion varied, but immigrants often viewed the Swedish church as a sign of stability in their community as well as a place to meet other Swedes like themselves. Symbolically, these churches stood as imposing structures, indicating an immigrant people who, in some measure, could shape and influence their own neighborhoods. Churches gave an air of respectability and continuity to their otherwise changeable lives. For example, Herman Olson asked his brother, Ivar, in a letter home, "How is mother? She maybe wonders if I go to church at all. I've been in Swedish church several times. Last Sunday I went with Mother's uncle. The old man gets on well, fat as a pig."[52] Herman believed that his mother would view his time in Chicago more favorably if she knew he occasionally attended a Swedish church, realizing that Chicago was not as foreign as she might believe it to be.

The Lutheran faith played a significant role in the life of Anders Gustafsson, representing traditional values that linked his past to his present circumstances in Chicago. In his letters to Sweden, Anders noted, "Here at our church, *Immanuals Församling*, we have an excellent minister, [who] preaches both in Swedish and English. If parents would only raise their children in the fear of the Lord, there is certainly no lack of available education in Christian ways here . . . we have two services every Sunday, as well as evenings of hymn-singing . . ."[53] Despite his belief that some Swedes in Chicago had "forgotten the church and the word of God and the priest," Anders observed that "Over 2000 people belong to [our Swedish church in Chicago]. . . . So [for] those who will hear the word of God, there is plenty of opportunity."[54] In the midst of a city that offered new ideas and possibilities, Anders Gustafsson clung to the church as a sign of stability and tradition in the Swedish community, and lamented the fact that not all immigrants felt the same way.

Like Ellen Winblad, many immigrants linked their social life with the life of the church. Betty Johnsson—enjoying community life before her premature death—told her parents about the time a group of nearly two hundred Swedes took a train ten and one-half miles out of the city to a park. The group stayed the entire day, bringing food with them and enjoying each other's company. The picnic was an annual event: "Once a year during the summer time the minister announces in the church so as many Swedes as want to can go. So we had Swedish preaching there. There were two ministers, not including our own, among the congregation."[55] In some cases, gatherings of Swedes in Chicago were larger than anything that could be experienced in Sweden's rural parishes, and provided a context for friendship and marriages. Large crowds and community spirit characterized many assemblies.[56] Furthermore, church meetings and other celebrations provided the perfect opportunity for future spouses to meet. In a fictional yet descriptive account of Swedish Chicago by a man using the pseudonym Sven Stubbe, the author provided some amusing observations about the mating process in the church:

> As [soon as] the young people are married, they disappear from the church, despite the fact that they got to know each other in the "Youth Education" [group] at church. . . . Old unmarried girls, ugly as sin, can find their future husbands here. Outside on the street you cannot speak to girls; here in the church you can become acquainted with them. The churches are America's marriage bureau.[57]

Certainly church records corroborate that many couples met at Swedish churches in Chicago after migrating from different regions of Sweden with their families or as single young adults, and married in those churches. Some made lifelong commitments to membership in those churches, others transferred their membership

FIGURE 6. A North Side Mission Church Picnic in Chicago's Lincoln Park in the 1880s (later known as the First Covenant Church). These types of gatherings were common for the various Swedish churches in Chicago, helping to reinforce Swedish community ties in the city. Courtesy of Covenant Archives and Historical Library, North Park University, Chicago.

to other churches in Chicago, and still others dropped out of church activities once they had met their match.

Whether sponsored by the churches, secular clubs, or just informal gatherings in neighborhoods, social events kept young immigrants busy. Birthday parties provided the perfect excuse to celebrate their common life together. Betty Johnsson wrote to her brothers and sisters about the various parties she attended during the Christmas season. Herman Olson and his new wife Frida also wrote about his birthday celebration. The weather was warm, so they enjoyed homemade beer and some schnapps. "Nearly everyone makes beer here, you can buy malt and hops and brew it yourself. We make it together with Albert, about 25 liters per week. We drink it all; it is 7 times better than the warm, bad water during the summertime."[58] Many immigrants took part in some of the larger community festivals where they could celebrate their shared ethnic heritage. All of these social events highlighted the network of strong personal relationships created by Swedish immigrants in Chicago, relationships that were reinforced through Swedish organizations and celebrations. Immigrant letters overflowed with excitement about new friends and festive parties, painting a stark contrast to life in rural Sweden and helping in some ways to justify the move to Chicago.

FINDING A MIDDLE GROUND

As is evident in their personal correspondence with family members in Sweden, Swedish immigrants in Chicago maintained strong transatlantic ties. These points of connection created concrete lines of communication between Chicago and Sweden. Swedish immigrants briefed their relatives at home about economic conditions in Chicago, as well as about the religious and social climate of the city. When they could, Chicago's Swedes assisted relatives back home who desired to emigrate. Immigrant letters show how time spent with family and friends in the city was an important aspect of urban immigrant life. Living circumstances and health conditions became less tenuous over time, but immigrants continued to look to strong networks of friends and family to ease their adjustment into city life.

Although the city was very large, Swedish immigrants found ways to make it more personal, and in doing so, forged a middle ground between Sweden and America. Institutions created by Swedes provided an important backdrop to their everyday lives and added a sense of stability, familiarity, and respectability to the city. Ties with family left behind remained important, even after someone emigrated from Sweden, but over time new primary relationships supplemented the old, and the churches and other social organizations provided the context for these new connections. Family already in the city, church and club connections, and social networks created in Chicago were not only comforting, they were essential to the survival and well-being of the typical immigrant. The security net created by churches and fraternal organizations provided necessary institutional support for an otherwise precarious existence—and they continued to provide such support even as the newcomers moved within the city of Chicago. Swedish immigrants in Chicago brought their traditions with them, not merely transplanting them, but transforming and re-creating them into a Swedish American identity that proved meaningful in their new circumstances.

CHAPTER 3

CHURCH GROWTH IN SWEDISH CHICAGO

The motivation for this step [of building a new Lutheran church in the Lake View neighborhood], which we will take with the knowledge and approval of the mother church, is the same as was made effective by other Swedish Lutheran Churches built in different parts of the city of Chicago and its suburbs. . . . A sound mission work in Christian and churchly spirit is needed [in Lake View] and we seriously doubt that such can come to stand with a less organized congregation. . . . Our . . . work shall carry on.

—Johan Enander, on behalf of the founders of Trinity Lutheran Church,
in a letter to the Immanuel Lutheran Church congregation
explaining their need for a new church, 1883[1]

Swedish churches were an integral part of the Swedish immigrant community, as evidenced by the extensive network of religious institutions built by Swedes in Chicago. Swedes took advantage of Chicago's young, malleable urban environment to create associations that allowed them to carry on familiar religious traditions, to modify them according to their new residential circumstances, and to make their churches responsive to the kinds of needs revealed in immigrant letters. When Swedes began to move from their older ethnic enclaves in the 1880s and settle in new, suburban neighborhoods of Chicago in subsequent decades, they replicated diverse religious denominations and the theological debates that went along with them in a number of outlying regions. This served to extend the Swedish community throughout the Chicago area and to provide a context for mobility within the city. Through their churches—and organizations within those churches—Swedish immigrants created concrete networks of affiliation that gave many of them a much-needed sense of relationship with other church-going Swedes. As Dag Blanck points out, the very act of joining a Swedish American church represented a deliberate decision on the part of members to actively engage in Swedish American community life.[2] Ethnicity was thus not merely an issue of heritage, it was more importantly a matter of choice and effort, as measured by the number of churches built by Swedish settlers throughout Chicago.

Churches created in Swedish Chicago reflected expressions of religious fervor among the immigrants as well as the desire to project a positive image of Swedes in America. As Raymond Breton argues, this duality is the very essence of ethnic identity. Ethnic affiliations within immigrant communities, he contends, are the spontaneous creation of immigrants at a grassroots level and, at the same time, are consciously created by elites within the group.[3] This generalization also holds true for Swedish churches in America—an obviously important part of community life. Once created, Swedish churches and denominations became linked with national subcommunities to which members held strong loyalties. Leaders of these national denominations confronted social, political, and moral issues head-on, deliberately creating an image of Swedes as a group that fully embraced white American Protestant values. Even as they aided in the adjustment process, by 1920 the churches also mirrored the transition of the Swedish community in Chicago: an American-born, English-speaking generation of Swedish offspring grew to outnumber the Swedish-born immigrants in the city. This generational transition resulted in the forging of a new, American-based Swedish identity.[4]

The religious outlook of Swedes in Chicago was directly rooted in nineteenth-century theological developments in Sweden, and Swedish churches in Chicago provided channels through which familiar religious debates could be continued and adapted to new circumstances. The interplay between the Swedish Lutheran Church and the dissenting free church movement in Sweden played itself out among immigrant churches in America. To religious Swedes—the majority of whom came from rural, agrarian backgrounds—the Swedish churches validated their decisions to leave their homeland by assuring them that an important aspect of their past had been re-created in Chicago. Despite the fact that churches were vehicles through which traditions could be maintained, they were not mere duplicates of their Swedish counterparts. Theological debates, the process of church expansion, and the creation of organizations within the church all were affected by an urban context in which every institution needed to be created from scratch. Swedish churches in Chicago developed a voluntary character very different from that of the Church of Sweden, where membership was automatic at birth and funding was generated by the state.[5] An examination of how Swedes built their churches, how those churches spread into new enclaves throughout the city, and how organizations within the churches created an all-encompassing church community reveals how these Swedish immigrants shaped their new lives in America. These institutions helped immigrants adapt to urban life and maintain particularistic strains of their religious identity in a city known for its diversity.

RELIGION AS A DIMENSION OF IMMIGRATION

A number of historians have recognized the importance of the religious dimension of the immigration experience, although they disagree about whether religion represented conservative or progressive tendencies within an immigrant community.[6] Oscar Handlin emphasizes traditional elements in the relationship between immigration and religious expression; in stressing the disorienting effect of immigration upon individuals, he argues that the immigrants' religion added a dimension of continuity to their otherwise uprooted lives. To Handlin, immigrant churches in the United States were an extension of their old-world roots, conservative and backward-looking.[7] Timothy L. Smith disagrees, suggesting that immigrant churches contributed to the preservation and the revision of inherited religion. He writes, "Immigrant congregations served diverse family, group, and individual interests. They were not transplants of traditional institutions but communities of commitment and, therefore, arenas of change."[8] Furthermore, these communities sharpened the boundaries between the committed and the noncommitted, within and among immigrant groups. Scott E. Erickson applies this idea to the Swedes when he examines the founding of new Swedish denominations in America. He argues that "The Swedes . . . made a choice (commitment) to join an ethnic religious body. They did not inherit a tradition when they arrived in America. They invented a new tradition" that was essentially Swedish American. Denominations arose to "draw boundaries around voluntary associations" in order to guarantee the survival of the churches themselves as well as the ideas they embraced.[9] The churches were, in other words, direct products of Swedish immigrants living in a new environment where they could create their own institutions.

For many of the Swedes in Chicago, religion undoubtedly provided continuity in their lives, but the Chicago context after 1880 demanded significant innovation. Churches responded to the needs of a newly urban people who were actively engaged in the world around them. Chicagoans as a whole believed churches lent credibility to their city. In 1897, the *Chicago Tribune* asserted the respectability of Chicago, claiming that "The Queen City of the lakes outdoes all other cities in the number and variety of its religious and educational institutions."[10] Religious organizations and the institutions that they spawned were expected to create a civilized environment for a city with a reputation for lawlessness. The ethnic context from which many churches arose was a significant ingredient of religious institution-building.[11] Ethnic churches played an important role in Chicago's growth and expansion, and they added a meaningful dimension to the experience of immigrants in the city. In a large city speckled with a variety of ethnic enclaves, churches became points of connection for like-minded immigrants and provided an institutional mediation between the immigrants and their urban surroundings.

Certainly not all Swedes in Chicago joined churches after arriving in the city; however, churches were undoubtedly the strongest ethnic institutions in the Swedish community. Membership in the mainline Swedish churches ranged from 21 percent of the Swedish population in 1890 to 36 percent in 1920.[12] These figures

Table 1a. Membership in Chicago's Swedish Churches, 1880–1920

Denomination	1880	1890	1900	1910	1920
Augustana Lutheran	2461	4231	5784	9776	11,056
Mission Covenant	—	871	1719	2503	4596
Swedish Baptist	208	2091	2390	2897	3018
Swedish Methodist	715	1705	2154	2563	2307
Total Membership	3384	8898	12,047	17,739	20,977

Table 1b. Church Membership as Percentage of Swedish-Born Population in Chicago

Denomination	1880	1890	1900	1910	1920
Augustana Lutheran	19.0%	9.8%	11.8%	15.0%	18.9%
Mission Covenant	—	2.0%	3.5%	3.8%	7.8%
Swedish Baptist	1.6%	4.9%	4.9%	4.5%	5.2%
Swedish Methodist	5.5%	4.0%	4.4%	3.9%	3.9%
Total Membership	26.2%	20.7%	24.7%	27.3%	35.8%
Total Swedish Born	12,930	43,032	48,836	65,035	58,563

Table 1c. Church Membership as Percentage of Swedish Stock*

Denomination	1880	1890	1900	1910	1920
Augustana Lutheran	—	6.8%	5.6%	8.4%	9.1%
Mission Covenant	—	1.4%	1.7%	2.1%	3.8%
Swedish Baptist	—	3.4%	2.3%	2.5%	2.5%
Swedish Methodist	—	2.7%	2.1%	2.2%	1.9%
Total Membership	—	14.3%	11.7%	15.2%	17.3%
Total Swedish Stock	—	62,235	103,220	116,740	121,326

*Swedish Stock includes Swedish-born and their American-born children.

do not include other immigrants who attended Swedish American churches but did not join them, nor does it include less formal denominations that did not record their membership data. Hence, the impact of Swedish religious institutions upon the Swedish population in Chicago was very significant—even greater than the statistics themselves suggest. When Swedes moved to new areas of the city, they started new churches before they began other ethnic associations. These churches were not always unified in their attempts to provide community leadership; rather, the very diversity of options for religious affiliation reflected the often divisive nature of theological debates within the Swedish community. The end result was a broad array of Swedish American churches to which members attached a great deal of loyalty. Congregations and denominations became, in Timothy L. Smith's words, important "communities of commitment" for the Swedish immigrants.[13]

RELIGIOUS DEVELOPMENTS IN SWEDEN AND SWEDISH AMERICA

The religious identification of Swedes in Chicago was rooted in the theological debates and social developments of nineteenth-century Sweden, manifested and adapted in the new land. Swedish immigrants, influenced by Lutheran traditions and pietistic undercurrents, established and joined churches in keeping with their particular religious outlook. The Augustana Lutheran Church became the largest Swedish denomination and was most closely related to the Church of Sweden. Other denominations, including the Evangelical Covenant Church, drew more heavily upon pietistic influences. Although based in Swedish religious developments, all Swedish churches in America operated independently from their counterparts in Sweden and developed characteristics of expansion that reflected the growth and movement of the Swedish population.

The Church of Sweden, Lutheran in nature and firmly linked with the Swedish state, served as the official interpreter of the Bible in Sweden and gave visual evidence of the hierarchical nature of the relationship between laity, clergy, and crown. Pietistic influences that stressed personal devotion and relationship to God and a living faith originated in seventeenth-century Germany and posed a threat to the state church as these ideas gained popularity in Sweden. The Crown issued the Conventicle Decree of 1726, the strongest of several such acts, which prohibited private religious gatherings and represented an early attempt by the state to retain control of religious thought and expression. Nevertheless, the church's position as religious authority did not go unchallenged. The *läsare* (reader) movement, made up of people who met to read and study the Bible in informal conventicles, increased in popularity in the early nineteenth century despite the decree prohibiting such meetings. Religious revivalism spread in the 1830s and 1840s, gaining a widespread following and leading to the repeal of the Conventicle Decree in 1858. Revivalism had a democratizing effect upon Swedish society as it encouraged laypersons to take leadership positions in religious settings, undermining the hegemony and hierarchical relationships evident in the state church.[14]

Swedish revivalism received a boost from outside influences. George Scott, an English Methodist who arrived to Sweden in 1830, built upon the momentum of the pietistic *läsare*. He furthered the revivalistic sentiment with his preaching and by organizing missionary efforts and temperance organizations. After a fund-raising trip to the United States, Scott returned to Sweden and began publishing *Pietisten* in 1841, a religious newspaper that became influential in the free church movement. Although he was eventually forced to leave Sweden in 1842, Scott's influence continued through subsequent leaders, such as Carl Olof Rosenius and P. P. Waldenström, both of whom became editors of *Pietisten*. Baptists also made their way to Sweden, and between 1848 and 1859, four thousand adults were baptized, a sharp departure from infant baptism endorsed by the Church of Sweden.[15]

Most *läsare* in Sweden remained part of the Church of Sweden, however, until their separatist tendencies could no longer be contained. As Karl A. Olsson points out, spontaneous revivalism in Sweden eventually gave way to a more structured religious movement. Theological differences could no longer be confined to a unified Swedish church, and in 1878, the Free Church Conference decided to form its own denomination, the Swedish Mission Covenant Church. This new group stressed the greater importance of congregation over denomination, but its very formation revealed the inherent tension between the two positions as the denominational structure linked the local churches. Seven years later, the Swedish Evangelical Mission Covenant Church in America would organize in a similar fashion but, as Olsson notes, "the social circumstances in which the two groups were born and were to live their lives were vastly different."[16]

In addition to the free church movement, two other social movements in nineteenth-century Sweden—the labor and temperance crusades—provided an important step in the modernization of the Swedish state. Torkel Jansson argues that voluntary associations created by these social movements filled a potentially dangerous vacuum during Sweden's transition to modern capitalism. The crucial point Jansson stresses is "the new idea of coming together regardless of given and fixed relations, the principle of voluntary contribution."[17] Sven Lundquist points out that the free church, temperance, and trade union movements gave ordinary people a political voice and promoted dialogue over revolution. The Swedish popular movements created a horizontal solidarity in the form of the congregation, lodge, or trade union, to replace the vertical relationships of the old society, such as master-servant or priest-parishioner. Associations helped create a new

value system by channeling "dissatisfaction in the struggle for power" and establishing collective goals of a religious, moral, or political character. The popular
movements provided a new morality during a time of immense change. By 1920,
the free church, temperance, and trade union movements were nearly equal in
strength, involving almost one-third of the Swedish population.[18]

Swedish church growth in America, while drawing on these Swedish theological and social developments, occurred in a context of institutional freedom. The
majority of church-going Swedes in America attended an Augustana Lutheran
Church, the largest Swedish denomination established in the United States. The
history of Swedish Lutheranism in America began in 1848 when the first Swedish
Lutheran congregation was formed in New Sweden, Iowa, closely followed by the
founding in 1850 of the Andover, Illinois church by Lars Paul Esbjörn. Esbjörn,
an ordained pastor in the Church of Sweden, had been influenced by the *läsare*
movement while in Sweden, as had his coworkers, Ture Nilsson Hasselquist and
Erland Carlsson. Their sympathy with pietistic and liberal influences jeopardized
their chances for promotion within the Swedish church system. That fact, combined with a belief in a divine call to serve Swedes who had resettled in the new
land, spurred them to move to America.

Although these men always served as defenders of the Lutheran tradition and
doctrine, they faced vastly different conditions in America from the well-established church structure of Sweden. Esbjörn became an itinerant minister, traveling to a number of frontier towns in the Middle West, organizing congregations,
building churches, and making preaching tours. Hasselquist followed him to
America, and eventually became the first president of the Augustana Lutheran
Synod in 1860. At the urging of Hasselquist and Paul Andersen, a Norwegian
pastor in Chicago, Erland Carlsson accepted the call to serve Immanuel Lutheran
Church in Chicago—the first Swedish Lutheran congregation in the city. These
men, trained and educated in the Swedish church, founded a denomination
that combined their Lutheran heritage and a strong allegiance to the Augsburg
Confession with an independence from the Church of Sweden rendered by the
frontier conditions in America.[19]

Because their numbers were relatively small, Swedes joined with other
Lutherans to form the Evangelical Lutheran Synod of Northern Illinois. This
assembly, formed in 1851 and made up of Germans, Norwegians, and Swedes,
soon ran into conflicts over doctrine and education of the clergy. Dissention,
coupled with the increasing migration of Scandinavians to the United States,
led to the withdrawal of the Scandinavian conference and the formation of the
Scandinavian Evangelical Lutheran Augustana Synod in North America in 1860.
Ten years later, the Norwegians withdrew from the Augustana Synod and joined
previously established Norwegian synods, leaving the Swedes in complete control.

The Augustana Lutheran Church stood independently, supported by neither the Church of Sweden nor the other Lutheran churches in the United States. After 1856, Swedish American Lutherans did not receive any more ministers from the educated Swedish clergy, nor was the Swedish Church tempted to help the plight of those who had deserted their homeland. The Augustana Synod recruited their members in much the same manner as did their free church counterparts and educated their clergy at seminaries of their own creation. As George Stephenson points out, "Nothing could be more unhistorical than to designate the Augustana Synod as the 'daughter' of the Church of Sweden. The founders, to be sure, brought with them the Augsburg Confession and the symbolical books, but even these took on a new meaning . . . and in polity and practice the Augustana Synod has far more in common with Congregationalism and Presbyterianism than it has with European Lutheranism."[20]

The Episcopal Church was the only American denomination that stressed its similarity to the Church of Sweden. The St. Ansgarius Episcopal Church in Chicago, formed in 1849 by the Swede Gustaf Unonius and inspired by the Episcopal churches in the New Sweden colony in Delaware, was the first Swedish congregation in Chicago and the most successful Swedish Episcopal Church in mid-nineteenth-century America. Although a very important part of the early Swedish community in Chicago, the St. Ansgarius Church never found a strong following among the immigrants who arrived in the decades of large-scale migration after 1870. Moreover, the Episcopal denomination never shared the spontaneity of the other Swedish denominational movements. The Episcopal Church represented a movement in which the clergy took the initiative to form congregations, and it never reached deeply into the roots of the Swedish people. Those who joined often did so as a reaction against the strong moralizing tone voiced by the other Swedish denominations.[21]

The Methodist and Baptist movements met with success in Sweden and in America. The Methodist missionaries to Sweden furthered the nineteenth-century revivalism there, and the first Swedish Methodist Church in America, Olof Hedtrom's Bethel Ship in New York, predated the first Swedish Lutheran Church. Baptists founded their first church in Sweden in 1848 and their first Swedish church in America in 1852. Of the two, the Baptists met with the greatest success with early Swedish immigrants, stressing congregational independence and revivalism. While revivalism was also present in the Methodist churches, the hierarchical nature of the Methodist church structure did not appeal to many immigrant Swedes, who were skeptical of church authority. In addition, some Methodists preached perfectionism, which ran counter to the Lutheran belief in the depravity of human nature. Both the Baptist and the Methodist efforts initially represented American denominations reaching out to Swedish immigrants, and the Swedish churches received financial support from the missionary funds of their American counterparts. While contributing to the early successes of these churches, this close relationship eventually challenged the independent status of the Swedish congregations. The Baptists and the Methodists also had difficulty competing with the hold of the Lutheran tradition on the Swedish people.[22]

Not all Lutherans, however, felt comfortable with the establishment of the Augustana Lutheran Synod. Many of those who considered themselves to be followers of Rosenius and inheritors of the Swedish *läsare* tradition believed the Augustana synod replicated the stagnancy of the Church of Sweden. In an attempt to purify the Lutheran Church, they formed loose mission societies and held informal prayer meetings similar in style to the conventicles in Sweden. These Mission Friends believed the "inner call" of a person to the ministry was adequate qualification for lay ministers to practice and frowned upon the formality of the Lutheran worship service. In this setting, the Augustana Synod became the defender of traditionalism and the critic of spontaneous revivalism. Even the nonconformists needed to organize—if only to have the authority to license their own pastors—and in 1872 the Scandinavian Lutheran Mission Synod in the United States was organized under the leadership of a Dane, Charles Anderson.

The formality of nonconformist religion increased further with the formation of the Swedish Evangelical Lutheran Mission Synod in 1873 as part of the Synod of Northern Illinois. The formation of the Swedish Evangelical Lutheran Ansgarius Synod closely followed in 1874, becoming part of the Lutheran General Synod. In 1885, these latter two synods united to form the Swedish Evangelical Mission Covenant in America, an entirely separate denomination that adopted no formal creed, followed no established liturgy, nor believed in clerical vestments. C. A. Björk became the first president of the Covenant Church of America, a cobbler by training and preacher by profession. Overall, the Mission Covenant Church benefited from the new waves of Swedish immigrants arriving to the American shores. Its creation paralleled that of the Mission Friends in Sweden, but it acted as a completely independent agent without support from Swedish or American denominations.[23]

Swedish religious sentiment splintered even further in the next decade. Many revivalists disliked these denominational developments, claiming that the new unions usurped the authority of individual congregations. The leader of the disaffected, John G. Princell, refused to accept the Covenant Church. He believed that the most biblical form of Christian union was that of the local congregation.[24] Eventually, even Princell recognized the advantages of organizing and took part in the forming of the Swedish Evangelical Free Church in 1908. The Salvation Army also made great inroads among Chicago's Swedish population.[25] Many Swedish churches in America, especially those following the free church tradition, tended to be more lay-oriented and revivalistic than the Church of Sweden, giving the church a more democratic flavor. Overall, Swedes found ways of developing and replicating their own particular religious affiliations as they built more than seventy-three churches in Chicago between 1880 and 1920. This network of religious institutions extended throughout the suburbanizing city and provided a vehicle for relational, ethnic identification and solidarity using a language that Swedes could understand. Churches became an amalgam of Swedish theological developments, their American modifications, and the experience of living in Chicago.

THE PROLIFERATION OF SWEDISH CHURCHES IN CHICAGO

An examination of the creation and expansion of congregations in the Augustana Lutheran and Swedish Covenant churches provides a picture of the religious component of building Chicago's Swedish community. The mother congregations in the older Swedish enclaves, once the heart of the Swedish community, spread their influence to a number of daughter churches in the outlying neighborhoods. The stories of the birth of these new churches show the specific ways in which the Swedish community sustained itself even as it dispersed, and how immigrants maintained denominational ties as they moved from one location in the city to another. Churches supported family relationships, and in the case of many young female domestic workers, provided a family substitute and a safe haven for new social relationships. Through their various organizations, churches filled their members' free time with activities, in the process creating an all-encompassing religious subcommunity. Additionally, the social and moral agenda set by Swedish churches on the national and local levels reflected the desire of community leaders to embrace American Protestant values, distance themselves from Catholics and nonwhites, and help their fellow Swedes in times of economic and spiritual duress.

In order to examine the details of church growth among Swedes, this study narrows the focus to include only the Augustana Lutheran and Covenant churches. Concentrating upon these two groups does not negate the importance of other Swedish denominations. It does, however, acknowledge that the Augustana Lutheran and Covenant churches were created with little influence from American denominations and thus provide an excellent case study to observe how Swedes built their churches. Furthermore, by 1920, these two church groups represented the largest denominations of Swedes in Chicago, with membership encompassing roughly 27 percent of the Swedish population in the city. The Augustana churches remained the largest Swedish denomination in Chicago with more than twice the membership of the Covenant churches, but the Covenant had also made significant inroads among the Swedes by this time. Both denominations followed similar patterns of church growth and development, creating a network of congregations that extended the Swedish community throughout the city of Chicago and changed the nature of religious affiliation in response to evolving American conditions.

Augustana and Covenant Churches

The Augustana Lutheran and Covenant churches held different places on the spectrum of Swedish religious expression. The Augustana churches defended the Augsburg Confession, stressed an educated clergy and formality of worship, and accepted infants as members through baptism. Most of their pastors were Swedish-born, highly educated men, with nearly one-third having earned their doctorate in divinity, philosophy, or sacred theology at prestigious American schools such as Harvard, Yale, Northwestern, and the University of Chicago. Augustana pastors usually attended Swedish American undergraduate institutions created by the Augustana Synod, such as Augustana, Bethany, Gustavus Adolphus, or Upsala Colleges. This level of academic achievement separated Lutheran pastors from their largely working-class parishioners and directly followed the educational practices of the Church of Sweden, whose pastors had attended Uppsala University in Sweden for over two hundred years.[26]

By contrast, the Covenant churches were pietistic gatherings of confessed believers who rejected religious creeds, accepted lay leadership within the church, and emphasized greater freedom in worship practices. Most of the men who served Covenant churches did not receive as much formal education as the Augustana pastors; most believed that spiritual conversion and a call to serve the ministry were adequate credentials for a man to become a church pastor. This attitude was largely a reaction to the perceived formality and spiritual impoverishment of the Church of Sweden, a feeling that some Covenanters transferred to the Augustana Lutheran Church in America. Thus, the perspective of this dissenting Swedish church in America was rooted in an aversion to Swedish religious tradition. Despite the suspicion toward education, the Covenant established North Park College and Theological Seminary in Chicago early in its history as a location to train and educate its clergy. Overall, Covenanters believed their denomination struck a balance between congregational autonomy and denominational unity.[27]

Undoubtedly theological leanings contributed to an immigrant's decision to join one particular church over another; evidence also suggests that premigration experiences played a role in this decision. A comparison of church records of Swedish congregations in Chicago with records in Sweden indicates that the majority of both Covenanters and Lutherans came from agricultural backgrounds in Sweden.[28] There were, however, significant regional variations in their places of birth. Over one-half of the Covenant membership sample originated from the central Swedish counties of Värmland, Jönköping, Skaraborg, and Östergötland. These were regions where the free church movement had achieved great success among the population, and evidently pietistic influences followed the immigrants to Chicago. By contrast, fully one-quarter of the Lutherans sampled came from Halland County, on the southwest coast of Sweden, and another 15 percent came from Kalmar County on the southeast coast, areas where the free church movement was relatively weak. Without a doubt, exposure to nonconformist theology in Sweden made joining a Covenant church in Chicago a logical and comfortable choice for people already exposed to such ideas.

These regional differences between Lutherans and Covenanters played a role in the socioeconomic background of the immigrants. Within the agricultural sector, Covenanters were more likely to come from farm-owning families, and Lutherans more often originated from families of tenant farmers, a much more common situation in southwestern Sweden, where many large estates remained in the hands of the nobility.[29] These tenant farmers rented the land upon which they lived and worked for large landowners, making rent payments in cash. Lower in status and less common in both church groups were the crofters and field hands. Crofters rented their land, but they usually occupied smaller plots than the tenant farmers and paid rent with a percentage of their crops or with labor in the landowner's fields. The field hands were young men who lived in a farm owner's home and worked his fields for wages.[30] Roughly one-fifth of the members of both groups had fathers employed in specialized trades common in villages and larger urban areas, and fewer than 6 percent held military or white-collar positions. Hence, the overwhelming reality for both Covenanters and Lutherans is that they came from rural areas and, like most immigrants, were financially insecure. Although farm owners were slightly better off than tenant farmers, their children were just as unlikely to inherit a significant amount of land from their parents, making the economic differences in their background negligible.

The Mother Churches

Both the Augustana Lutheran and the Covenant churches began their work in Chicago with the establishment of a single mother congregation located in Swede Town. Before 1880, these churches, along with other early churches in the older Swedish enclaves on the West Side and South Side, provided the backbone of religious leadership in Swedish Chicago. By the twentieth century, their influence spread to new churches as their members moved to neighborhoods throughout the city, taking their denominational ties with them but leaving the older churches behind. In this way, Swedes shaped their particular urban experience and created strong ethnic institutions that were at the heart of the Swedish community in Chicago but no longer located in the old centralized Swedish enclaves.

In 1880, the largest, most influential, and best-attended Swedish church of any denomination was the oldest Swedish Lutheran Church in the city, Immanuel Lutheran Church, founded in 1853 in Swede Town. By 1881, church membership reached a total of 1,276, representing nearly 10 percent of Chicago's Swedish-born residents. Through the 1880s, Immanuel Lutheran held a place in the Swedish community very similar to that of the local churches in Sweden. Swedes in Chicago looked to this church and others like it to perform sacred rituals in a familiar church setting and language. Immanuel's location in the heart of the largest Swedish enclave in the city assured its prominence in the Swedish community as long as the Swedish population remained centralized in that particular area. But as demographic changes embraced the Near North Side of Chicago and it lost its importance as a center of Swedish settlement, the membership and activities of Immanuel Church diminished. Total church membership reached an all-time high in 1887 when Immanuel Church was only thirty-four years old and membership numbered 1,558. After that year, the number of members steadily declined, dropping to 986 in 1917. The following year, when most Swedes had left their old North Side enclave behind them, Immanuel Lutheran Church moved northward to the Edgewater neighborhood near Andersonville and merged with the Evangelical Lutheran Bethel Church. The Bethel Church had been started in 1907 by the Augustana Lutheran Mission Board as an English-speaking mission in Edgewater. Immanuel Church, as a Swedish institution, had outlasted the old neighborhood's needs, and it followed its people to a newer Swedish subdivision, uniting with a church that was not as much Swedish as it was Swedish American.[31]

The internal operations of Immanuel Church from 1880 through 1917 reflect the institution's changing role in the community and the aging of its membership. The decade from 1881 to 1890 represented the peak of parish activity, especially in terms of couples married and babies baptized. Many young, single Swedes arrived in Chicago and subsequently found their mates and were married in one of the Swedish churches, and Immanuel Church filled this role more than any other single church. Thousands of Swedish immigrants looked to the church in times of joy and sadness—to bless their marriages, baptize their babies, and bury their loved ones—much as they had done in their native country. The availability of these rituals in Chicago added a sense of continuity in many immigrants' lives. By the time the church decided to move to its new location in 1918, marriages in the church had dropped by nearly two-thirds since the 1880s, and baptisms decreased by more than three-fourths during the same period. Once these immigrants and their children died or moved out of the old neighborhood, the church followed its members, reflecting the remarkable fluidity of American urban life.[32]

FIGURE 7. A 1907 calendar advertising the Evangelical Lutheran Immanuel Church in Chicago in Swede Town at the corner of Sedgewick and Hobbie Streets. Immanuel Lutheran Church served as a hub of the Swedish community in Chicago for many years, providing a location for Swedish marriages, baptisms, and funerals. The image quotes part of Psalm 122:1: "'Let us go to the house of the Lord!'" Courtesy of the Archives of the Evangelical Lutheran Church in America.

The North Side Mission Church became the mother church to the rest of Chicago's Covenant Churches, eventually playing a role similar to that of Immanuel Lutheran Church. The small congregation began in 1868 as a mission society within Immanuel Lutheran Church with the blessing of its pastor, Erland Carlsson. Originally calling themselves "the Evangelical Lutheran Mission Society of Chicago," they represented one of four such societies in the United States. In 1869, members of the mission society purchased land and completed a building on North Franklin Street near Whiting Street, on the near North Side of Chicago.

Initially, this congregation remained tied to the Lutheran Church, and no one was permitted to preach the word of God unless he adhered to the Lutheran doctrine and the Augsburg Confession, prerequisites to Lutheran affiliation. As time passed and the congregation grew, the Mission Friends, as they called themselves, took on their own distinctive characteristics and grew more independent of Immanuel Church, placing great emphasis upon a fellowship of believers and spiritual renewal. To push the split even further, the Immanuel Church barred Mission Friend colporteurs from its pulpit. In 1870, the North Side Mission Church became incorporated under the laws of the state of Illinois as the "Evangelical Lutheran Missionary Association of Chicago" and began licensing its first preachers. The North Side Church provided an important source of leadership for Mission Friends throughout the Middle West of the United States and played an important role in the formation of the Swedish Evangelical Mission Covenant Church of America in 1885.[33]

The Chicago Fire destroyed the North Side Mission Church in 1871 and caused a major setback for its members. Not until 1873 was a new church building erected on the same site. Attendance at the North Side Mission Church grew rapidly in the early 1880s, fueled not only by the expansion of Swedish population in the city but also by increasing revivalistic sentiment in Sweden and in Swedish America. The church's anniversary booklet, *The One Hundred Years*, notes that "Many of the new arrivals had recently been converted in Sweden but the unconverted also attended the church services which provided an opportunity for making friends and for social fellowship."[34] Growing attendance and the slight northward migration of the Swedes resulted in the construction of a larger church edifice in 1887 on the southwest corner of Market (Orleans) and Whiting Streets. On special occasions, the auditorium could seat two thousand people, "which was said at the time of its completion to be the largest assembly place in America for Swedish people."[35] Early church leaders became heavily involved with the Covenant denomination. C. A. Björk, the congregation's second full-time pastor, served the church from 1877 to 1894 while also serving as the first president of the Covenant Church of America. He resigned as pastor when his job as president became a full-time, paid endeavor. Members such as A. F. Boring, C. G. Peterson, Otto Högfeldt, and John Hagström also served in leadership positions in the independently owned but denominationally oriented publication, *Missions-Vännen*.

As long as the Swedish population remained centered in this enclave, the North Side Mission Church thrived. In 1889, the first year the Covenant churches reported their membership figures, 500 people belonged to the North Side

Mission Church. Church membership peaked in 1898 with 556 people, a number claimed to be about one-third the number that actually attended Sunday morning services. During the next two decades, however, church membership steadily declined, and by 1920, only 346 people belonged to the church.[36] Like Immanuel Lutheran Church, the North Side Mission Church eventually fell victim to changing neighborhood demographics and a diminishment of interest among second-generation Swedes. In 1924, the North Side Mission Church, by then known as First Covenant Church, moved to the southwest corner at Albion and Artesian Avenues in West Ridge, an area located to the northwest of Andersonville. Evolving residential patterns mandated that the church relocate; another Swedish institution had outlasted the Swedish residents in the area.

The Spread of Swedish Churches to New Chicago Neighborhoods

As the Swedish population in the city grew and spread into outlying neighborhoods, the number of religious institutions serving those people likewise increased. In the process, the power and influence of a single church such as Immanuel Lutheran or First Covenant transferred to a larger number of smaller churches. In 1880, four Augustana Lutheran churches and three congregations of Mission Friends existed in Chicago, located in the main hubs of Swedish population on the North, South, and Near West Sides of the city. The membership in Lutheran churches alone numbered nearly 2,500, a figure representing 19 percent of the Swedish-born population in Chicago. By 1920, Swedish Lutherans and Covenanters had built forty-six churches in Chicago with a total membership of nearly 16,000.[37] Although membership at Immanuel Lutheran Church and First Covenant Church declined after the 1890s, these two churches were not dead institutions. Their lives continued to flow through the new congregations their members helped create throughout the Chicago area. Swedes in Chicago became adept at building new churches to fill their spiritual and social needs—a task largely unprecedented in their Swedish upbringing.[38] The institutions themselves reflected changes in the urban landscape, as they grew, matured, and aged with the Swedish population in the city.

The creation stories of these daughter churches are quite similar: the mother churches helped plant them, sometimes with financial aid and often by supplying the core of charter membership. As early as 1868, Immanuel Lutheran Church helped seed the new Salem Lutheran Church—located in the South Side Swedish enclave of Douglas/Armour Square—with the gift of three lots valued at one thousand dollars. A number of Immanuel's members who lived in the area transferred their membership to the Salem Lutheran Church, helping establish a base for the new congregation. By 1881, membership of Salem Lutheran Church reached 660, and it peaked at 935 in 1894 when the church was twenty-six years old. After that point, membership declined steadily, and by 1920, only 250 members appeared on the church's register.[39] As Swedes left the neighborhood behind, the church there could no longer survive. New churches in new subdivisions located farther south in the city subsumed the role of the Salem church.

The Salem Lutheran Church lost many members to the Bethlehem Lutheran Church, founded in 1876 by Swedish Lutherans in the up-and-coming South Side neighborhood of Englewood. Johan Forsberg, one of the church's founders, observed that

> Englewood was then a suburb of Chicago and quite a number of Swedish people had settled there. Among them was a family named Anderson. Mr. Anderson was a painter and was known as Painter Anderson. . . . The Anderson Family had built a fine big home and were very good friends of the pastor of the Immanuel congregation, Pastor Erland Carlsson. The Andersons invited Pastor and Mrs. Carlsson to come and have afternoon coffee with them, and before Pastor Carlsson was ready to leave he suggested that they have general prayer, and the neighbors were invited to come in and take part. A goodly number came, in fact so many that the large home could hardly accommodate them all.[40]

After that meeting, Erland Carlsson asked Johan Forsberg to begin pastorate work in the Englewood area. A number of early members became personally involved in building a church structure. As Forsberg later surmised, "We have here a concrete example of what God had done and can do through the coffee cup in the mission work."[41] Membership of Bethlehem Lutheran Church grew steadily until 1916, when 726 people belonged to the church and population growth in Englewood stabilized.[42]

The creation of the Covenant churches occurred in much the same manner and followed the same trends as did the Augustana Lutheran churches: meetings began in people's homes or in other non-Swedish churches until the congregation could afford to build its own church. Prior to 1880, the Mission churches in the Chicago area were located in the mainline Swedish hubs. In addition to the North Side Mission Church, two South Side churches began in 1877, the Mission Church in Douglas Park on the corner of Rockwell and Parmelee (Twenty-third Street), and the Tabernacle Church, on South LaSalle and Thirtieth Street. The Tabernacle, a popular spot for revivals and pietistic preaching, reached a peak of 456 members in 1896, only nineteen years after the congregation was founded. The Mission Church in Douglas Park never grew as large as its neighbor. Its

Table 2. Swedish Churches Established in Chicago Until 1920

	Church	Year Established	Neighborhood
Before 1880:	St. Ansgarius Episcopal	1849	Near North
	Immanuel Lutheran	1853	Near North
	First Methodist	1854	Near North
	First Baptist	1866	Near North
	Salem Lutheran	1868	Douglas/Armour Square (A.S.)
	North Side Mission Church	1868	Near North
	Gethsemane Lutheran	1870	West Town
	Second Baptist	1874	Douglas/A.S.
	Haven Street Methodist (then Third Methodist)	1874	Douglas/A.S.
	Bethlehem Lutheran	1875	Englewood
	Second Methodist	1875	West Town
	Mission Tabernacle	1877	Douglas/A.S.
	Douglas Park Covenant	1877	Douglas/A.S.
1880–1889:	Bethany Lutheran	1880	South Chicago
	First Swedish Free Church	1880	Near North
	Zion Lutheran	1881	Lower W. Side
	Bethany Covenant	1882	Englewood
	Third Baptist	1882	South Shore
	Fourth Baptist	1882	Roseland
	Trinity Lutheran	1883	Lake View
	Colehour Covenant	1883	South Chicago
	Elim Free Church	1884	Douglas/A.S.
	Fourth Methodist	1884	Englewood
	Fifth Avenue Methodist	1884	5th Ave-33rd?
	Humboldt Park Covenant	1884	Humboldt Park
	Elim Lutheran	1885	Pullman
	Roseland Methodist	1885	Pullman
	Englewood Baptist	1885	Englewood
	Forest Glen Methodist	1886	Forest Glen
	Englewood Methodist	1886	Englewood
	Lake View Covenant	1886	Lake View
	Humboldt Park Methodist	1887	Humboldt Park
	Elim Methodist Church	1887	Lake View
	Ravenswood Covenant	1887	Ravenswood/ Lincoln Sq
	Saron Lutheran	1888	Logan Square
	South Englewood Covenant (Oakdale)	1888	S. Englewood
	Parkside Covenant	1888	South Shore
	Moreland Covenant	1889	Austin
	St. Paul Lutheran (English)	1889	Austin
	Lake View Swedish Baptist	1889	Lake View
1890–1899:	Bethel Lutheran	1890	Englewood
	Salem Baptist	1890	Lower W. Side

	Gustav Adolf Lutheran	1891	Gr. Crossing
	Bethesda Lutheran	1891	East Side
	Bethany Methodist	1891	Ravenswood/Lincoln Sq
	Humboldt Park Baptist	1891	Humboldt Park
	Austin Baptist	1891	Austin
	Ebenezer Lutheran	1892	Andersonville
	Moreland Methodist	1892	Austin
	Grand Crossing Covenant	1892	Greater Grand Crossing
	Maplewood Covenant	1892	Logan Square
	Austin Trinity Methodist	1893	Austin
	Emanual Methodist	1893	Lower W. Side
	Tabernacle Baptist	1893	South Chicago
	Austin Covenant	1894	Austin
	Messiah Lutheran	1895	Austin
	Lebanon Lutheran	1896	Hegewisch
	Messiah Lutheran (English)	1896	Lake View
	Brighton Pk/McKinley Pk Meth.	1896	Brighton Pk/McKinley Pk
	Cuyler Covenant	1897	Lake View/North Center
	Concordia Lutheran	1898	North Center/Cuyler
	North Park Covenant	1898	North Park
	Elim Baptist	1899	South Shore
1900–1909:	Tabor Lutheran	1900	South Chicago
	Madison Avenue Methodist	1900?	Hyde Park
	West Pullman Methodist	1900	Pullman
	Salem Methodist	1900	Hermosa
	Nebo Lutheran	1901	Portage Park
	Cragin Covenant	1901	Belmont Crag.
	Irving Park Covenant	1902	Irving Park
	Libanon Lutheran	1903	Belmont Crag.
	Augustana Lutheran	1903	Hyde Park
	Irving Park Lutheran	1903	Irving Park
	St. Johns Lutheran	1904	Avondale
	Englewood Hill Covenant (Ogden Park)	1905	Aub. Gresham
	Capernaum Lutheran	1906	Chatham
	Immanuel Baptist	1907	Ravenswood/Lincoln Sq.
	Messias Lutheran	1908	W. Englewood
	Grace Lutheran (English)	1909	Englewood
	Bethel Lutheran (English)	1909	Edgewater
	Edgewater Covenant	1909	Edgewater
	Edgewater Baptist	1909	Edgewater
1910–1920:	Matteus Lutheran	1914	Aub. Gresham
	Hyde Park Methodist	1914	Hyde Park
	Auburn Park Methodist	1915	Aub. Gresham
	Olavus Petri Lutheran	1917	Albany Park

membership reached a high of 142 people in 1904 after twenty-seven years of existence. By this time, changing neighborhood characteristics once again curtailed the life of Swedish congregations in the older Swedish enclaves of Chicago.[43]

As Covenanters moved to Chicago's developing neighborhoods, they found ways to start congregations and to eventually build new churches. The Evangelical Covenant Church of South Chicago provides a fairly typical example. Located in a heavily industrial section of the city, the church was surrounded by five steel mills and many smaller industries—companies that provided work for church members and brought new people to the area. In this area of South Chicago, Swedish Christians of various backgrounds—Lutherans, Mission Friends, and Methodists—first formed the Free Swedish Mission Church. This church began meeting at the Swedish Baptist Church, then moved to the First Evangelical Church. Members constructed their own building in 1889, and in 1892, the church joined the Covenant denomination.[44]

Other Covenant churches followed similar patterns of development. The Covenant Church in Blue Island began to meet in a home, then transferred locations to a Congregational church, a Methodist church, and a vacant store. After the congregation formally organized, work was begun on a new building.[45] The Lake View Covenant Church's history was similar: prayer meetings began in homes in the early 1880s, in 1884 they rented a German church and started Sunday school, in 1886 they formally organized the church, and in 1887 they erected a new structure.[46] The Ogden Park Covenant Church began services in a Presbyterian church and started a Sunday school, and then moved the preaching and teaching to a home in the area. When that became too small, they rented a hall, then moved to a store, and, when the people had been meeting for eleven years, the congregation formally organized.[47] Members of the Covenant Church in Irving Park constructed the church edifice themselves four years after the congregation started to meet and three years before the church was legally incorporated.[48] In 1890, several Swedes in the West Side neighborhood of Moreland "assembled at Leonard Larson's [home] . . . to confer about Christian Mission work in this area."[49] After opening the meeting with prayer, the group decided to organize a congregation and incorporate under Illinois law. Although many Augustana Lutheran churches grew from similar situations, the Mission Friends believed most strongly in the importance of the congregation and in the informality of the gatherings.

In these humble meetings, small groups of Swedish immigrants acted out their beliefs by creating concrete organizations that institutionalized their faith. Even though the gathering places often varied, church membership remained consistent until demographic changes overtook the neighborhoods in which they were located. As long as new Swedes moved into an area, the Swedish churches there continued to grow and thrive. When the Swedish presence in a particular area declined, so did church membership, and some churches did not continue to grow beyond their first two decades. Those churches begun before 1900 that continued to increase in membership through the decade of the 1920s had been built in areas that continued to appeal to Swedes, such as Lake View, Grand Crossing, and Andersonville. On average, membership in Lutheran churches peaked within twenty-seven years of their establishment. A decline in church membership did not necessarily reflect a dying institution, but it did signify that the initial impetus for joining and affiliation had begun to reverse itself. It also reflected a remarkable mobility among the Swedish population of the city.[50]

A corollary to this same trend also held true: Swedish churches could not grow in an area until they were demographically supported by incoming Swedes. For example, the Ebenezer Lutheran Church, established in the region of the city that came to be known as Andersonville, remained quite small for the first ten years of its existence. Started in 1892 with a membership of twenty-eight, the total number of church members had only reached fifty-six a decade later. Within another ten years that number had grown to 770, and by 1930, when Andersonville was a thriving Swedish community in Chicago, membership at Ebenezer reached 1,259 people. By that time, Ebenezer superseded Trinity Church in Lake View as the city's largest and most active Swedish Lutheran Church.[51]

This pattern of slow growth also held true for the Nebo Swedish Evangelical Lutheran Church in Portage Park. Begun in 1902 with forty-four members, the church's founders attempted to create a Swedish Lutheran subdivision based on a new college and seminary, named Martin Luther College. A church anniversary booklet stated that "in the Martin Luther Subdivision, Pastor Sven Sandahl saw a haven for his countrymen."[52] Unlike the more successful North Park College on Chicago's North Side, the Martin Luther College project never materialized as intended, and the neighborhood grew only slowly.[53] At the time of the establishment of the church and school, the Portage Park area was not connected to the city by transportation routes and lacked sewers and electricity. Swedish settlers found other areas of the city more attractive, but eventually, after 1910, the church membership began to grow. Membership reached 250 in 1920, and by 1930, 634 people belonged to Nebo Lutheran Church. Some Swedish Lutheran churches never prospered, however. The Lebanon Lutheran Church in the Hegewisch neighborhood peaked in 1904 with ninety members when it was only eight years old; Capernaum Swedish Lutheran Church reached its largest membership, fifty-four altogether, in 1908, its second year of existence.[54]

When observed from the perspective of individual immigrants, churches provided a context for urban mobility. According to an anniversary reflection, after members of First Covenant Church left the old Swede Town neighborhood, they "joined other Covenant churches in Chicago or in more distant places."[55]

The Covenant Church in Edgewater, a respectable community on the North Side, received many of these membership transfers. Founded in 1909, the church grew to 251 members by 1920. More than half of these members transferred their affiliation from other churches—the vast majority from other Covenant churches in Chicago.[56] Lake View Covenant Church supplied roughly one-third of the members who transferred to the Edgewater church. Since Lake View Covenant Church was itself a spin-off from First Covenant Church, Edgewater Covenant was in actuality a third-generation Swedish church in Chicago. Several people even kept their Covenant affiliations as they moved to Chicago from Michigan, Wisconsin, or southern Illinois, and others transferred directly from Covenant churches in Sweden. Whether the move to Edgewater represented a second or a third move within Chicago, the movement took place within a context of Covenant church connections. Furthermore, the majority of these people had lived in the United States for more than one decade, indicating that their ethnicity and their religious identification thrived during their time in America. Although residential movement for the Swedish immigrant was commonplace, it was not haphazard.

Swedish churches in Chicago became powerful symbols for traditional values in the Swedish community, even while many of them projected religious ideals that departed significantly from the Church of Sweden. Not only did churches attempt to preserve and propagate Swedish American religious values—in all their variety—they also tried to supplement the family structure of Swedish immigrants. For example, when Trinity Lutheran Church was founded in the Lake View neighborhood in 1883, its charter membership was comprised of twelve married couples and their thirty-one children. These people undoubtedly believed that their families would be strengthened by the presence of the Swedish Lutheran church in their new neighborhood, an attitude repeated in many other congregations. When Trinity Lutheran built a new church structure in 1897, they designed it to hold over one thousand people and saw it as a center of community life. The church building itself was an imposing structure in the new suburb—its steeple loomed over the street below with Swedish inscriptions carved upon its edifice. The architect, Erick G. Petterson, and the construction foreman, John F. Johanson, were both Swedes, and the building closely resembled a parish church in Sweden. Trinity Lutheran—and many of the other Swedish churches in Chicago—thus served as a powerful visual symbol of a traditional past in a setting that was anything but traditional.[57]

The Preservation and Adaptation of Religious Traditions

Churches built by Swedes in Chicago created all-encompassing community organizations. Church activities and organizations expanded the scope of the churches, bringing them into the everyday lives of their members. Swedish immigrants initiated Sunday school and youth programs to transmit important religious values to their American-born children. In the United States, Protestant churches developed Sunday schools as a means of educating children from all social classes in moral and religious guidelines. Although Sunday school itself had no Swedish precedent, the diverse ethnic and religious conditions of American society encouraged Swedes to embrace this American institution as a means of passing on their inherited Swedish religious culture to the next generation. Sunday school taught religion to young Swedish Americans in a Swedish context, reflecting an effort among the immigrant generation to preserve their linguistic and ethnic traditions.[58]

With the support of the immigrant generation, the popularity of Swedish American Sunday schools soared. Attendance in Immanuel Lutheran Church's Sunday school reached 1,200 in the 1880s, a number that remained fairly consistent for the following decade. The North Side Mission Church's Sunday school, always an important part of the church's mission, reached an attendance of 1,200 people in 1900. Sunday schools were also used for purposes of evangelism, reaching out to the children of less-religious Swedes. The Edgewater Covenant Church actually began as a Sunday school mission of the North Side Mission Church in 1907, preceding the incorporation of the church itself by two years. Even though Sunday schools were begun with the intention of preserving the immigrants' ethnic and religious heritage, they succumbed to pressures of a Swedish American generation by making the transition to English up to two decades earlier than the rest of the church.[59]

Congregations established Young People's Societies soon after they founded the churches themselves, often for evangelistic purposes. Like the Sunday schools, these groups conducted their meetings in English and attempted to reach out to the teenage children of immigrants to involve them in the church's activities. For example, at Trinity Lutheran Church in Lake View, several young women founded a young people's group in 1895 called "*Senapskornet*" (the mustard seed). They met in different homes and raised money for foreign missionaries. In 1905, young men were allowed to join, and soon the group became the Young People's Society.[60] The Young People's Society at Colehour Covenant Church was decidedly evangelistic in nature. The group's constitution stated that its purpose was "to enlist the young people in the service of our Lord and Savior, Jesus Christ."[61] The Young People's Society at the Covenant Church in Douglas Park required its members to "testify for Christ before becoming members."[62] The organization distributed tracts, provided needy families with coal and shoes, and sent contributions to the American evangelist Billy Sunday. At Moreland Covenant Church, meetings were characterized by singing, Bible reading, and a lesson by

FIGURE 8. Hundreds of children posed in 1903 for this picture of Immanuel Lutheran Church's Sunday school classes. Sunday school was an American invention embraced by Swedish immigrants as a means of educating their children in Swedish religious traditions. Courtesy of the Archives of the Evangelical Lutheran Church in America

the pastor, and the group was divided into coffee, missions, program, literary, and membership committees. If members indicated that they had fallen away from a "solid relationship with God" they would be dropped from membership.[63] Thus young people's societies drew their members closer to the church while at the same time perpetuating religious and secular divisions within the larger Swedish community in Chicago.

Certainly the Swedish churches felt the tension between a Swedish-speaking church and an English-speaking society early, particularly when their children increasingly identified with that larger external society. Many Swedish churches offered Swedish language school for several weeks during the summer in preparation for a Swedish confirmation service; adults wanted their children to learn the Swedish language and be familiar with the traditions of their native land. In contrast to the hopes of the church leaders, the memories of the Swedish American youth who took part in these language programs were often quite negative. Although many children attended Swedish school during the summers, Sarah Swanson remembers that "the young people didn't want to learn Swedish."[64] At North Park Covenant Church, Swedish class met five days a week from nine o'clock in the morning to noon for two months. Walter Enstrom recalls how the children used to misbehave in class. "We were taught Swedish, and it was a Swedish out of the Bible. It was with a religious background, and we kids rebelled because it was our summer vacation."[65] A generational conflict existed between the immigrant parents, attempting to preserve aspects of their Swedish heritage and pass them along to the next generation, and their children who saw themselves as more American than Swedish.

The Augustana Lutheran Synod was the most aggressive in confronting the tension between the Swedish and English languages in their churches. In 1880, the Augustana Synod passed resolutions urging as many of its pastors as possible to be fluent in both Swedish and English, noting that bilingualism was especially important in urban churches where interaction with non-Swedes was often necessary. The Augustana Lutherans affirmed that their primary language was Swedish, but they also recognized the growing importance of English among their offspring. In 1909, the synod established a separate Association of English Churches. The purpose of this Association was to "perpetuate the faith of the fathers in the English language and serve the best interests of the Evangelical Lutheran Augustana Synod" and "to devise and execute plans for aggressive English work." In 1915, the association reported that "It is generally recognized now that the success of our English work is not detrimental, but rather strengthening for our mutual cause and work." The report went on to state that "the language question does not hereby need to be forced. In spite of all that may be done, [the] onward progress [of the English language] is irresistible. We have no desire to hasten it, but rather hope that it may not be too rapid."[66] Through these English missions, the Augustana Lutherans sought to establish churches steeped in the Swedish Augustana tradition that reached out to an English-speaking generation. In this effort they attempted to stay one step ahead of the erosion of the Swedish language to make sure that it did not also lead to a decline in religious values.

In addition to clubs and programs that reached out to the Swedish American youth, many organizations within the church strongly appealed to women. During the late nineteenth century, fraternal societies grew in popularity, but their secular focus and male orientation alienated many women. By contrast, churches offered havens to women—particularly young single women—from potential dangers of their urban surroundings. Like their American counterparts, Swedish churches

FIGURE 9. A Ladies Aid Group at North Park Covenant Church on Chicago's northwest side, taken shortly after the church's founding in the 1890s. Women's organizations such as this one were prevalent throughout Swedish Chicago, offering their members friendship while reinforcing particular community connections. Courtesy of Covenant Archives and Historical Library, North Park University, Chicago.

often registered more female than male members. At the Covenant Church in Edgewater, for example, for every single man there were two and one-half times as many single women, many of whom worked in affluent American households in the surrounding area. Married men were more likely to attend church than single men, but they were still outnumbered by married women. Women's organizations within the churches were an important means of revenue for church projects and sources of fellowship for the women involved. Most women's societies were actually sewing circles where women used traditional handiwork skills learned from their foremothers to raise money for mission work and the erection of church buildings. Thus traditional crafts of embroidery and sewing were used for new purposes in Chicago.[67]

Organizational activity within the churches often filled their members' lives, creating a comprehensive religious community. In addition to young people's and women's societies, other groups attempted to convert and recruit nonreligious Swedes. Immanuel Lutheran Church formed a Tract Society in 1889 for the purpose of distributing religious tracts, organizing new churches, and serving a variety of parishioner needs.[68] The Covenant Church in Blue Island sponsored annual Fourth of July picnics, serving lemonade from large tubs and ice cream to everyone in attendance. These celebrations offered a Christian alternative to other forms of entertainment available that day and competed directly with the activities of the Swedish secular societies. At the same time, they provided an ethnic context to the celebration of an American tradition. Overall, churches and their internal organizations were a creative amalgam of the attempt to preserve religious traditions on the one hand and urban adaptation on the other.

The Growth of Swedish Denominationalism

The development of Swedish American churches in Chicago paralleled the emergence of national denominational structures, creating a local community and connecting it to a national network of affiliated churches. Dag Blanck explains this spectrum of Swedish ethnic affiliation as a "continuum [of ethnicity] . . . stretching from what can be called an 'everyday' level to a 'higher,' more elite level." Everyday ethnicity, Blanck argues, was "rooted in the ethnic neighborhoods." The elite level of ethnic expression was created by community leaders who intended it to be "national, transcending the neighborhoods and regionalism of Swedish America." While Blanck contends that ethnic identity was "actively constructed or invented" by elites, this process of invention was also taking place at the grassroots level, especially with regard to Swedish American churches.[69]

As already shown in this study, Swedish immigrants built their churches from the bottom up, and in doing so they created important expressions of their ethnic

identity. These churches were, in turn, the foundation of the national denominations. Any opinion rendered or cause undertaken by the denomination as a whole
needed to have the support of the majority of delegates to national meetings—
usually local church pastors and lay leaders. Hence, the national denominations
were integrally linked to local congregational communities. Denominational
leaders addressed problems internal to the Swedish American community by
creating missions and institutions to assist newly arrived immigrants and others
who fell on hard times. Leaders also expressed opinions on issues external to the
community—they took moral stands on American social issues and frequently
petitioned appropriate politicians for action. In doing so, church leaders, with the
support of local congregations, effectively conveyed the notion that Swedes were
desirable immigrants who promoted middle-class, Protestant American values.[70]
Essentially, they emphasized their whiteness, and hence their fitness for acceptance into the American ethnic and political mainstream.

A key issue that concerned many Swedes—an issue internal to the Swedish
community as a whole—was the plight of immigrants arriving in America who
had no associational or familial connections. The Augustana Lutheran and
Covenant denominations set up immigrant missions in New York and Boston to
assist Swedish newcomers with food and lodging immediately after their arrival
in America. As the Augustana Synod's Annual Report of 1880 noted, so many
"Immigrants . . . [are] landing from the Fatherland here to America, [that] it has
become necessary . . . to go meet them with advice, help, and leadership."[71] The
report of the Covenant Church's Immigrant Mission in New York in 1887 stated
that the mission attempted to protect immigrants, many of whom did not know
the English language, from the "merciless immigration officials."[72] Newcomers
might also be exploited by unscrupulous countrymen who were willing to take
advantage of them for financial gain. The Lutheran Church particularly saw itself
as the primary church responsible for all Swedes, and sent a missionary, Axel B.
Lilja, to work among Swedish immigrants arriving at Castle Garden, which operated as an entry depot for European immigrants in New York between 1855 and
1890. The secretary and superintendent at Castle Garden commended Lilja, writing that "The sick, the poor and those needing guidance and aid receive [Lilja's]
personal care and attention. He is daily to be found among the arriving immigrants, serving them with unwearying zeal and aiding them in every way that lies
in his power."[73]

As time passed and regulations regarding entry into the United States became
increasingly strict, the Lutheran mission began to provide more legal assistance
to Swedish newcomers. In 1911, the report from Ellis Island indicated that the
mission was especially sensitive to the needs of those detained because they were
designated as "L. P. C.," or liable to become a public charge. During the year,

the mission sent 82 telegrams and 195 letters on behalf of these people.[74] When immigration fell during the First World War, these missions shifted their focus to homeless and needy folk already in the cities. Thus, in situations where new Swedish immigrants were particularly vulnerable—when they initially arrived in an American port and when they encountered physical hardships and sickness—churches stepped in to help their own people. By so doing, they provided a safety net that not only helped individual Swedes, but also protected the reputation of the Swedish community as a whole.

A secondary purpose of the Immigrant Missions was to proselytize among Swedish immigrants, and in this area the Covenant and Lutheran churches competed with each other. Missionaries from the Covenant Church attempted to convert newcomers through the distribution of evangelical tracts and personal conversation. They also assisted immigrants already converted to pious beliefs with spiritual and physical assistance. An important objective of the Lutheran Immigrant Mission was to "Serve the Augustana synod through . . . introducing immigrating country-men to our churches" as well as to provide overnight lodging, food, information, and to "advance . . . funds for continuing their journey" for the most needy.[75] As exemplified by these missions, the competing religious persuasions among Swedish immigrants in the late nineteenth century manifested themselves even as Swedes attempted to help each other through the most difficult aspects of migration.

Swedish denominations also created a wide range of institutions and missions in Chicago to help their constituents once they had settled in the city. These organizations helped religious subcommunities—in this case Swedish American denominations—approach what Raymond Breton calls "institutional completeness."[76] From congregational gatherings where Swedes shared worship and friendship, traditions and common experiences, to national denominations that supported colleges, hospitals, and nursing homes, Swedish American churches embraced their members in all phases of life. For example, the Lutheran Church built Augustana Hospital in Chicago to treat Swedes and others who needed medical care. The denomination built homes for the elderly and children in Joliet, Illinois, just outside of Chicago. The Covenant Church's Home of Mercy was intended to aid helpless widows, orphans, and the sick. The Home evolved into Swedish Covenant Hospital and offered more expansive care. North Park College provided educational opportunities for Covenant youth and future clergy. The Lutherans and the Swedish Methodists offered homes of refuge for young, single women traveling and living alone in the city.[77] These types of institutions, built and supported by Swedish American denominations, offered Swedish immigrants social support and charity in times of need, a function that became even more important during the Great Depression of the 1930s. Furthermore, by creating

FIGURE 10. The Covenant Home of Mercy, pictured in 1886, was an early example of the ability of Swedish immigrants to build institutions that provided safety nets for, in this case, Covenant Church members. The home eventually became Swedish Covenant Hospital. Courtesy of Covenant Archives and Historical Library, North Park University, Chicago.

such a comprehensive array of supportive institutions, these churches in Chicago played a role once filled by families and local parishes in Sweden.

Swedish denominations were also very interested in issues external to their community, particularly religious and social matters addressed by other Protestant denominations. Missionary efforts concentrated on proselytizing in China, Africa, the Indian Territory, and among the Mormons, who had achieved modest success in converting fellow Swedish immigrants. Augustana Lutherans conducted missionary work among Jews in Chicago and spoke openly against the Catholic Church, accusing it of using its influence to "control the political situation wherever possible in local, state, and national politics, thus making the State subservient to the Church."[78] Conversely, friendly relations were maintained with like-minded Protestant groups. Warm greetings were exchanged between Swedish Lutherans and German Lutherans, and the Augustana Synod supported the American Bible Society in its efforts "to place the Word of God in the homes of all the people of this country and to give it to the world."[79] The synod also elected representatives to an Inter-Church Conference to explore the possibility of "a federation of evangelical churches only, already in fraternal relations and in substantial agreement as to fundamental Christian doctrines."[80] In attitude and behavior, Swedes resembled white Protestants who had lived in the United States for generations and, at some level, considered non-Protestants to be a threat to their own identity.

The largest social and moral issue tackled by the Swedish churches was their unequivocal support of the American temperance movement. Swedes carried a strong temperance tradition to America from their homeland—a tradition democratic in character and supported by individuals across class lines. In America, however, the temperance movement reflected a greater sense of class division than in Sweden as industrial and middle-class business leaders sought to promote temperance among workers in order to further the expansion of the industrial economy.[81] Although the Augustana leaders argued that "pure wine must be used for sacramental purposes," they also believed that the "Church is the divinely ordained society for the promotion of genuine temperance reform." Furthermore, they asked their pastors to preach "at least once each year on the duty of temperance."[82] Denominations passed resolutions when temperance votes came up in the various states, reflecting an ongoing interest in the issue on the part of the Swedish American churches.

Augustana Lutherans and Covenanters also strongly supported the Anti-Saloon League, a group that attacked the urban saloon as a breeding ground for social unrest and vice. The Anti-Saloon League was concerned not only about working-class drinking, but also about the free exchange of ideas that took place in urban, particularly immigrant, saloons during workers' leisure time. Religious Swedes, by supporting the American prohibition movement, suggested that they were also concerned about working-class unrest and saloons as competing urban institutions, reflecting a decidedly middle-class American perspective on the issue. Through their support of the American temperance crusade, Lutheran and Covenant Swedes distanced themselves from nonreligious Swedish immigrants. Not only did they alienate nonabstaining Swedes of all social classes, the churches also alienated many working-class Swedes who were strong advocates of temperance reform due to the churches' close affiliation with antilabor American temperance organizations.[83]

Both the Augustana Lutheran and Covenant denominations firmly supported the American government when conflicts arose. As ethnic Americans, religious leaders were very sensitive about projecting a patriotic image. In 1898, the Augustana Synod passed resolutions supporting the United States' cause in the Spanish-American War. Although not denying their immigrant past, these Swedes expressed their loyalty to the United States in language similar to that of the nation's founders themselves. The war "for human liberty and for the sacred rights and great principles upon which human liberties rest" led them to ask "God's blessing . . . upon [the president] and upon the army and navy of the Republic . . . and victory to the cause of righteousness, liberty and justice."[84] They wanted to leave no doubt about their patriotic fervor.

World War One proved to be a more delicate matter, since Swedes were closely identified with and often lived in close proximity to German immigrants. In 1916, the Covenant denomination sent a resolution to the Congress and the president of the United States to put a "timely and legitimate stop to the exportation of arms and ammunition to belligerent nations, which is a traffic in human blood for the sake of monetary gain."[85] Overall, most Swedish Americans—like most Americans—opposed America's involvement in the war before 1917. When American involvement in the war became a fact, the denomination sent a telegram to the White House to assure the president of their patriotism and support. Given the close relationship between Swedish and German Lutherans, the Augustana Synod boasted of its loyalty in no uncertain terms: "The synod rejoices over the spirit of loyalty to our government manifested by our people and especially by those of them who freely offered their lives in the service of the nation. That so many Augustana Synod boys occupy soldiers' graves in foreign lands bears solemn and eloquent testimony to the Synod's contribution toward the winning of the war waged for justice and humanity. . . . With rejoicing we welcome our returning young men."[86] At such a sensitive time when hyphenated ethnic-American identities were called into question, Swedish immigrants wanted to put a definite emphasis upon their American loyalties.[87]

On the national level, the Swedish Covenant and Lutheran churches as institutions remained in the American Protestant mainstream, both by the intentional efforts of their leaders and by the ideological orientation of their members. By working to rid the nation of the scourge of intemperance and by defending the American flag, leaders in the Augustana and Covenant denominations protected the reputation of the Swedish immigrants and projected an image of an immigrant group easily compatible with white American middle-class values. Furthermore, the building of educational institutions, hospital facilities, and urban missions of various kinds suggested the prosperity of an immigrant people. The intent was to distance Swedes from the immigrants arriving from southern and eastern Europe, and more generally from all types of immigrant radicalism. At both the local and national levels, these approaches ultimately aided religious Swedish immigrants in adjusting to their lives in America and in creating important aspects of a Swedish American identity.

TRANSITIONS IN RELIGIOUS IDENTITY

The pattern of the growth and expansion of Swedish churches in Chicago was the same for all denominations: institutional development followed population movement into Chicago's sprawling new neighborhoods. As long as Swedes remained in an area, the Swedish-speaking churches there flourished. Ethnicity remained an important part of Swedish identity, but the ethnic institutions themselves could not sustain all of the immigrants' needs, nor could they hold the Swedes in a particular area of the city. Much greater trends would lure the Swedes to new areas: rapid population growth in older areas of Chicago, the increasing ethnic diversity of the city, improved transportation networks, and the dispersal of jobs to newer and more scattered areas of Chicago. New subdivisions beckoned newcomers with opportunities for home ownership and increasingly easy access to jobs, and the move there reflected the upward mobility of the Swedish community. Once the Swedish population moved, so did their churches. As one member of the Covenant Church in Humboldt Park remembered: "The area around Humboldt Park had [by 1879] become part of the city, and the streets were laid out. . . . More and more people moved west, therefore it also became necessary to move the [mission] work."[88] Churches provided a context for immigrant mobility.

Swedish denominations became subcommunities of the Swedish population in Chicago, and more expansively, of Swedes in the United States. At the same time, they reflected the tensions of Swedish American institutions and the transition that was occurring in the larger Swedish community. New immigration from Sweden—halted during the First World War—never resumed the proportions of immigration in the 1880s and the early 1900s. As the Swedish-born population in Chicago declined by 7 percent from 1910 to 1920, church-building among Swedish Lutherans and Covenanters declined significantly.

The language issue was at the heart of the transition: although English made some inroads in churches prior to 1920, especially among youth organizations and among specifically English-speaking congregations, the fact that Swedish remained the dominant language of the churches limited their appeal to the immigrants' children.[89] As immigrant institutions, the churches reflected an over-all aging of the Swedish immigrant population and needed a new agenda if they were to continue to thrive in the postimmigration period. When the churches moved toward a greater reliance upon the English language after World War One, the immigrants effectively passed church leadership on to a new generation, hoping to preserve their ethnic and religious identity while recognizing that the future belonged to their American-born children and grandchildren.[90]

VIKINGS, ODD FELLOWS, AND TEMPLARS

Voluntary Association in Sweden and Chicago

> A spark still lives of the primeval fire,
> Within the Northman's bosom. Nurse it, then
> Each noble son of an heroic sire!
> What scions of a high-born race! What men!
> The clash of shields is past, but hearts beat higher,
> And fame shall flash from out of the North again.
>
> —From the Initiation Ritual of the Swedish fraternal order Independent
> Order of Svithiod, harking back to their Viking heritage, 1923.

Like the Swedish churches, Swedish clubs and organizations allowed for continuity in ethnic expression in a very diverse city. The growing, sprawling city of Chicago provided a flexible urban environment that allowed those who settled there to map out their own organizational network, and thus create their own community. Between 1880 and 1920 Swedes did just that, founding over 145 social organizations throughout Chicago. These clubs functioned in a similar fashion as the churches: they were places where immigrants' Swedish heritage intersected with their need to create primary relationships with other like-minded Swedes. Voluntary associations provided a forum for Swedes to combine Nordic traditions with new urban realities, and were often infused with an ethnic symbolism that gave Swedish immigrants an identity separate from other groups in Chicago. Although these organizations provided a means for preserving ethnicity, most were not intended to be replicas of clubs known to the immigrants in Sweden. On the contrary, Swedes created associations to meet their needs for social interaction, intellectual growth, recreation, and financial security in their new American home, Chicago.[1]

Swedish associational life between 1880 and 1920 reflected a remarkably diversified and adaptable pattern of affiliation. Per Nordahl, in writing about Swedish radicalism in Chicago, notes that "there was a constant struggle between different perceptions of what it meant to belong to a specific ethnic group and how best to make use of [a group's heritage] in its new context."[2] The most obvious and deeply felt subdivision within the Swedish community occurred between religious and secular organizational camps. But the divisions and debates in the community were not merely bipolar, they were multifaceted. As pointed out in the previous chapter, religious Swedes were divided by a variety of disagreements over denominational structures and theological interpretations. The more secularly oriented Swedish organizations also split up the community, usually along lines of ideology, class, and gender. The issue of drinking, for example, divided temperance clubs from the imbibing fraternal lodges. Political and ideological differences separated trade unions from social clubs. Class differences manifested themselves in the separation between working-class fraternal orders and the more elite organizations that sought to unite and speak for the entire Swedish community. The most basic division within the secular side of community life was that of gender. As they were founded, most fraternal orders only opened their doors to men, forcing women to create their own organizations or peripheral clubs and reinforcing the separation between men and women evident in late nineteenth-century America. This chapter will explore the rapid growth and development of neighborhood-based voluntary associations; the next chapter will delve into the efforts of more elite Swedish associations to create a strong, united Swedish presence in Chicago and to unify Swedish organizations in the city.

THE CONTEXT OF VOLUNTARY ASSOCIATION

The creation of Swedish voluntary associations in Chicago was part of an international process that affected people in all modern, urban, industrial societies. In the past, historians and sociologists understood these associations as replacements for the security once found in the church, family, and traditional community. Industrialization, according to this argument, weakened traditional institutions and spawned the need for new types of personal association. More recently, scholars have asserted the resilience of traditional institutions in modern society and argued against the belief that industrialization led to a decline in the importance of the family and a disintegration in communal affiliations.[3] Furthermore, as pointed out earlier in this study, traditional institutions such as family and

church were not static nor were they always backward-looking; they adapted to
fill the needs of an immigrant population living in a foreign society and culture.
Voluntary associations also played an important role in urban immigrant communities. Richard Oestreicher points out that the tendency to voluntarily associate helped workers maintain control over their lives in terms of ethnic culture,
family, work, and community involvement.[4] Roy Rosenzweig, in his study about
workers in Worcester, Massachusetts, argues that ethnic communities provided
workers with an arena in which they could influence their own lives. He notes
that organizational infrastructures within ethnic communities "offered Worcester
workers a sphere in which they could carry out a mode of life and express values,
beliefs, and traditions significantly different from those prescribed by the dominant industrial elite."[5] Voluntary associations were thus creative instruments to
assist immigrants in adapting to the American industrial milieu.

The structure of voluntary associations in Sweden and the United States was
very similar—those such as fraternal and temperance orders were based on international infrastructures and models. The meaning of those associations in the
larger urban context differed significantly in each country, however. Arnold M.
Rose defines a voluntary association as a group of people who "finding they have a
certain interest (or purpose) in common, agree to meet and act together in order
to try to satisfy that purpose."[6] In Sweden, voluntary associations united people
according to philosophical views or social standing, much as in Rose's definition.
In Chicago, Swedish organizations took on an ethnic dimension not necessary in
Sweden's homogeneous society. Swedish voluntary associations in Chicago differ-
entiated Swedes according to status, interest, or viewpoint; they separated Swedes
from other groups in the city according to national heritage, language, and traditions. Both status and ethnicity served to strengthen voluntary affiliations, creating tightly knit subcommunities within the Swedish enclaves. The sum of these
ethnic organizations created a cultural system in Swedish Chicago that attracted
people's interest and loyalties while at the same time diminishing ideological or
class affiliations with members of other ethnic groups.[7] Over time, voluntary associations mirrored larger changes within the Swedish community. By 1920, they
witnessed a generational divergence in affiliation patterns and a tension in their
hybrid, Swedish American identity.

SWEDISH BACKGROUND

Swedish immigrants arriving in Chicago in the late nineteenth and early twentieth centuries had been exposed to a strong tradition of voluntary association in their homeland. In addition, some individuals had direct experience of

membership in particular clubs and organizations. As noted in the previous chapter, church affiliation often depended upon exposure to particular religious ideas in Sweden. Per Nordahl also concludes that on the other end of the spectrum, free-thinking Swedes in Chicago replicated organizational and personal affiliations they had experienced in Sweden.[8] In the same fashion, immigrants who joined temperance and fraternal orders in Chicago often had been exposed to similar types of organizations in Sweden. Influences traveled in both directions, however. The formation of temperance and fraternal societies in Sweden paralleled the creation of similar associations in the United States and were often based directly upon American prototypes. In both countries, the growth of voluntary associations accelerated as each society became increasingly urban and industrial.

In Sweden, the impulse for people to organize into voluntary associations began in the early nineteenth century. These associations evolved from small clubs to large networks of organizations that connected people from around the country. Torkel Jansson points out that "voluntary association was a suitable tool for solving social problems," helping to fill the void between the crown's system of poor relief and private philanthropy, neither of which was adequate in a country that was moving away from the confines and predetermined social relationships of preindustrial society.[9] The Evangelical Society became Sweden's first voluntary association in 1808, formed to spread religious publications throughout Sweden. Other associations that stressed temperance, philanthropy, and general education became more commonplace by mid-century. For example, the Society for the Promotion of Monitorial Education was formed in 1822, the Swedish Missionary Society in 1835, and the Swedish Temperance Society in 1837. These organizations were based on a notion that the root of poverty's eradication and the solution to society's problems lay in education of the public.

Swedish voluntary organizations grew after the mid-nineteenth century and expanded beyond the upper classes. In the mid-1840s, people from the middle strata of society began to form educational circles and workingmen's associations, influenced from abroad and centered in urban areas. Organizations that offered sickness and burial funds also spread after mid-century as a means of creating financial security for workers. These early associations were the forerunners of the large-scale organizations that grew in popularity in Sweden after the 1860s. By the late nineteenth century, voluntary associations based upon principles of general assembly and equality attracted large numbers of people. These massive movements centered on the free church, temperance, and trade union issues, and were frequently national organizations with localized congregations, lodges, or chapters. Jansson argues that the formation of these types of associations contributed to the modernization of Swedish society in a nonrevolutionary fashion. The major focus of this chapter will be upon the temperance and, more extensively, the fraternal movements in Sweden and in Swedish America.

The temperance movement in Sweden grew remarkably during the nineteenth century, evolving from small elitist clubs to vast working-class organizations. As Jansson points out, the founders of the Swedish Temperance Society never intended to "promote associations of people throughout Sweden."[10] The main purpose of the Temperance Society when it was founded in 1837 was to influence the clergy to promote abstinence among their parishioners. Many times, church members joined under duress, pressured to do so by their parish minister. This elite effort at controlling lower-class behavior resembled American efforts at temperance reform. As an effort to impose social change from above, its impact was limited.[11]

The Swedish temperance associations of the late nineteenth century, founded upon international organizational paradigms, differed significantly from these early efforts. In 1879, Olof Bergström, a Baptist preacher, founded the International Order of Good Templars (IOGT) in Sweden, based directly upon and affiliated with the Independent Order of Good Templars in the United States. This organization promoted membership throughout Sweden, encouraging members of the working class to improve their lives through temperance and education—themes also evident in the up-and-coming trade union movement. By the following year, ten active lodges had been established in Sweden. The movement spread quickly, reaching 58,014 members by 1888, and peaking in 1910 with nearly 160,000 members in more than 2,000 lodges. The IOGT gained strength from Sweden's traditions of temperance and voluntary association among ordinary workers, who made up the vast majority of Templars.[12]

By the turn of the twentieth century, the temperance movement split ideologically as it simultaneously spread from urban into rural areas. The IOGT began in Göteborg, Sweden's second largest city, but soon the largest districts in the Order were Skåne, Östergötland, Östersund, and Dalarna.[13] As it grew, the IOGT struggled with ideological issues about whether or not to embrace socialism—a political doctrine increasingly popular among Swedish workers. Initially resistant to socialist ideas, the IOGT leaders gradually accepted more radical ideology. Their willingness to do so led to the creation of a more conservative, rival organization in 1888, the National Good Templar Order. Other temperance advocates who believed that the IOGT was not radical enough founded the Verdandi Temperance Order (*Nykterhetsorden Verdandi*). Additional temperance organizations included the Motorists' Total Abstinence Association, Sweden's Teachers' Temperance Association, and the White Band—a branch of the Women's Christian Temperance International.[14] Overall, the temperance movement made deep inroads into the Swedish population, and the formation of affiliated lodges allowed large numbers of individuals to participate in the cause. Thus, by the late nineteenth century, the temperance movement in Sweden had a strongly democratic, worker-oriented flavor, distinguishing it from the American prohibition movement, which John Rumbarger argues was an effort by America's capitalist class to control worker behavior and expand industrial production.[15]

The expansion of the IOGT lodges in Göteborg gives a prime example of the manner and speed with which these organizations took hold in Sweden. The first IOGT lodge, Klippan Number One, was established in 1879, and soon thereafter, several smaller groups broke off to form new lodges. During the decade of the 1880s, at least thirty-nine new lodges formed in Göteborg's district of the IOGT, followed by more than forty additional lodges during the 1890s. Charter membership of these new clubs ranged from eight to forty-seven members, and included both men and women. In 1881, "children's temples" were begun in the district, hoping to enlist young people in the cause of temperance. The names of most of the lodges were Nordic in origin, such as *troheten* (the faith), *broderska- pet* (the brothers' cause), "Svea," a name applied to the country of Sweden, and "Gustaf Vasa," after one of Sweden's most famous kings. The American influence crept in, however, and some lodges took on the names "Amerika," "John Ericsson," after the Swedish immigrant in America who designed the Civil War–era iron-hulled steamship the *Monitor*, and "Georg [sic] Washington."[16] Although activities centered upon particular lodges, IOGT members were part of an organization with impact beyond a particular town or community. The manner in which the IOGT in Sweden spread in urban areas paralleled the Templar's efforts in Swedish America, and placed the Swedish IOGT at the front of the International Templar Movement.

Although not nearly as extensive as temperance associations, fraternal societies also met with some measure of success in Sweden. The International Order of Odd Fellows and the Vasa Order of America, both foreign in origin, established branches of their organizations in Sweden. Heavy on symbolism and ceremony, the Swedish division of the International Order of Odd Fellows was founded in 1892 in Stockholm, and the first lodge was called "John Ericsson." Odd Fellowship actually originated in Great Britain in the late eighteenth century and at that time represented a working-class effort to resist the negative impact of the early stages of the Industrial Revolution. As the order spread to the United States, it evolved into a middle-class organization whose members valued respectability and sober behavior. This was the character of the group that in turn came to Sweden, where its main purpose was "to spread brotherly thoughts in the world and friendship among people . . . to educate others about love for God and for others . . . [and] to aid mankind's common circumstances and thereby accomplish improvements."[17]

A close examination of the first Odd Fellow lodge established in Göteborg reveals an organization far removed from Sweden's tradition of working-class voluntary associations. In 1895, one of the organizers of the original Stockholm Odd Fellow lodge moved to Göteborg and started the lodge "Gustaf II Adolf." The organization provided sickness and death benefits to members, but the membership of the lodge did not come from the stratum of society that most needed such benefits. A membership roster of this particular lodge during its first twenty-five years of existence indicates its members were among the most educated and highly trained men in the city. This was not a laborers' lodge: the majority of members worked in some aspect of business, and a significant number held positions in technical fields, the health professions, shipping, and manufacturing. A smaller portion worked in education, law, and journalism, and only one member registered his occupation as farmer. Women were not admitted to the Order. The total membership in this lodge grew slowly from 91 in 1895 to a peak of 180 in 1920.[18] Undoubtedly, this group was a coalition of many of the city's leaders; it was a social fraternity embracing the status quo rather than an activist association created to mitigate social problems.

A similar organization, the Vasa Order of America, established its first lodge in Sweden in 1921. The bylaws of this society stated that it would work in Sweden "for the order's noble purpose and worthy goals . . . especially . . . for similar sentiment between Swedes in America and Sweden."[19] This group—like the Odd Fellows and the Templars—was based on an organizational structure imported from abroad. The Vasa Lodge insured members against sickness and death and created solid links between the United States and Sweden. Although no comprehensive portrait of membership exists, a list of the officers in 1924 indicates that the leadership included a business director, a professor, a wife, and an editor. In contrast to the Odd Fellows, women were welcomed into membership and even elected to positions of leadership, not a typical scenario among fraternal orders.[20] The Vasa Order represented an effort by Swedes living in America to embrace those left behind in Sweden within the same organizational umbrella. It never, however, reached deeply into the Swedish population.

Voluntary associations in Sweden flourished during the period when the country was experiencing population dislocation caused by the early stages of industrial growth. Temperance associations such as the IOGT were particularly popular in Sweden, and represented a worldwide effort to eradicate the influence of alcohol upon society. The Odd Fellows and the Vasa Order, although not matching the success of the temperance groups, also reflected organizations with direct transatlantic relationships. Thus, many of the Swedes who arrived in Chicago in the late nineteenth and early twentieth centuries had been exposed to voluntary associations in Sweden, and some even had direct experience as members of such organizations. As Per Nordahl points out, organizations such as the IOGT had been "founded in America decades earlier, been exported to Scandinavia and re-shaped according to Swedish norms and ideals, and finally re-exported back to America with the emigrants."[21] In Chicago Swedish voluntary associations took on additional significance. Not only did these organizations allow immigrants to affiliate with others who shared similar interests and viewpoints, they also incorporated an ethnic dimension that served to reinforce the immigrants' Swedish identity and distinguish them from other groups in the city.

SWEDISH ASSOCIATIONS IN CHICAGO

Between 1880 and 1920, Swedish organizational life in Chicago flourished. The growth of voluntary associations allowed Swedes to create strong ethnic organizations where newly arriving immigrants could connect with Swedes already established in the city. Swedes created organizations based upon their interests in sports, music, temperance, social security, or simply their desire to unite with other Swedes for socializing and fellowship. Fraternal associations—the most successful among Swedish secular organizations in Chicago during this period—joined members into sickness and death beneficiary societies in addition to providing them with important social interaction. These social connections were at times reinforced by women's auxiliaries and children's lodges, providing lodge-connected activities for entire families.[22] The result was a complex web of Swedish organizations in Chicago, uniting various small neighborhood lodges and clubs into citywide and national associations. The presence of such a range of Swedish organizations in Chicago added to the diversity of opportunities for affiliation available within the Swedish community.

As Swedes first settled in Chicago, their relatively small numbers led to the formation of many pan-Scandinavian associations. In 1870, the Swedish population was slightly less than the Norwegian, numbering 6,154 and 6,374 respectively. Such small numbers created a need for cooperation between these groups, particularly when founding organizations.[23] According to Ulf Beijbom, approximately forty Swedish and pan-Scandinavian organizations existed in Chicago prior to 1880 and nearly half of them included Norwegians and Danes in their membership. He characterizes these early organizations as being the "bourgeois immigrants' alternative to the church."[24] The cultural program and social activities of these organizations were more important than providing assistance to other immigrants, an agenda that neglected the needs of the average, newly arriving Swede. As the Swedish population in Chicago doubled during the 1870s and continued to grow in subsequent years, it surpassed the number of Norwegians living in the city. As Odd S. Lovoll has noted, the growth in the number of Swedes along with the increase in Swedish-Norwegian political tensions assured the success of strictly Swedish (or strictly Norwegian) organizations in Chicago, and conversely, made pan-Scandinavian associations problematic.[25]

In the late nineteenth century, large-scale Swedish organizations grew in Chicago, just as they were doing in Sweden. Swedes arrived in Chicago in ever-larger numbers, having been exposed to the spread of voluntary associations in Sweden and finding them useful in their new surroundings. Although few of the forty organizations documented by Beijbom thrived beyond 1880, other newer Swedish associations flourished. In fact, between 1880 and 1920 Swedes built more than 145 ethnic lodges and clubs in the city of Chicago. Membership in the Svithiod and Viking Lodges alone involved nearly 20 percent of the Swedish-born population in Chicago by 1920.[26]

Table 3a. Membership Statistics of Chicago's Svithiod and Viking Orders, 1880–1920

Organization	1880	1890	1900	1910	1920
Svithiod	200	557	2814	4876	6344
Viking	—	542	986	4284	4997
Total Membership	200	1099	3800	9160	11,331

Table 3b. Membership as Percentage of Swedish-Born Population in Chicago

Organization	1880	1890	1900	1910	1920
Svithiod	1.55%	1.29%	5.76%	7.49%	10.82%
Viking	—	1.26%	2.02%	6.59%	8.53%
Totals	1.55%	2.55%	7.78%	14.08%	19.35%
Total Swedish-Born	12,930	43,032	48,836	65,035	58,563

Table 3c. Membership as Percentage of Swedish Stock

Organization	1880	1890	1900	1910	1920
Svithiod	—	.89%	2.73%	4.18%	5.22%
Viking	—	.87%	.95%	3.67%	4.12%
Totals	—	1.76%	3.68%	7.85%	9.34%
Total Swedish Stock	—	62,235	103,220	116,740	121,326

Note: Club membership statistics do not exactly correspond with the census material that appears by decade, thus statistics from the closest available date are used. For the Svithiod Order, those dates are 1885, 1893, 1910, and 1921. For the Viking Order, the dates are 1892, 1900, 1910, and 1914.

Swedes formed many types of secular organizations in Chicago, ranging from small recreational clubs to large fraternal orders. The structure of the organizations themselves was not unique to the Swedish community, but the content of the meetings and the characteristics of membership infused these voluntary associations with Swedish distinctiveness.

Sports clubs contributed to the vast array of organizational options in Swedish Chicago. The Swedish sports clubs were loose affiliations of men who gathered for purposes of recreation and athletic competition. Demonstrations and contests also provided opportunities for social activity and exhibitions of Swedish pride. Axel Werelius, who later became a doctor and founded the South Shore Hospital, began the first Swedish American gymnastics club in 1894. The group called themselves "Lings Pojkar" (Ling's Boys) after Pehr Henrik Ling, founder of a gymnastic system based on scientific muscle development. This club gave its first demonstration to the thunderous approval of a North Side audience. Dances were often held after gymnastic demonstrations, turning them into major social events in the community. The club visited parks and other recreational areas, where Dr. Werelius remembered that Swedish "swains and maidens . . . met, frolicked, danced . . . and played other homeland games sometimes till early dawn."[27] Similar athletic groups formed in other parts of the city where Swedes resided and served as a focal point for social activities.

In order to centralize some of the athletic events in the Swedish community, North Side athletic groups formed the Chicago Swedish Athletic Club in 1913, later known as the Swedish American Recreation Club of Chicago. On the South Side, the athletic clubs merged to form the Swedish-American Athletic Association in 1914. The object of the latter organization, as stated in its charter, was to "promote clean amateur athletics of all kinds and social welfare for its members."[28] Both of these organizations sponsored teams in track and field, soccer, boxing, wrestling, bike racing, and swimming. These groups competed with similar teams sponsored by the Greek Olympic Club, the German Turners, and the Norwegian and Danish-American Athletic Clubs.[29] They combined recreational interest with national pride and friendly competition against other ethnic groups in the city.

Swedish musical groups played a dual role in forging both an "everyday" ethnicity and a more elite, consciously created ethnic identity.[30] Singing clubs provided musical and social outlets for Swedish immigrants, and in doing so, promoted Swedish culture in the city. The vast majority of these singing clubs limited membership to men, creating a subculture within the Swedish community based on fraternal relationships and manly performances.[31] Members of the Svithiod Singing Club, founded in 1893 for the purpose of creating "a Society for the cultivation of the Voice and other Social Amusements," performed musicals, entertained at picnics, parades and soirees, and competed in citywide singing competitions.[32]

FIGURE 11. The Svithiod Chorus, pictured in 1896, offered Svithiod Lodge members the opportunity to reinforce fraternal relationships through music while also promoting Swedish culture in Chicago. Courtesy of Swedish-American Archives of Greater Chicago, North Park University, Chicago.

Larger musical societies were in an even better position to preserve and promote Swedish music. The chartered purpose of the Swedish Singers Union of Chicago was fairly narrow: to encourage "the study and practice of music among its members" and "to cultivate and foster Social, Moral and Intellectual ideals among its members." Likewise, the primary aim of the American Union of Swedish Singers was the "cultivation and promotion of singing, music, and good fellowship."[33] Another early organization, Föreningen Freja, evolved into the Swedish Glee Club in 1889 and then incorporated as the Swedish Club of Chicago in 1923. It owned and operated a clubhouse at 1258 North LaSalle Street. By that time it focused on promoting Swedish culture and social interactions.[34]

The underlying purpose of all of these musical organizations was much more expansive, however. They all asserted a positive Swedish identity in a new homeland. Participants—perhaps subconsciously—used their festivals to establish a favorable impression of Swedish Americans as compared with other ethno-racial groups. A souvenir program from a concert of the American Union of Swedish Singers claimed that the group's ambition was "to cultivate Swedish male chorus singing and to make Swedish elements of culture known and appreciated in this country," and a concert program of the Svithiod Singing Club stated the club's purpose was "to carry forth in this country that native love of song, inherent of their Motherland, and develop it to a like efficiency over here."[35] Furthermore, H. Arnold Barton notes that men's choral societies served an important function of raising the cultural level of their members, most of whom came from relatively humble backgrounds. Barton writes that "The singers turned out in evening dress and white visored caps of the type worn by graduates of the elite *gymnasium* back home." Their activities were quite formal, focusing on "banquets, balls, and ceremonies . . . [and] placing a premium upon dignified and genteel behavior." The musical selections they performed became a vehicle for cultural education, for the audience as well as for the performers, because "the repertory required familiarity with literary Swedish and proper pronunciation of both Swedish and English."[36] Hence, Swedish singing societies offered participants and spectators opportunities to remember, celebrate, and reinvent their Swedish cultural heritage while creating important relationships among Swedes in the city.

Swedish theater productions added another dimension to the expression of Swedish culture in Chicago. Condemned by pietistic churchgoers, the Swedish theater was embraced by secular clubs and more liberal thinkers. According to Henriette C. K. Naeseth, the Swedish theater in Chicago emerged out of the same conditions as did the social clubs, singing groups, and lodges. She notes that "A sense of strangeness, a dislike of loneliness, [and] the handicap of an alien language" contributed to the popularity of the Swedish theater.[37] Voluntary associations also contributed to the success of the Swedish theater in more direct ways.

FIGURE 12. This banquet was held in conjunction with a Swedish musical festival in 1905. Organized by the "Swedish Ladies of Chicago," this postcard highlights the formality of many such occasions, emphasizing the genteel setting and dignified behavior of participants. Courtesy of Swedish-American Archives of Greater Chicago, North Park University, Chicago.

The Svea Society sponsored Chicago's first Swedish theatrical presentations in the late 1860s. By the early twentieth century, groups with political or ideological agendas, such as temperance lodges or socialist clubs, often produced their own plays. More frequently, social clubs and lodges supported the theater by regularly attending and enthusiastically publicizing performances as a means of light-hearted entertainment.[38]

Small troupes of actors emerged to stage these productions. The Swedish Theater Society (*Svenska Teatersällskapet*) was active in the first two decades of the twentieth century. The society was made up of experienced Swedish actors who themselves were Swedish immigrants in Chicago. These actors frequently were joined by performers directly from Sweden who were touring the United States. Turner Hall, located on the near North Side of the city, frequently served as the venue for Swedish plays. Audiences there typically ranged from five hundred to two thousand people. When the number of people attending performances did not meet expectations, the secular Swedish press chided readers and encouraged them to attend, while churches discouraged their members from doing the same. The popularity of the theater among less-religious folk was also encouraged by other factors. Beer and refreshments were served before and after performances, and when the play was over, the tables and chairs were cleared and the dancing began. Frequently the party continued into the early morning hours.[39]

During the 1920s and 1930s, a generational shift occurred in the Swedish theater in Chicago. A new group formed, the Swedish Folk Theater (*Svenska folk-teatern*), made up of new Swedish immigrants and fueled by a growing sense of Swedish nationalism in both Sweden and America. Particularly popular were productions of *Vermländingarne* (The people of Värmland), a play that Lars Furuland claims "deserves the name of Swedish national drama in the United States."[40] The play deals with themes of the declining significance of class distinctions, love for the homeland, and regional linguistic dialects—all wrapped into the form of a folk comedy that struck a chord with an immigrant audience. On a lighter side, touring vaudeville-style shows such as *Olle i Skratthult* (Olle from Laughtersville) entertained Swedes by presenting a varied repertory of jokes, Swedish songs, and poems recited in a Värmland dialect. The leader of this group, Hjalmar Peterson, poked fun at immigrant life and provided an often romanticized link with the home country. Peterson always performed in Swedish, but other performers blended Swedish and English—a formula that could only work if the audience understood both languages.[41] By the end of the 1930s, the popularity of Swedish theater in Chicago began to fade as the number of first-generation Swedes living in the city diminished.

As with the musical and theatrical societies, the temperance movement projected a positive image of Swedes—particularly common laborers—while offering social connections for people with similar interests. Drawing on its success in Sweden, the Independent Order of Good Templars grew rapidly in Chicago. From early in its history, the IOGT welcomed women to its ranks and after 1887, it admitted persons of all races and creeds. In addition to temperance, the IOGT supported an agenda for workers' rights to education and self-improvement, and for the "Elevation of Mankind, for Democracy, for the Equality of Sexes and Races, for International Brotherhood."[42] All of these positions placed the Templars to the political left of the dominant, more conservative wings of the American temperance movement. Even the Prohibition Party—a third political party in America founded in 1870 to critique the nation's new capitalistic order—became more conservative in subsequent decades. As many disaffected Republicans joined the Prohibition Party in the 1880s, its pro-labor, anticapitalistic rhetoric was toned down in favor of a platform that viewed the laboring class as an object needing to be reformed rather than an ally in reform. By the turn of the century, American temperance reformers focused on the urban saloon as the source of the drinking problem in America: by eliminating the saloon, corporate leaders could better control workers' leisure time and enhance their productive capacity. This position was as much anti-immigrant as it was antilabor and antiliquor.[43]

By contrast, the Independent Order of Good Templars actively recruited the nation's immigrant workers, and the Scandinavians proved especially receptive due to their familiarity with the temperance movement in general and the IOGT in particular. The establishment of separate Swedish lodges assured the participation of Swedish immigrants and added to the Order's success, giving the lodges an ethnic as well as an ideological focus. From 1882 until 1907, Swedes formed thirteen Good Templar lodges in Chicago, and in 1907, the Swedish Templars created the Scandinavian Grand Lodge of Illinois, a separate Scandinavian wing of the American Good Templars. The Swedish IOGT lodges in Chicago competed with other secular societies and churches for the attention of Swedish immigrants. They established youth lodges in which the primary language was English in order to reach out to their offspring, formed sports clubs and singing societies to provide a nondrinking alternative for people seeking such activities, and purchased a park in Geneva, Illinois where social activities could take place in an alcohol-free environment. The Templars also provided lifelong care for their members by establishing homes for the elderly in Park Ridge and Evanston, Illinois. In these ways, the IOGT created a lifelong, all-encompassing safety net for its constituents. In doing so, it approached Raymond Breton's condition of "institutional completeness."[44]

The bonds created by the IOGT members in Sweden survived the Atlantic crossing more intact than did those for other secular associations, with the possible exception of socialists and political radicals.[45] Fully three-quarters of Chicago's

Swedish Good Templar leaders transferred their membership from IOGT lodges in Sweden, and some had already joined a number of different lodges before arriving in the United States. For example, in 1881 J. A. Runnberg first joined the Templars in the town of Kågeröd in Sweden's southern county of Skåne. He transferred his membership to a lodge in Helsingborg and finally joined the lodge "Idoghet" in Chicago after emigrating in 1891. Runnberg became a leader among Chicago's Templars, and his wife and daughters were also active IOGT members. Another Templar, Gust F. Ockerman, brought his IOGT affiliation with him wherever he moved. He joined three lodges in Sweden before emigrating and two in Chicago as he moved in the city, a pattern fairly typical of Swedish Templars in Chicago. E. Knut Hessling also joined his first Templar lodge in the Swedish province of Dalarna, then affiliated with IOGT lodge Hoppets Här #441 after arriving in Chicago. Hessling commented in the IOGT anniversary publication: "I love the Order because for thirteen years it was my only home. Now I've been married for three years, so I have twin homes. . . . I was born, have lived, live, and shall die a Good Templar."[46] Like the Swedish churches in Chicago, membership in the IOGT provided a personal context to immigrant mobility and complemented familial relationships, cultivating a strong sense of loyalty to the lodge among its members.

Even more popular than the IOGT, fraternal organizations became the most successful prototype of secular Swedish associations in Chicago with the advent of grand lodges and the expansion of their branches throughout the city. Ulf Beijbom attributes the growth of Swedish American fraternal orders to their provision of social assistance in unstable economic circumstances. He notes that in the 1890s, the fraternal orders' increased emphasis upon death, sickness, and unemployment benefits increased their appeal to many Swedish newcomers.[47] These organizations started as small clubs centered in the older Swedish enclaves in the city. After the 1880s, they grew with the Swedish population in Chicago and extended activities to new Swedish neighborhoods. The success of these associations unified two opposing trends: to expand organizational tendencies characteristic of urban society, and the need for Swedish immigrants to create small, local lodges in a new and growing American city. These neighborhood-based lodges allowed for more localized participation, connection, and control for individual members.

The Independent Order of Svithiod and the Independent Order of Vikings both began in Chicago as single clubs, then expanded to National Grand Lodges with local branches. Their largest period of growth was from 1890 to 1906 when thirteen Svithiod lodges and fifteen Viking Lodges were founded. After that point, lodge formation among these groups slowed, as only three Svithiod lodges and three Viking lodges came into being from 1907 until 1920. These two organizations were the largest Swedish fraternal orders in Chicago.

Because they also originated in Chicago, they provide perfect case studies for an analysis of the structure and content of fraternal lodges and will be looked at in greater detail later in this chapter.

The other two major fraternal orders that met with success in Chicago were the Scandinavian Fraternity of America (SFA) and the Vasa Order of America (VOA). The SFA had its roots in three different organizations named "The Scandinavian Brotherhood of America." One of these groups began in Butte, Montana in 1889, and the other two were initiated in Warren, Pennsylvania in 1894 and 1900. These three organizations eventually united in 1915 at a meeting in Chicago, forming the national SFA. By that time, nine lodges had been formed in Chicago with a membership of nearly 1,500, fairly evenly divided between men and women. The SFA attempted to unite persons of Scandinavian origin and overcome political differences between the Nordic countries, believing that "all worthy descendants of the Vikings are bound together in one grand chain of noble fraternity."[48] The Order encouraged members to lead temperate lives, and some members in this lodge were also active in the International Order of Good Templars.[49]

In a similar fashion, the Vasa Order of America was imported from elsewhere in the United States. Originating in New Haven, Connecticut in 1896, the VOA arrived in Chicago in 1908. Between 1908 and 1918, twenty-three Vasa lodges were founded in Chicago, three of them for women and the rest limited to male membership. After 1916, many local men's lodges began to admit women. The VOA paralleled other fraternal orders by offering sickness and funeral benefits to members while emphasizing the importance of fraternal comradeship. It stressed the moral, intellectual, and social growth of its members and encouraged them to be worthy representatives of the Swedish nation.[50] Thus, in their own fashion, both the SFA and VOA attempted to forge a positive image of Swedish immigrants in their adopted homeland.

Each fraternal order in Chicago had an initial surge of growth at its establishment, which shortly tapered off to a pattern of slower, steady expansion. Once lodges were established, some degree of entrenched leadership and membership existed, and often it became more appealing for individuals seeking organizational affiliation to link up with newly formed fraternal orders where they could wield greater influence in the life of the lodge. In all, fraternal lodges provided newly arriving Swedish immigrants with a sense of security, offering financial insurance during sickness and death and—in more pleasant times—companionship and friendship.

The Swedish Engineers Society, founded in Chicago in 1908, offered professional affiliation for more socially elite Swedes. Chicago attracted engineers of all kinds—people who found work designing and building much of the new construction around the city—and Swedish engineers were no exception. The purposes of the Swedish Engineers Society of Chicago, according to Byron J. Nordstrom, were "professional, educational, ethnic, cultural, and social."[51] Early member Henry Nyberg also remembers that the group sought to promote the standing and reputation of Swedish engineers in the city, particularly compared to "the Irish, the German, and a few other nationalities [present in the city] at that time."[52] Members celebrated holidays together, held social events, and sponsored educational programs. Along with sports, musical, temperance, and fraternal societies, the Swedish Engineers added to the diverse network of Swedish organizations in Chicago, which, like the churches, assisted immigrants in adapting to life in an American city.

SVITHIOD AND VIKING LODGES

The creation and expansion of Swedish fraternal orders in Chicago—groups such as the Independent Orders of Svithiod and Vikings—took place within the larger context of American fraternalism. Mark C. Carnes points out that the last third of the nineteenth century was referred to by contemporaries as "the Golden Age of Fraternity."[53] Hundreds of insurance societies came into existence between 1880 and 1900, most of them offering cheap insurance, secret rituals, and common fellowship. American men joined these fraternal orders for a number of reasons. Certainly tangible benefits such as business contacts and insurance policies provided enough incentive for many people to join. But as Carnes points out, most urban historians claim the overriding reason men became members of fraternal orders was to combat the impersonal environment of the city by providing "cohesive social networks" and the opportunity to "re-create the face-to-face relationships and values formerly associated with family and community." In this manner, "the orders became a source of stability amidst the social chaos of modern life."[54] While not discounting these motivations, Carnes instead emphasizes the fact that the ritual itself attracted men to fraternal orders, and that rituals were "closely linked to issues of gender." He argues that "fraternal ritual provided solace and psychological guidance during young men's troubled passage to manhood in Victorian America."[55] Victor W. Turner notes that the use of ritual often occurs within a society undergoing a perceived crisis, and according to Carnes, late nineteenth-century America was just such an arena of crisis for the middle-class male. Complex rituals encouraged middle-class men to retreat into a secret place where they could bond with each other and take refuge from the changing world around them.

What is missing from all of these analyses is the importance of ethnicity in drawing men to fraternal orders. Mary Ann Clawson argues that from the 1860s to the 1880s, fraternalism in America was characterized by cultural pluralism as American lodges welcomed immigrants to their ranks. After the 1880s, as nativism in the United States increased, American fraternal orders became more ethnically exclusive.[56] This trend created a greater need for ethnic-based fraternal orders and fed the popularity of the Swedish lodges in Chicago in the late nineteenth century. But even more than their exclusion from American groups, working-class Swedish immigrants were drawn to their own fraternal orders because of the lodges' ethnic distinctiveness. Through club meetings and secret rituals, Swedish immigrants could retreat to a place where they could build important contacts with those who shared similar economic and social conditions. They could also celebrate their common Nordic heritage in the language of their native land. Swedes not only used fraternal lodges as a refuge from the multiethnic metropolis surrounding them, they also employed them as a means of adapting to their adopted country. Their mutual assistance programs assured that no member would fall upon hard times. Overall, they protected the reputation of Swedes in the city and promoted a strong sense of Swedish brotherhood.

The rest of this chapter looks at the histories and rituals of the Svithiod and Viking lodges as a window into the world of Swedish fraternity. These Orders were founded in Chicago and typified the genre of the Swedish American fraternal order. Although they resembled their American counterparts, the creation of these clubs arose spontaneously from the immigrants themselves. Four particular aspects of Swedish fraternalism will be examined: the working-class origins of the Swedish fraternal orders; the social connections and context for mobility created by the lodges; the importance of ritual; and changing notions of gender within the organizational structure of the orders. Swedish fraternalism, as reflected in the Svithiods and the Vikings, was largely a working-class movement in which members cared for each other by providing social security in a potentially uncertain urban environment. As lodges expanded throughout the city, they provided a context for the mobility of their members. Svithiods and Vikings were not anti-Christian, but their club rituals and moral understandings distinguished them from the more pious, churchgoing Swedish immigrants. Instead of focusing on Christian symbolism, their ritualistic meetings drew heavily upon Viking mythology and infused members' actions with grand cultural importance. Bastions of Swedish manhood, the Viking and Svithiod rituals celebrated the separate world of men within the community and reflected the gender divisions of late nineteenth-century America. Over time, the fraternal orders themselves reflected the transition of the community as they struggled over issues of language purity, national loyalty, and gender exclusivity.[57]

The Origins

The origins of the Svithiod Order were quite humble. On December 3, 1880, eight men assembled at Bowman's Hall at 370 West Chicago Avenue for the purpose of founding a fraternal beneficiary organization, and nine months later, the state of Illinois granted a charter to The Independent Order of Svithiod of Chicago, Illinois.[58] The charter claimed the purpose of the organization was "assisting its members when sick" and "upon the decease of any member to levy an assessment upon every member . . . payable to the widows, orphans and devisees of said member," and finally "for educational and social purposes which trustees . . . may see fit to establish."[59] The founders deliberately selected Svithiod as the name for the new order. Ancient Icelandic sagas referred to the land and people of Sweden as Svithiod, hence the name harked back to a glorious Nordic past.[60] During the first decade of Svithiod's existence, the club remained centralized in Swede Town. By 1885, membership reached two hundred and soon thereafter, the club devised a system of branch lodges which multiplied the number of actual lodges and spread them throughout the city. In 1893, membership numbered approximately 750, and in 1900 it approached 3,000. Within another twenty years, that number had more than doubled.

The formation of the Viking Club on January 7, 1891, challenged the dominance of the Svithiod Order on the Swedish associational scene, and, like Svithiod, it grew rapidly after its founding. The original lodge was started by a group of young men who usually gathered informally for recreational purposes in a small park on Clark Street near Oak Street. They founded their own lodge, The Vikings, in the Swede Town home of two bachelor brothers, Carl and Gustaf Carlson. Nine other men were present, all of whom became the charter members of the Independent Order of Vikings. Chartered for the purpose of "sociability and benevolence," the organization's membership consisted of thirty men by the end of 1890, and the following year, membership figures skyrocketed to about five hundred members.[61] The Grand Lodge was formed in 1892 for the purpose of organizing subordinate lodges. In 1900, membership neared one thousand, quadrupling in the next decade to over four thousand members by 1910.

Swedish fraternalism in Chicago, as manifested in the Svithiod and Viking lodges, was essentially a working-class movement that created a tight brotherhood of membership. The Chicago lodges differed considerably from the Odd Fellow Lodges established in Sweden, from many nonethnic American fraternal orders, and from the social clubs formed in Swedish Chicago prior to 1880—all of which were mostly upper middle-class in character.[62] Timothy J. Johnson points out that between 1916 and 1920, the membership application registers for the Svithiod Order indicated that nearly one-fifth of the members were machinists and one-tenth were carpenters. A significant number of members were clerks, painters, bricklayers, and tailors, and other occupations represented to a lesser extent included lawyers, bookkeepers, architects, bank tellers, as well as piano makers, general laborers, janitors, and salesmen.[63] The occupational profile of the members joining the Viking Lodge Odin between 1900 and 1915 similarly included mostly blue-collar workers involved in Chicago's building and industrial sectors. More than one-quarter of the Viking members were carpenters, and over one-third were involved in some facet of construction. Other occupational categories included general nonskilled workers, machinists, grocers, teamsters, tailors, and blacksmiths. Two members were medical doctors and served as the lodge's physicians.[64] These fraternal groups were not elite organizations; rather, they represented an association of average Swedish working men who sought fellowship with people like themselves.

In fact, evidence suggests that the Swedish immigrants who joined fraternal orders came from strong working-class roots. Although church and club membership were not mutually exclusive categories, differences in background may have accounted for some of an immigrant's decision about which organization to join. A comparison of membership applications of the Messiah Lutheran Church, the Austin Covenant Church, and the Viking Lodge Odin—all located in the West Side Swedish neighborhood of Austin—indicate that lodge members were more likely to come from nonagricultural families than were church members. Nearly one-third of the Viking Club members had fathers in Sweden who were skilled or semiskilled workers, compared with roughly one-fifth of the fathers of churchgoers. This difference meant that, although the majority of all Swedes in Chicago came from rural backgrounds, members of the Viking lodge were more likely to have had urban, working-class experience in Sweden. Church members, by contrast, were more often the first generation in their family to live off the farm on either side of the Atlantic. Swedish fraternalism was a newer type of voluntary association compared to the churches, and those who joined were less bound by tradition.[65]

Even more than in their demographic background, the fraternal orders further distinguished themselves from the churches and temperance organizations in their attitudes toward alcohol consumption. At times, the lodges enacted some limitations on alcohol abuse. In 1904, the Viking Grand Lodge noted that life insurance statistics proved that alcohol abuse and a higher rate of death was evident in occupations associated with the manufacture or sale of spirits. Hence, the Order moved to prohibit people in those occupations from joining and charged such persons already in the Order with higher assessments.[66] This caution did not, however, connect the Lodge to prohibition or to a curtailment of drinking practices. In a debate held on the subject of prohibition in Viking Brage Lodge #2, a physician and a lawyer teamed up on each side to argue the issue. The general consensus of the group sided against prohibition, which placed this group directly against many of the other Swedish organizations, particularly the churches and the IOGT.[67]

Overall, the fraternal orders carved out a new niche in the Swedish community, offering fellowship and association to less religious, less traditional immigrants. In *Runristningar*, a history of the Independent Order of Vikings written in 1915, the author noted that in terms of organizations, until 1890 "the church had the field completely for itself," obviously discounting the importance of earlier, smaller secular clubs. He noted that the churches benefited from "the immigrants' longing for something Swedish to join especially after staying among so many strange nationalities," and the Swedish American churches were more powerfully linked with Swedish immigrants in America than was the state church with Swedes "back home." The impetus for the creation of the Viking Lodge and other fraternal orders came from those who wanted "something outside church activities" and thus associated with the "like-minded in organizations of different character."[68] The result was an amazingly diverse associational life in Swedish Chicago.

Forming a Brotherhood

To young single men, lodges became a family substitute and provided a safety net in times of trouble. As the lodges grew and matured and the members themselves aged, the lodges supplemented family relationships and activities. When a member fell on hard times, or when they died far away from the place of their birth, lodges took care of the necessary arrangements for their members. The growth of fraternal orders and their expansion throughout the city created a cadre of loyal members who retained their membership as they moved to new homes in the city. Like the churches, they created a context for the urban mobility so common in industrial society. As fraternal orders—and their members—continued to age and mature, they established homes to care for elderly members and, like the Swedish churches and the Templar lodges, approached a condition of institutional completeness.[69]

Friendship and the cultivation of close personal relationships were undoubtedly important ingredients of lodge membership. The initiation ritual of the Svithiod Order included a recitation about friendship:

> A man of friends bereft, though he may be strong,
> Like an oak despoiled of bark, survives not long!
> With friends, he thrives as tree in the forest groweth,
> Refreshed by brooks and safe from the storm that bloweth.[70]

The relationship went beyond mere friendship, however, as members bonded together in times of crisis. The minutes of the regular Svithiod Club meetings revealed the priorities of the group and the informal way in which benefits were paid in the first decade of the club's existence. On January 14, 1882, the balance in the treasury was a mere $350, and funds grew slowly and unevenly in the early years of its existence.[71] In August 1882, the lodge decided to build a more official burial fund. Members paid initiation fees ranging from three to ten dollars and monthly dues of twenty-five to fifty cents. The Order paid three to five dollars per week to members who were sick and waived their dues for the duration of their illness. Members received this benefit for up to four months, and if their illness continued, the Sick Committee would help secure a place for the patient in a public hospital. When more funds were needed, the most common way to levy fees in the organization's earliest years was to pass the hat and collect money from the club's members. The importance of friendship was particularly evident when someone died, as club members attended the funeral, marched to the grave site accompanied by a band, and often lingered until the next morning.[72] The bond of brotherhood among these men gave them an important sense of belonging, providing them with strong, personal connections beyond their immediate family.

The agenda of many Svithiod meetings included the planning of parties and other social activities, but the biggest priority registered in the minutes was to keep track of sick and dying members. The group delegated this task to an appointed Sick Committee, which reported its news to each full meeting. In this manner, the lodge played an especially important role for its single members. On January 28, 1882, the group collected $10.93 for "Brother A. Magnuson who had an accident and burned his hand." That same meeting the Order paid $5.00 for the hospital stay of Brother Simon Hallberg, one of the Order's founders and its first president. On July 7 of that same year, thirty-two-year-old Hallberg died after a six-month bout with pneumonia, undoubtedly a shock to his fraternal brothers. Since Hallberg was a bachelor, fellow Svithiod members took care of his personal affairs. The group passed a resolution on July 29 that extended sympathy to all those who grieved his passing, thanked a Mrs. Nelson on 74 Milton Avenue who cared for him while he was sick, and paid for his funeral expenses. Club members also took an active part in planning and participating in Hallberg's funeral. When Adolf Valentin Lindberg died at the age of twenty-six in 1886, the nearest relatives were unknown, so the Lodge wrote to the pastor in his home parish in Malmö to notify his relatives there of his death. Another member, Charles Olander, died in 1890 without relatives in America. The Order paid for his funeral expenses and extended its sympathy to his family in the "Old Country." These types of activities gave an extra dimension of security to members' lives: although many were without relatives in the United States, the Svithiod Order acted as a surrogate family in assisting the brothers in times of distress.[73]

Although joining a Svithiod or Viking lodge in America was a new experience and replaced family connections for many single members, in some cases ties of kinship and friendship originated in Sweden and were reinforced by lodge membership. In a sample of membership data from the Viking Lodge No. 8 Odin, 25 of the 191 men included in the sample had brothers in the same lodge. In one case, five Hemwall brothers from Maglehem Parish in Kristianstad County joined the Odin Lodge, and a friend from a home on the same farm not only joined with the Hemwalls, he also took their same last name upon arrival in America. In many other cases, men joined the lodge with others from their home towns. Seven men from the Vessige parish in Halland County belonged to the Odin Lodge. Two were brothers, and all of them were born within eleven years of each other and so were undoubtedly well acquainted. Karl Axel Young and Frans Victor Young also came from different homes on the same farm in Dingtuna parish, Västmanland County. They knew each other well and chose the same last name after arriving in America. The club's membership records reveal numerous such examples of friends and family members joining the lodge's secret brotherhood. Hence, joining a lodge was not done randomly but reflected part of an individual's personal choice to build new friendships and reinforce already established relationships through lodge affiliation.[74]

The expansion of fraternal orders throughout the Chicago area provided a framework for many immigrants as they moved to new areas of the city. Like the churches, new lodges sprung up in new Swedish neighborhoods, usually after congregations had already been founded.[75] The history of Svithiod's Verdandi Lodge #3 reveals the nature of actual lodge formation and maturation. In 1890, eight men of Svithiod Lodge #1 founded Verdandi in one of the member's homes in Lake View. The group referred to Svithiod Lodge #1 as its mother lodge, much as church members considered the denominational churches in Swede Town as the mother churches. Many of those who began Verdandi originated from Kronobergs County in Småland, further strengthening the initial bond between members. The Verdandi #3 lodge grew rapidly, especially when the group moved its meeting place deeper into the heart of the Swedish settlement in Lake View.[76]

In a similar fashion, in October of 1892 the second Viking lodge—Brage #2— began operations on the Near North Side of the city.[77] Started in a basement flat that doubled as a tailor's shop, this lodge soon became one of the strongest groups in the Viking Organization. This development did not threaten the mother lodge, but was seen as an extension of its operations. In fact, two of Brage's charter members were among the founders of the original lodge, and returned to it after Brage was well on its way to becoming an active and self-sustaining lodge. Membership in the Brage lodge reached 1,503 in 1920.[78]

Thus, as the city grew and its Swedish population dispersed into newly developing neighborhoods, Swedish settlers brought their fraternal organizations with them. Just as in the churches, members of the older lodges became charter members of the new ones. The rate at which particular lodges grew depended on the area of the city in which the lodge was located, and external factors such as the rate of immigration, as well as the less tangible and more difficult-to-measure internal dynamics of the lodge itself.

In Chicago, lodge affiliation often followed immigrants to their new homes. Even within neighborhoods, immigrants changed residences often, and as they did so, they remained tied to particular lodges. One address book, containing names of 496 members from Svithiod Lodge #1, indicates that 60 percent of the members moved at least once between 1880 and 1892, and many moved several times. One member moved as many as ten times, and each time his new address was duly registered in the official book. Forty individuals moved to other regions in the Chicago metropolitan area, four returned to Sweden, and eight moved to another place in the United States. Relatively few left the area with no forwarding address: the lodge lost track of only eighteen of its nearly five hundred members.[79] Overall, Swedes maintained their organizational affiliations as they moved. The associations many of them cultivated transcended their residential mobility and created strong personal networks of connection in the city.

As the fraternal orders matured and their members grew older, they found new, more expansive ways to help their constituents. With the establishment of the Vikings' Valhalla Association in 1909, the Independent Order of Vikings and the Independent Order Ladies of Vikings began plans to care for their elderly members and widows, orphans, and other dependents of deceased members. According to the charter of the Vikings' Valhalla Association, its purpose was to establish "A Bureau for the Care of the Aged and Infirm. A bureau of Hospital Service and Medical Aid. A Bureau of Employment. A Bureau of Legal Advice."[80] Four men and three women signed the charter, and by 1913, the group purchased an estate of forty-three acres in Gurnee, Illinois, for the purpose of establishing a Home for the Aged. The Viking Order thus attempted to attract, keep, and take care of members for life. The nature of the benefits they offered met members' long-term needs by giving tangible relief and security as they aged.[81]

Rituals and Masculinity

Not only did fraternal orders create important social connections in the city, the ritual engaged in by the clubs created a secret world separate from the members' wives and families, and from religious groups who particularly frowned upon such activities. The initiation ceremony of fraternal lodges bonded members into a brotherhood sealed by secret rituals. For example, after questioning an incoming member of a Viking lodge, a herald introduced the newcomer as a "stranger from the high north, descendant of the Vikings." Through a series of rituals, the stranger soon became more familiar to the group. A song welcomed the new member "in our circle and chamber." The officers reminded him about the importance of secrecy and trust, stating that "a Viking never breaks his promise." After swearing in the new member, the lodge continued by singing the following song:

> Now have Odin and Tor, Frej and Balder and Njord,
> In Valhalla, high up in the blue;
> Now have Freja and Nanna and Frigg heard your word!
> That you promised, you hold and believe!
>
> Listen now, you, who raise up the Viking exploits,
> You, our faith is bright as steel.
> To those magnificent runes, to the chieftain's feats
> On our high-sounding ancestral goal.[82]

The Viking's first chieftain—the second in command of the organization—then spoke to the group, encouraging members to pursue their intellectual development, for the good of the order and the good of society. He emphasized that the Vikings would provide help for members in times of sickness, and when "Odin chooses to call [you] to the peaceful Valhalla." The First Chieftain further stressed the importance of friendship, claiming that the man who died alone was as a "stem in the dessert with peeling bark. But the man with friends enjoys life, as a tree in a grove." This fraternal brotherhood was to be impenetrable by outside influences, and the secret ritual was not to be divulged to outsiders.

The symbolism of Swedish fraternalism heavily depended upon the Swedes' Viking heritage to the exclusion of Christian traditions and rituals. References to a glorious past paralleled similar trends in the American fraternal movement. Mark Carnes notes that "no idea was more commonplace, nor more palpably untrue, than the fraternalists' claim of ancient and venerable origins." The purpose of such claims was to "confer legitimacy upon institutions of recent origin."[83] It also had the unifying effect of distancing the lodges from contentious religious discussions of the day. The Svithiod Order's bylaws stated that a candidate for membership shall "acknowledge belief in Almighty God, creator and protector of all," and its ritual stated that Svithiod membership did not "interfere with . . .

FIGURE 13. The Independent Order of Vikings started lodges throughout Chicago, bringing men together in bonds of fraternal brotherhood. This picture of the "Harald" Lodge from 1915 shows members dressed in Viking regalia used to reinforce notions of Sweden's proud history. Courtesy of Swedish-American Archives of Greater Chicago, North Park University, Chicago.

religious beliefs."[84] Religion was only important in a traditional sense, however; it did not reflect any pietistic influences among the members. Instead, political and religious issues were not to be addressed during meetings, lest they disrupt the group's unity and brotherhood.

By contrast, the ritual embraced Viking symbolism, as the following words from the Svithiod songbook clearly indicate:

> Round the banner, comrades, gather
> Now in Svithiod's hall;
> Hand in hand we stand united,
> If we rise or fall.
> Balder make us mild and gentle,
> Thor give strength for strife,
> Odin grant us light and wisdom
> For the tasks of life!

"Truth and courage, now and ever,"
Be our battle-cry,
And our sacred cause will triumph,
If we live or die.
Raise aloft our noble standard,
Ever may it wave,
High and higher, lowered only
At a comrade's grave.[85]

By glorifying a distant, Viking past, the Svithiods and Vikings found unifying symbols that celebrated a common Nordic heritage.

The Svithiod and Viking brothers also conducted a ceremonial ritual at the burial of fellow members. After a clergyman led the regular burial service, the Svithiod leaders performed their own rituals. After the coffin had been lowered into the grave, the chairman would stand on the right side of the burial site and the vice chairman on the left, grasping hands over the grave. Two other members held a spear over the grave and another an axe, and the lodge's chaplain recited a long liturgy that stressed the importance of shared burdens and united experiences. Throughout the recitation and the closing prayer, the chaplain invoked the spirit of fraternalism and prayed to God as the Creator, Protector, and Father.

Clearly absent were Christian references, except that the order of ceremony allowed for hymns such as "Nearer, my God, to Thee," or "Jesus Lover of my Soul." It also spelled out, however, a song with little Christian sentiment for the more secularly minded members:

Learn thou to live thy life aright,
Before the light forsakes thee;
For ere thou knowest, comes the night.
And lurking death o'ertakes thee.
Put thine own house in order, then,
And sleep in peace to rise again,
When heaven's trumpet wakes thee.[86]

The Viking Order also created a highly formalized ritual for the burial of dead members. Viking imagery permeated the Order's ritual to a greater degree than in the Svithiod Order, with no reference made to Christianity. While some members may have preferred a religious funeral, those who followed the Viking ritual book were buried in a fashion fitting for a true Viking. The formal procession began with the musicians, followed by the marshal, the flag bearer, the lodge's leaders, and finally the other lodge members. Members formed the letter V around the grave, with the chieftain standing in the middle of the V and presiding over the ceremony. Brotherly love overflowed, as the Order bid farewell to one of its own.[87]

Thus the importance of rituals moved beyond the realm of secret brotherhood and into a more public arena. Not only was this true for burial rituals, it was also true in public celebrations. By the turn of the twentieth century, fraternal lodges maintained a high profile in the Swedish community, clearly evident when the Vikings' Brage Lodge erected a Viking Temple in Lake View with the cooperation of other Viking lodges. A large celebration took place on the day the cornerstone of this new clubhouse was laid, October 17, 1909. A parade through the streets of Lake View marked the occasion on a grand scale, with over two thousand Vikings marching in the parade and three thousand other Swedes waiting for them on the corner of Sheffield Avenue and School Street where the building would be erected. When the Viking Temple was dedicated the following year, entire families became involved in the celebration. Adults attended the official dedication ceremony on a Friday evening, and a ball was held the following evening. On Sunday, the Vikings held a celebratory feast for entire families. Memoirs of the event note that "More than half of the public was made up of children. It was the day of the papas, mamas, and the children, and they had their fill of ice cream, coffee and cakes."[88]

The Gendered Dynamics of Club Life

In the late nineteenth century, secular associational life in Swedish Chicago was a male-dominated world. Fraternal orders, sports and recreational clubs, and professional associations all focused their internal activities and recruiting efforts upon men. Social gatherings and dances included women, but the primary functions of the club catered to men. The exception to this rule was the Good Templars, a group devoted to promoting temperance that had always included women— but this organization was more ideologically focused than were the larger social clubs. Mark C. Carnes points out that through American fraternal orders, men attempted to distance themselves further from the sphere of women, especially from the realm of Evangelical Protestantism that was dominated by women. They hoped to create an arena in which they could remove their sons from the influence of their mothers and initiate them into their own male fraternity. Rituals engaged in by the club members created a secret world separate from their wives, families, and the rest of the Swedish community.[89]

Initially barred from membership in the large, male fraternal orders, women had few organizational options outside the churches. The Ladies Society Ingeborg, founded in 1890, was one of the few early organizations aimed primarily at women that followed an agenda similar to those of the male fraternal orders. Formed as a sick benefit society for women of Swedish birth or descent, over the years it served a total of 3,400 members until it disbanded in 1958.[90] A more typical pattern of association occurred when women's organizations arose as peripheral groups attached to a particular men's club, often joined by the wives, sisters, and daughters of club members. These women's auxiliaries focused their activities on traditionally supportive roles, including organizing social events, decorating club-houses, and preparing meals when called upon to do so.

One such affiliated women's group was the Ladies Associate Club, formed in 1898 as a group attached to the strictly male Svithiod Singing Club. The group later changed its name to the Ladies' Guild and held meetings in the men's club room once per week. These women assisted in raising funds for the acquisition of property for the Svithiod Singing club by participating in festivals and bazaars, including a yearly event called the Värnamo Market. After the purchase of a club-house in 1899, the women attempted to extend their authority. The Ladies' Guild demanded one-third interest in the new building and declared a willingness to assume one-third the risk, or else they threatened to withdraw their support from the club. The men unanimously refused their demands for power-sharing, coun-tering "the Ladies' Guild of the Svithiod Singing Club is sincerely invited to hold its meetings and gatherings, and also to use the large lounge on the second floor of our new clubhouse . . . as long as the Ladies' Guild exists under the name 'The Ladies' Guild of Svithiod Singing Club.'"[91] The message was clear: the women were relegated to subordinate status and seen as only peripheral to the club's activi-ties. As a result, twenty-six of the women resigned in protest. The Ladies' Guild continued to exist on a more limited basis, and eventually revived in 1906 when the conflict had been forgotten. Although contributors toward the clubhouse and participants in many of the club's events, the Ladies' Guild never influenced the Svithiod Singing Club's policy-making, which remained firmly in the hands of the men. The women, however, empowered by their contributions to the larger group, had stepped out of their peripheral and more traditional role to challenge the club's male leadership.

By the 1890s, many American fraternal lodges had added women's auxiliaries, and after the turn of the twentieth century, this trend spread to the Swedish com-munity as well. Both the Svithiod and Viking Orders had, by this time, started affil-iated peripheral women's clubs. The relationship between the men's lodge and its women's auxiliary was usually cooperative but sometimes rocky. Ladies of Brage and Ingeborg Ladies of Drake, both formed in 1905, were auxiliaries linked with the Brage and Drake men's Viking lodges. The impetus for founding the Ladies of Brage in particular grew out of frustration over members' wives assisting in organizing entertainment and fund-raising for the Brage Lodge, but having no control over how the proceeds would be spent. Women who had helped raise six hundred dollars by holding a bazaar, withdrew their support, split the money with the Brage Lodge, and formed the Ladies of Brage, where they would have more direct control over the actions of their organization. These women remained independent, but later continued to help the Brage Lodge with fund-raising projects.[92]

Not all women were content with playing an auxiliary role, and interest in forming their own independent orders grew among wives, mothers, and sisters of the members of the men's lodges. The Ladies Independent Order of Svithiod was founded in 1903 in Chicago, and soon its lodges spread throughout the city. The Independent Order Ladies of Vikings was formed the following year under the same format as the men's Viking lodges. Like the men's groups, these women's lodges allowed women from similar backgrounds and with similar interests to gather for social purposes while also giving them a sense of financial protection. The Bylaws of Valkryia Lodge No. 1, the first of the Independent Order Ladies of Vikings lodges, claimed the purpose of the organization was "in sisterly harmony and working together among women of Swedish descent" to provide sick and death benefits to its members. If a member died without any family in Chicago to make arrangements for her burial, the club would step in and fill this familial role.[93] By 1933 the Ladies Independent Order of Svithiod had paid out over $300,000 help to sick members and over $125,000 in burial help. It had also donated $10,000 to various social causes the lodge members had deemed worthy. Within a decade of their formation, each of these women's orders had started ten separate lodges in Chicago, and their popularity continued to grow in the early decades of the twentieth century.[94]

The growing popularity of women's lodges put pressure on the men's organization to admit women as full members or lose the women's assistance with activities of the clubs.[95] The Independent Order of Svithiod modified its bylaws to allow women as full-standing members in 1916, but women's clubs were to remain in separate lodges. The change was not made without considerable debate and resistance, although in retrospect much of this controversy faded with time. An article about the Svithiod Order in the 1927 *Swedish Blue Book*, a directory of Swedish Americans in Chicago, claimed that including women on equal terms as men "has proven of material benefit to the lodge work, particularly in its social activities."[96] Otto Hanson reminisced in 1933 that the decision to admit women as full-standing members "has proven to be one of the most beneficial amendments made to the Constitution."[97] Agda C. Nordlund was the first woman to be admitted as a member in May of 1916, and in June, Alpha No. 50 became the first all-woman Svithiod lodge. Other women's lodges were founded, and within a few years, some of the men's lodges began admitting women.[98]

Many women preferred to keep their own separate lodge structure, where they could retain power over the internal affairs of the organizations, but due to growing financial pressures, a few lodges from the Independent Order Ladies of

Svithiod applied for membership with the larger Independent Order of Svithiod. The purpose of the Order now became "to unite in one fraternity men and women of Swedish birth or descent and their families for mutual assistance."[99] The group was very conscious of the Swedish reputation in the ethnically and racially diverse city, promoting in its members traits of "honesty, industry, respect for law and order, and love of liberty and justice with which our people of Swedish birth and descent can in such great measure contribute to the welfare of America."[100]

The Viking Lodges remained firmly dominated by men for over a decade longer than the Independent Order of Svithiod. In 1919, when pressure increased for women to be equal members in the organization, the Viking's Brage Lodge unanimously defeated the motion to allow members of the Independent Order Ladies of Vikings to attend meetings. The Viking Order itself remained the most staunchly male organization of the entire range of Swedish fraternal orders, and did not admit women as full members until 1933. During the height of the Great Depression, the Viking Lodges felt pressure on a number of fronts. Not only did the economic climate create financial difficulties for the club, the decline in new immigrants arriving from Sweden meant there was no source from which to recruit new members. Furthermore, Carnes argues that the incentive for men to create a separate world of ritual diminished due to the loosening social mores of the 1920s. The best way for the Viking lodges to add numbers to their membership rosters was to begin to cooperate with women by admitting them into the organization. This action represented the declining notion that women must operate in separate spheres of activity from men. If Swedish ethnic identity among lodge members was to remain strong, men and women needed to work together. As women became full-standing members of secular organizations such as the Vikings, their visibility within the Swedish community grew

A Swedish and American Identity

As with the churches, the spread of Swedish fraternalism created a dual level of ethnic identity in Chicago. On the grassroots level, lodge members constructed their ethnicity through lodge activities and face-to-face relationships. On a more elite level, fraternal leaders consciously forged a new Swedish American ethnic identity by promoting an image of Swedes as immigrants with a respectable history, but also completely loyal to their adopted homeland.[101] Although lodges frequently conjured up romantic images of Sweden's past, they were fully grounded upon the fact that the members' future belonged to America. The initiation ceremony for Svithiod members exhorted newcomers to keep their word in the true Viking heritage, so that "In this great country of ours with a people of so many different races we endeavor to advance the interests of our Swedish people, make known their many merits and uphold their virtues." The ritual called for members to uphold the reputation of the "country up in the high North, which gave birth to our ancestors" but at the same time, urged members to "become loyal American citizens, and we believe that this is possible without their forgetting . . . the country from which they hail or the race from which they have descended."[102] Svithiod leaders believed that Viking and American traditions fit well together: "We are descendants of . . . an old, sturdy race, which did not tolerate deceit or endure oppression," claimed club rituals. These very Nordic qualities fit in nicely with the patriotic American emphasis upon the same virtue of liberty.[103]

The Viking Order also celebrated the way in which its associations successfully combined Swedish and American characteristics. The Order's official history noted that the large lodges encouraged "the preservation of Swedishness in America" while helping members and their families in times of duress. Writers commented that the Viking Order itself captured a particularly American aspect of the city in that something was always brewing: the club and the city were ever-changing and growing entities. The haphazard method of urban growth corresponded with the seemingly unplanned growth of the Viking Order, which proved that the founders were "inspired with a genuine American spirit together with the Viking power."[104] The growth of the lodges attempted in some way to personalize the city and to offer a connecting point for the creation of a Swedish and American identity.

TRANSITIONS IN FRATERNALISM

The organizational network created by Swedes in Chicago extended throughout the city and offered a newly arriving Swede a large choice for ethnic affiliation. Some of these organizations—such as sports and recreation clubs and many of the singing societies—remained loose associations of members and did not branch into new areas of the city, remaining in the locations where they were first organized. The Temperance and Fraternal Orders, however, created branch lodges that extended their influence into every Swedish neighborhood in the city. They took care of their members' social needs, providing health and death benefits and eventually building homes for elderly members. The club life itself allowed for the celebration of the members' Swedish heritage in the midst of a large, diverse, American city. The propensity to join secular associations rather than pietistic churches was influenced by an individual's background and ideological perspective. Overall, fraternal societies created a vibrant subcommunity within the Swedish population of Chicago. They provided forums for combining the immigrants' Swedish heritage with their need to create affiliations with other Swedes in the city.

As the subcommunity of Swedish secular societies grew, it reflected vast changes within the larger Swedish community. From 1880 to 1920, the opportunities for secular association increased immensely, as did the Swedish population in the city. In addition, more women joined similar societies as women's orders were established. Eventually, women were allowed to join previously all-male fraternal orders. This development gave women greater opportunities to become involved with organizations outside the religious sphere of Swedish community life. The Swedish community in Chicago offered many diverse organizational options to incoming Swedish immigrants, and once a person joined such an organization, he or she began to create a personalized world within their urban environment. Life in Chicago was thus perceived through an ethnic organizational framework to which immigrants attached strong loyalties and that served to differentiate the Swedish population in the city. After 1920, the trend of rampant institutional expansion drew to a close. Although the Svithiod Order continued to grow until 1927, by 1950 the membership reflected significant aging trends.[105] Organizational survival depended upon keeping the attachments to such organizations alive among the second generation, a task increasingly difficult to accomplish. Gradually, as immigrants aged and their children moved away from ethnic neighborhoods and lost interest in Swedish clubs and associations, membership fell into a decades-long decline.

CHAPTER 5

SWEDISH NATIONALISM IN A NEW LAND

Toward a Swedish American Identity

"There is no denying the fact that we belong, so to speak, to two nationalities, that we have two countries, and duties toward both."

—Officers of the Swedish Historical Society, 1908, on the tensions of being both Swedish and American

The creation and nurturing of proliferating neighborhood institutions reflected a Swedish population of increasingly diverse composition. A few organizations in Swedish Chicago attempted to overcome that diversity and perceived fragmentation by asserting and codifying Swedish identity and culture. In the 1890s, efforts began on a citywide basis to provide a degree of organizational unity with the creation of overarching Swedish associations. These organizations sought to preserve Sweden's heritage, promote its culture, and protect the reputation of Chicago's Swedish residents. In so doing, they served as a capstone to the reassertion of Swedish identity evident in the churches and fraternal associations. The formation of such groups drew on themes of Swedish nationalism and romantic notions of the Swedes' glorious history. These associations were not attempting to re-create a lost past, however; they were American-made, founded to add coherence to the Swedish organizational system in Chicago. They also attempted to separate the Swedish reputation from deteriorating urban conditions witnessed in many of Chicago's ethnic neighborhoods, particularly those dominated by southern and eastern Europeans, America's newest immigrant groups, and by the growing number of African Americans in the city. To use Matthew Frye Jacobson's terminology, Swedes were better able to "becom[e] Caucasian" and safely position themselves high on the American ethno-racial hierarchy by promoting their reputation and their contributions to American society. The very presence of groups often perceived as less desirable helped Swedes achieve assimilation into the white majority culture.[1]

By the early twentieth century, Swedes in Chicago created a number of elite associations that provided a forum for organizational life and the exchange of current ideas and debates. Never speaking with one voice, the leadership of these groups nevertheless established a core of Swedish immigrant leadership and worked for self-conscious continuity in Swedish ethnic identity. They created associations based not upon nostalgia, but upon their belief that such organizations would offer Swedish immigrants the opportunity for self-improvement and advancement, and they openly grappled with the tensions posed by forging a Swedish American identity. As Dag Blanck points out, "Swedish-American cultural patterns . . . exhibit[ed] a duality . . . drawing on cultural elements from both Sweden and the United States, while at the same time maintaining a distance from both."[2]

Swedish American identity formed around a core of elite associations and centralizing clubs, reflecting a remarkably complex periphery of specialized associations—secular and religious, social and ideological, cultural and regional. These groups achieved substantial membership and solidarity among a great part of the Swedish immigrant population of Chicago; however, none of the efforts at centralization could provide a unified Swedish voice in Chicago. Neighborhood-based organizations remained the most popular form of voluntary associations in the city, and, in aggregate, they remained the strongest and largest of the Swedish institutions.

THE GROWTH OF SWEDISH NATIONALISM

Swedish organizations in Chicago were all heavily influenced by the exposure of their members to themes of Swedish nationalism circulating in Sweden. In early nineteenth-century Sweden, prominent intellectuals and scholars probed deeply into Sweden's ancient Viking heritage. Great works such as Esaias Tegnér's *Fritiof's saga*, Erik Gustaf Geijer's *Vikingen*, and P. D. A. Atterbom's *Lycksalighetens ö* celebrated the Viking era and called on readers to live up to their noble history. These men did not encourage individuals to accept the status quo; rather, they spurred people to explore new ideas and experiences, very much in keeping with the nineteenth-century notions of liberalism and individualism. The importance of an educated and well-informed citizenry was an integral part of these ideals, and Sweden moved toward educational reform. In 1842, a new law mandated the establishment of a national system of primary schools, which resulted in Sweden achieving one of the highest rates of literacy in Western Europe. A more educated public responded to a wide variety of literary and ideological impulses, helping Sweden move—however haltingly—toward a more modern and democratic society.[3]

In the late nineteenth century, Sweden experienced a revival of nationalistic sentiment, often referred to as romantic nationalism. According to Franklin Scott, a number of forces contributed to this nationalism: "The increasing friction with Norway reinforced the Swedishness of the Swedes, the bloodletting of emigration made them fear for their national survival, and the ancient fears of Russian expansion were rearoused."[4] Literary trends reflected a combination of regional nostalgia and national patriotism, drawing on the classics of Tegnér and Geijer. August Strindberg created epic historical dramas; Verner von Heidenstam wrote popular historical-heroic fiction; Selma Lagerlöf depicted her native Värmland in many of her tales and adventures; and Erik Axel Karlfeldt noted the power of ancient folk life over the Swedish culture and characterized his home region of Dalarna as the most Swedish of provinces. Sweden's national anthem, "*Du gamla du fria*" (you ancient, you free), written by Richard Dybeck, also became popular during the 1890s. Overall, this outpouring of national romantic literature encouraged Swedes to take pride in their heritage, revived interest in old folk traditions, and reinforced notions of cultural grandeur. Swedish nationalism culminated with the formal split between Sweden and Norway into separate kingdoms in 1905.[5]

Themes of Swedish nationalism likewise found their way to the United States and were incorporated into views of American loyalty and patriotism, but it was not a seamless transition. According to H. Arnold Barton, national culture came late to Swedish-America because the period of the great migration was one of low national consciousness among the majority of Swedish peasants. "The emigrants' strongest emotional attachments," Barton writes, "were . . . to family, home, and native place (*hembygd*), rather than to the Swedish state and nation, against which they might feel powerful resentments over circumstances they felt had driven them out of the land."[6] Swedish American organizations, therefore, needed to help these Swedes reconnect to their Swedish traditions. Barton argues that these associations helped immigrants "create their own, new unifying myths and traditions, as the central rituals of organized ethnic life."[7]

Immigrant groups forged new myths and traditions in a variety of ways. Swedish American fraternal lodges, for example, held ceremonies that glorified the Viking heritage while extolling the virtues of their members being exemplary American citizens. Churches continued Swedish religious and musical traditions. The ethnic press promoted a Swedish American identity, and the Swedish colleges taught students about their cultural heritage while equipping them for a future in

America. In addition, the decade of the 1890s marked the creation of a number of nationalistic Swedish associations in Chicago and witnessed the celebration of citywide parades and ceremonies which drew attention to the Swedish presence in the city. All of these efforts reinforced the immigrants' Swedish identity. In some cases organizations introduced nostalgic sentiments, and in others they created new Swedish cultural expressions. By the turn of the twentieth century, such cultural expressions represented a revival and a largely re-created folk culture that was not only new in Swedish America but also largely new in Sweden itself.[8] The promotion of Swedish culture also gave these immigrants a Swedish cultural context for their activities in multiethnic Chicago, offering a means for differentiating themselves from other immigrants in the city while promoting their value to American society.

SWEDISH NATIONALISM IN CHICAGO

Efforts within the Swedish community to raise the profile of Swedes and to assert Swedish cultural expressions in Chicago increased in the 1890s. By that time, the large wave of Swedish immigrants who arrived during the previous decade had been absorbed into community life, and their numbers could be felt in all Swedish organizations. Recent arrivals mingled with aging immigrants who had lived in Chicago for decades. Many Swedes, particularly community leaders, increasingly felt alienated from their homeland and defensive about their decision to emigrate, giving them incentive to forge a new Swedish American identity of which they could be proud.[9] The decade also presented new challenges, as unemployment was on the rise and ever-greater numbers of immigrants crowded into Chicago, leading to a rise in anti-immigrant sentiment. Poor economic conditions and the increasing diversity of Chicago's population encouraged many Swedish organizations to take action to protect the image of the hardworking, honest Swedish worker. Swedes took advantage of events such as the erection of the monument to Carl von Linnaeus—the pioneering Swedish botanist—and the celebration of Sweden's Day at the Columbian Exposition to display the Swedish community's strength and to publicize Swedish cultural and national achievements. Throughout the decade, Swedes in Chicago combined their sense of nationalistic pride with a desire to publicize the quality and integrity of the Swedish immigrant.

These efforts at cultural promotion within the Swedish community in Chicago coincided with larger trends within European immigration history. During the 1890s, immigration from northern and western Europe diminished as migration from southern and eastern Europe grew. This shift alarmed many American citizens as they watched Italians, Poles, and Russian Jews crowd into poor, inner-city neighborhoods, replacing the Germans, Irish, and Scandinavians who left these poorer regions as their economic conditions improved. The recent arrivals from southern and eastern Europe soon came to be called the "new immigrants" by their contemporaries, racially distinct from earlier arrivals, and they seemed to personify the ills of urban industrial society. The fact that many of them were Catholic or Jewish accentuated their foreignness, and their obvious poverty concerned many Americans.

By contrast, the "old immigrants" from western and northern Europe were a known quantity: although Irish Catholics had met with discriminatory treatment earlier in the century, on the whole these immigrants had proven their ability to succeed in America. The economic depression of the 1890s coupled with the large influx of new immigrants led to a debate over the wisdom of an open immigration policy. In 1907, the US Congress established the Dillingham Commission to investigate what it perceived to be an immigration problem. Immigration restriction sentiment culminated in the passage of literacy requirements in 1917 and in the enacting of immigration quotas favorable to old immigrant groups in 1924. These actions embraced these older immigrant groups as firmly acceptable into white American society.[10] Against this backdrop, Swedes in Chicago did their best to distance themselves from the new immigrants and tout their exemplary American citizenship.

Swedish self-promotion was one of the important aims of the construction and unveiling of the Carl von Linnaeus statue in Chicago's Lincoln Park in 1891. Eric Johannesson points out that the statue was also intended to be a source of unity among Swedes in America; its promoters hoped to unify liberal and religious factions within the community by selecting Linnaeus as a subject, a pious man of international significance. In this goal they never succeeded, as most religious groups refused to become officially involved in the Linnaeus statue project. However, one of the chief promoters was an Augustana Lutheran leader, Johan Enander, editor of the Augustana Lutheran newspaper *Hemlandet* and well-known Swedish American journalist. The raising of the Linneaus monument was part of a larger movement among Chicago's ethnic groups to build statues of their own cultural or political heroes, and the entire effort by the Swedes mimicked the process of the Germans' building a Schiller monument in Lincoln Park five years earlier. Over fifteen thousand persons gathered for the dedication of the Linneaus monument and witnessed two keynote speeches, one in English and the other in Swedish, both of which stressed the prominence of Linnaeus and the value of being both Swedish and American. As Johannesson points out, "It was . . . important for Enander [who gave the Swedish speech] that Swedish ethnicity be bound to Americanism, like two sides of a coin."[11] The monument provided a gathering place for cultural activities in subsequent years.

Swedish nationalism and American patriotism also converged in the celebration of Sweden's Day on July 20, 1893, held in conjunction with the Columbian Exposition. Dag Blanck points out that the festivities surrounding this day united the Swedes in Chicago: Swedish nationalistic sentiment overcame ideological divisions among the people. Although secular groups took the lead in organizing and participating in the festivities, the religious press applauded their efforts, and Johan Enander once again played a prominent role in the day's activities. The party began with a parade that drew twelve thousand participants, many of them from Chicago's Swedish organizations, and floats and banners celebrated the history of Sweden and Swedish America. An estimated fifty thousand persons attended ceremonies in Jackson Park later in the day, and speeches emphasized Swedish contributions in the United States and the high quality of Swedish culture.[12] Both the Linnaeus and Sweden Day celebrations served to strengthen the Swedes' reputation in Chicago as a respectable and industrious people—an immigrant group that would contribute to the greatness of the city instead of depleting its resources and contributing to its problems.[13]

Chicago's American newspapers responded positively to these efforts at Swedish cultural promotion and applauded the dual Swedish American identity of these immigrants. At the dedication of the monument honoring Carl von Linnaeus, the *Chicago Times* took note of the great parade and demonstration. It claimed that "While intensely American in their social and political views, [the Swedes] are at the same time intensely Swedish whenever called upon to do honor to anything of which their country is justifiably proud."[14] The *Chicago Tribune* was even more laudatory toward the Swedes. In 1895, the newspaper marked the fiftieth anniversary of the arrival of the first Swede in Illinois. It extolled the characteristics of Swedes as model American citizens and pointed to what it perceived as their exemplary behavior:

> If the record of the Swedish-American citizens of Illinois does not contain the names of great statesmen, politicians, warriors, men of letters and science of worldwide reputation, neither does it contain the name of any great criminal or violator of the law. The Swedish emigrants came here with the intention of becoming good American citizens and of acquiring a home for themselves and their children—not to accumulate wealth and then return to their native country and there spend the money they had amassed here. As naturalized citizens no nationality stands higher in the estimation of the native-born Americans than Swedes.[15]

Thus, the press in Chicago furthered the efforts of the Swedish groups to represent the Swedish immigrant as an asset to American society. In so doing, it reaffirmed the American notion that old immigrant groups made good American citizens as compared to more recent arrivals to American shores.

Swedes in Chicago attempted to capture the enthusiasm evident in public events such as the dedication of the Linnaeus statue and Sweden's Day by creating organizations specifically designed to promote Swedish cultural identity. One such organization was the American Union of Swedish Singers (AUSS). Founded in Chicago in 1892, this group united Swedish men's choral groups from around the eastern and midwestern United States in anticipation of the celebration of Sweden's Day at the Columbian Exhibition the following year. The AUSS represented a departure from its parent organization, the United Scandinavian Singers of America, by its concentration upon purely Swedish traditions and music. The group claimed that while learning much from the Danes and Norwegians, the combination of three nationalities, each with its own traditions, was the group's Achilles' heel. Increased Swedish nationalism and the growing number of Swedes in America allowed for the creation of this strictly Swedish men's musical organization.

The AUSS officially incorporated in 1894 to provide for the "cultivation and promotion of singing, music, and good fellowship," with the added ambition of making "Swedish elements of culture known and appreciated in this country. . . ."[16] Although the AUSS was a national organization, the city of Chicago played an integral part in its early history. Not only was it founded in Chicago, the group held its first Singing Festival on Sweden's Day in 1893, and the experience of over three hundred Swedish men's voices singing "Hear us, Svea, mother of us all" made quite an impression upon the spectators.[17] Victor Nilsson, in a short history of the Union, noted the important place it held among Swedish associations: "Among country-men in America there exists no institution which, without political or religious connections, has reached a cultural achievement of such . . . meaning as that toward which our Swedish association so energetically and enthusiastically works."[18] Concerts of Swedish music gave Swedes renewed pride in their cultural heritage. They created a sentimental journey back in time, celebrated the spirit of Swedish national romanticism, and reaffirmed Swedish group identity in a pluralistic city.

Two other organizations attempted to perpetuate the unity evident in the celebration of Sweden's Day, capitalize on its momentum, and protect the welfare of Swedish immigrants in the city. One of these organizations, the Swedish Associations' Central Society, was chartered on August 17, 1894, in order to "unite the various Swedish Societies in Cook County and to promote the interest of their members."[19] The group invited representatives from all Swedish organizations into its membership, and its underlying purpose was to build a home for elderly Swedes who had no means for supporting themselves. This association was the first non-religious organization that attempted to provide such assistance to Swedish immigrants. Although the homes run by the churches often took in nonmembers, a need remained for other groups to supplement their efforts as many early Swedish immigrants to the city reached their senior years. In 1898, the group purchased a home in Park Ridge as its first Home for the Aged. In 1908, it officially changed its name to the Swedish Societies' Old People's Home Association and specified its purpose was "to build and maintain a home for aged indigent persons and other charitable purposes."[20] It thus became a mechanism for Swedish secular organizations to channel funds into an institution designed to care for the aging Swedish immigrant population. This support became a substitute for the care provided by extended families in Swedish society, a necessary provision for the first generation of a people living in a new land.[21]

The second organization originating in the aftermath of the Chicago World's Fair was the Swedish National Association (SNA), formed for "social, political, and benevolent purposes" on May 25, 1894.[22] A very specific event triggered the foundation of the SNA: on Christmas Day 1893, a young Swede was involved in an altercation with two Chicago police officers. Without apparent provocation, the policemen shot and killed the Swede. This single event served to create a feeling of affinity among the Swedes in Chicago, opening their eyes to abuses inflicted upon this young man and mobilizing them into action. Although the man had no relatives in the city, he belonged to the Viking Lodge Angantyr No. 4, and within five days, the Viking Lodge No. 1 organized a committee to deal with the issue. One member of this committee was Harry Olson, an attorney who subsequently assisted the public defender in the case. Two Swedish newspapers, *Svenska Tribunen* and *Svenska Amerikanaren*, joined forces with delegates of numerous Swedish organizations to see that these policemen would receive just punishment for their deeds.

Through this coordinated effort, the SNA came into being. According to *Runristningar*, the official history of the Independent Order of Vikings, the case itself became a "long-festering legal proceeding." Finally, in February 1895, the policemen were convicted and sentenced to several years' penal servitude in Joliet. *Runristningar* noted that the entire case cost Swedish organizations and individuals a total of eight thousand dollars, and further claimed that this "was the first time in Chicago that police officers were sentenced to jail for that kind of crime."[23] Undoubtedly, Swedes perceived an act against one young Swede as an act against their entire group and an insult to the Swedish character, which they believed should be held in such high esteem. The fact that the courts agreed indicated the degree to which Swedish immigrants as a group were viewed as acceptable and respectable by the white American establishment.

This episode represented a realization by a number of Swedes that no particular organization existed in Chicago with the specified purpose of protecting the rights of Swedish Americans and assisting the unemployed in securing work. The SNA set out to fill that void by actively addressing the problems of Swedes in Chicago, particularly through its Free Swedish Employment Bureau. On November 8, 1895, the SNA notified the various Swedish churches and societies in Chicago about the establishment of the Free Swedish Employment Bureau and invited them to send their representatives to an upcoming meeting at which officers for the SNA would be elected. Invitation letters claimed that every Swedish organization in Cook County, "be it of a social, religious, or political character, is entitled to representation at the Headquarters of our Association."[24] In 1896, the SNA refined and expanded its mission to include promoting "temperance, morality and temporal welfare among the Swedish-American people of Cook County," as well as maintaining a library and being of "mutual aid and assistance in enforcing the legal rights" of immigrants needing such help. It also changed its organizational structure to "establish branch societies of this association."[25] The scope of the group grew as it attempted to assist fellow Swedes in a systematic fashion and to serve as an umbrella organization for the wide variety of Swedish secular and religious associations in Chicago.

The timing of the establishment of the SNA reflected larger economic trends. The economic depression of the 1890s curbed the flow of immigrants from Sweden to America and made it difficult for those already living in Chicago to find work. Through its employment bureau, the SNA became a publicity agent for protecting the Swedish reputation in the city. Othelia Myhrman, an active leader in the International Order of Good Templars and one of the founders of the SNA, was put in charge of the Swedish Employment Bureau. Under Myhrman's capable leadership, the Bureau served an average of one hundred people every day except Sundays. In its eighteen years of existence, the SNA found employment for nearly one hundred thousand persons.[26]

The *Chicago Tribune* featured an article about the Bureau in 1896, aiding in the very publicity that the SNA hoped to achieve. The *Tribune* noted that the Bureau's waiting room was packed with people each day who were looking for a job within a very limited number of openings. The Bureau provided financial help for those who did not find work, but as the article stated, the general attitude among people there was that they would rather work than receive any kind of outside assistance. The Bureau sent out a pamphlet to prospective employers in order to publicize its cause:

> We take the liberty to call your attention to the opening of our employment bureau at No. 85 Washington Street, Room 1. We propose to furnish the best Swedish help,

male or female, free of charge to everybody. As it is a well-known fact that Swedish people are honest, industrious, competent and sober we feel confident we can fill any position, whether in factories, business houses, hotels, or private families, in the city or in the country. Trusting that you will give this notice your kind consideration, we are, yours very truly, The Swedish National Association.[27]

Overall, the bureau achieved its greatest success in finding work for men as general laborers and women as domestic workers, although it also secured positions in stores, factories, and with construction contractors.

Through the Free Swedish Employment Bureau, the SNA addressed the immediate needs of Swedes living in Chicago. Not only did it seek to elevate the Swedish character, it also attempted to thwart potential criticism against Swedes as a group by keeping them out of the ranks of the unemployed. The Swedish Associations' Central Society and the American Union of Swedish Singers also promoted Swedish welfare and cultural integrity during the economically depressed decade of the 1890s and beyond. Nationalistic celebrations such as raising the Linnaeus monument and celebrating Sweden's Day at the Columbian Exposition created the outward appearance of unity within the Swedish community. Swedes thus celebrated their common heritage while asserting their ethnic identity in the presence of other immigrant groups in the city. Underlying differences among Swedish community organizations remained, however, as the proliferation of neighborhood-based churches and lodges continued. Even so, the umbrella organizations founded during the 1890s provided a mechanism for communication among the plethora of Swedish associations in Chicago and helped to elevate the profile of Swedes in the city as an honest, hardworking group of immigrants.

THE FORGING OF A SWEDISH AMERICAN CONSCIOUSNESS

After the turn of the twentieth century, new organizations emerged that drew together significant elements of the Swedish population, building on the centralizing impulse begun in the 1890s. Although these efforts reflected an intentional appeal to a wide variety of Swedes, they also revealed the large degree of specialized Swedish interests. Swedes continued to organize and divide themselves according to cultural, intellectual, religious, musical, athletic, and ideological issues, reflecting the multifaceted and often divisive nature of Swedish community life in Chicago. Even so, as Barton points out, the Swedish community overcame "earlier internal conflicts" and focused instead upon "a growing sense of common identity and pride in a shared Swedish heritage."[28]

The preservation and invention of Swedish culture regained importance—especially as a new generation emerged that was less Swedish and more American than their parents, and as national romanticism spread in Sweden.[29] Cultural preservation was more than balanced, however, by a need for Swedes to establish their place as part of mainstream American society and assert their long-term commitment to their new country. Hence efforts by the educated elite in the Swedish community to unify organizations and to promote Swedish culture and historical identity, all took place in the context of a self-conscious attempt to forge a new, Swedish American identity.

Three particular associations founded in the early twentieth century affiliated citywide groups of individuals who gathered together for a specialized, overriding purpose. One was the Linnea Aid Society, founded in 1906. This organization united Christian women from a number of Swedish denominations to serve as a support for Englewood Hospital, and it soon expanded its goals to serve more general charitable and evangelistic purposes. The year it was founded, the Linnea Aid Society counted ninety-eight women in its membership. As the organization grew its work became more complex, and included membership, relief, sewing, clothing, and sick committees in order to better fulfill its goals.[30]

The second specialized association of this period was the Swedish Singers Union of Chicago. Formed in 1911, it was a local branch of the American Union of Swedish Singers. Its purpose was to serve as a local umbrella organization uniting the various male singing associations in Chicago. Groups which took part in the Swedish Singers Union of Chicago included the Glee Club Norden, and the Svithiod, Zephyr, Iduna, and Harmoni Singing Clubs.[31] Their efforts promoted Swedish musical traditions among their members, and in a broader sense, among their audiences as well.

The third organization, the Swedish-American Athletic Association, attempted to draw together sports groups around the city. Its object was to "unite men of Swedish birth or descent of sound health and good moral character," and to "promote and advance Swedish gymnastics and all indoor and outdoor sports or athletics, and in general work for the social and intellectual welfare and advancement" of the group's members.[32] These three organizations—although formed for very different purposes—each represented an attempt to unify groups of individuals around a specific interest or activity, thus operating as specialized umbrella organizations.

Throughout the first decade of the twentieth century the Swedish National Association remained the only organization that attempted to unite all Swedish Associations in Chicago. Yet however much it attempted to do so, the SNA could not successfully speak for the variety of interests represented in the Swedish community in Chicago. Ideological differences among the various Swedish associations eventually resulted in the creation of a rival organization in 1913, the Swedish National Society (SNS). Similar to its predecessor, the chartered purposes of the SNS were "To affiliate Swedish Societies and persons of Swedish birth and descent of Cook County; To extend charity and benevolence to worthy persons of Swedish birth or descent; To promote interest in Swedish song, literature and history; To cultivate and foster social, moral and intellectual ideals among its members, and to give entertainments for the accomplishment of its purpose."[33]

A major point of contention with its forerunner had surfaced prior to the creation of the SNS, however. The new group charged that the SNA had defied its charter by selling intoxicating liquors at its festivals and operating its labor bureau for profit. One month after its official incorporation, the SNS passed a resolution stating that "No intoxicating drinks shall be supplied at this society's meetings or parties," and in its bylaws, the society included a clause that the organization would work for the cause of temperance.[34] In response to this development, the SNA amended its charter in 1916, removing the previously stated objective that claimed it would work for temperance. Instead, the association would strive to "promote the interests and prestige of our nationality within the state of Illinois, and also, in the first place according to our ability to aid poor and needy persons of Swedish descent who have fallen into poverty and need through illness, lack of employment or other cause not self-occasioned."[35] By dropping the temperance clause in its original charter, the SNA completed the rift which the SNS had begun. The controversial issue of temperance thus destroyed efforts to unify the Swedish community.

Ideological considerations aside, there was undoubtedly plenty of need for charity work among Swedes in the city, and both organizations continued to exist. Those who began the SNS believed a more effective job of providing social assistance to Chicago's Swedes needed to be done. They added new life to efforts of unifying Swedish organizations of varying political and religious viewpoints, a solidarity that they believed was lacking within the Swedish community of Chicago. In addition to taking a stand against intemperate living, the SNS demonstrated its solidarity with labor by agreeing to honor the union label in all of its transactions; it began to publish a weekly newspaper named *National Bladet*; and it protested to the governor of Utah the death sentence given to the radical Swedish labor activist Joe Hill as an unjust punishment.[36] The SNS arranged Christmas markets and craft exhibits, and assisted in any crisis in which Swedish Americans were affected. A wide range of organizations sent delegates to the meetings.[37] Temperance took a back seat to charity work, as members of the Svithiod, Vasa, and Viking orders held leadership positions in the Swedish National Society of Chicago—members of organizations not known for adhering to the cause of alcohol reform.

FIGURE 14. In this 1916 postcard of the Swedish National Society's Christmas Fair, members are dressed in traditional Swedish provincial garb. This organization promoted temperance and supported the efforts of Swedish labor groups. Courtesy of Swedish-American Archives of Greater Chicago, North Park University, Chicago.

Perhaps the most elite organization in Swedish Chicago was the Swedish-American Historical Society, founded in 1905 by a group of well-educated leaders in the Swedish community who sought to unite Swedish intellectuals in Chicago and across the Upper Midwest. This group realized the historical significance of the great movement of people between Sweden and the United States, and its members acted to avert the potential loss of important documents and historical memorabilia. They claimed that their object was "to collect and preserve for future generations a library of books and manuscripts relating to Swedish men and institutions on the American continent, or written by Swedish Americans, and a museum containing objects, or photographs of objects, of interest on account of their associations with immigrants from Sweden or their descendants."[38]

The Swedish-American Historical Society also intended to promote the study of Swedish history and culture in American universities, to issue publications relating to Swedes in America, and to establish a library of books about Sweden and Swedish-America. In 1908, the organization changed its name to the Swedish Historical Society of America because leaders learned that another association had already been incorporated in the United States under the previous name, and this group wanted to remain distinct.[39] Although Swedish was the group's original primary language, in 1907 the members decided to make English the official language, largely to expand the scope of the group to include second-generation Swedes and scholars who were not familiar with the Swedish language. By 1911, membership reached 216 persons.

This society of highly educated and professional Swedish Americans attempted to form an organization that would, in time, serve as an intellectual center for Swedes in America. Although founded in Chicago, its constituency included people living in a variety of American states. It counted among its members an elite group of clergymen, professors, and publishers. A list of Chicagoans involved with the Historical Society in 1907 included many leaders in Swedish churches and secular associations. A number of Augustana Lutheran pastors, including Carl A. Evald, A. P. Fors, Victor Tengvald, and L. G. Abrahamson, belonged to the Society. Johan Alfred Enander, renowned publisher and speaker at the Linnaeus and Sweden Day celebrations, was the most prominent member of the group with Augustana Lutheran connections.

The list of Chicago members of the Swedish Historical Society included a number of highly esteemed educators of various backgrounds. One such member was Anton J. Carlson, who received his bachelor's and master's degrees at Augustana College and his doctorate from Stanford University, was a professor at the University of Chicago, and served for a time as the president of the American Association for the Advancement of Science. David Nyvall, a pastor in the Covenant Church and professor and president at North Park College, was also active in the organization.

Another key member was C. G. Wallenius, a Swedish Methodist pastor, newspaper editor, and professor at the Methodist Seminary in Evanston, Illinois. The active leadership provided by men from different denominational backgrounds shows a willingness among elite Swedes to move beyond sectarian squabbles.

Officers in the Historical Society included three men who wrote and published a two-volume book entitled *The History of Swedes in Illinois*: Ernst W. Olson, Anders Schön, and Martin J. Engberg, a partner in the Engberg-Holmberg Publishing Company. Two Chicago attorneys also belonged to the Historical Society: Carl R. Chindblom, who did his undergraduate work at Augustana College, and who in 1918 was elected to the US House of Representatives; and Joseph G. Sheldon, who served as the Grand Master of the Independent Order of Svithiod.[40] The vast majority of these men were Swedish-born and had become well established in the Swedish American community in Chicago.

The Swedish Historical Society of America hoped to move Swedes beyond the romantic and emotional notions of their Swedish heritage so evident in the celebrations and organizations of the 1890s. Because its membership included the leaders of a variety of organizational interests in Chicago, they hoped their activities would prove to be a unifying force in the Swedish community. At the suggestion of David Nyvall, the Historical Society decided to hold a conference in Chicago of Swedish American schoolteachers and college professors. The minutes of a council meeting on March 25, 1908, revealed the aspirations it harbored regarding the impact of such a conference:

> It is believed that such a conference would do much to solidify the members of our nationality in America; it might perhaps even be a step towards the bringing about of that close relation between Swedes in this country and in Sweden that is so earnestly desired in our old fatherland, and that without working contrary to the well understood interests of our adopted country.[41]

The minutes went on to acknowledge the split identity of the Swedish American people, with loyalty and duty to both Sweden and the United States. These intellectuals hoped to strike a balance between their Swedish heritage and their American surroundings. They were not attempting to regain a romantic past; rather, they desired to combine both the Swedish and the American aspects of their identity by forging a Swedish American consciousness. In 1921, The Swedish Historical Society moved its headquarters to the Twin Cities in Minnesota as leaders there came to dominate the organization.[42]

After 1910, a different kind of effort began in the Swedish neighborhood of Lake View to unify persons in the Swedish community around ideas of self-improvement. Instead of attempting to publicize the superiority of Swedish cultural values and work practices outside the Swedish community, the Cooperative Temperance Café Idrott and the Swedish Educational League focused their efforts within the Swedish population. These organizations pushed Swedish workers to improve their own lives through temperance and self-education. They were both worker-oriented and had strong ties to the Swedish socialist movement, but they also attracted the interest of Chicago's more elite Swedes. Although supportive of free-thinking attitudes, a few of Chicago's religious leaders found an acceptable and welcoming forum for their ideas in the Swedish Educational League, and many churchgoing persons used the Café Idrott for leisure and social purposes.[43]

The founders of the Cooperative Temperance Café Idrott combined their interests in self-education and temperance. In an interview in February of 1928, the manager of Café Idrott remembered that fifteen years earlier, "about fifty Swedish[-born] boys decided they wanted some sort of a club where they could meet, eat, read, and talk. They did not enjoy pool halls and wanted some place where smoking and drinking were not allowed. They decided to rent an apartment, buy furniture on the installment plan and hire a woman to take care of the place."[44] In order to finance this enterprise, they charged an initiation fee of five dollars per member. They took the name "Idrott" from a Viking athletic contest—a name which in the Swedish language also means "sports." The manager of the club pointed out that these men not only wanted "a place to eat and talk but they wanted a common place of meeting to keep their interest in their mother country, in Swedish books, and in Swedish customs."[45] To this end, they created the largest nonacademic library of Swedish books in Chicago.

Soon, the members of the Café Idrott realized the club needed to have a building of its own. As a move toward that goal, they applied for legal incorporation in the State of Illinois on March 23, 1917, and thereafter began to raise building funds. Their charter stated that the group was formed "to work for the principles of total abstinence from intoxicating liquors, and in connection therewith to operate one or more reading rooms for its members where refreshments and non-intoxicating liquors may be served."[46] In 1919, the group's leaders circulated a letter to Swedish societies and lodges in Lake View, attempting to enlist their support in purchasing a building, and another letter was sent to its members asking for subscriptions for a financial program that would allow them to open a "restaurant without spirits, a library and reading room."[47]

The fund-raising effort proved successful, and in 1923, the Cooperative Temperance Café moved into its new building on Wilton Street near Belmont Avenue. The entire operation included, on the first floor, a dining room, an assembly hall, and a bakery; and on the second floor, a café, and a clubroom. In addition to the outstanding library collected by the organization, the café kept copies of the Swedish daily papers, the various American Swedish weekly papers, as well as English literature and magazines available for its clients' perusal. The café soon became a popular meeting place in Lake View for Swedes from all corners of the Swedish community.[48] Café Idrott represented a worker-oriented attempt to draw together strands of the Swedish community in Chicago, solidifying the Swedish presence in the city by providing a meeting place for the community's many constituents.

Café Idrott was a perfect place for the Swedish Educational League (SEL) to hold its meetings.[49] The group's cofounders—Gustaf L. Larson, Ludvig Holmstrom, Nils Linnberg, and Carl Person, with C. G. Wallenius of the Methodist Seminary serving as educational advisor—began their work within the Jupiter Lodge of the International Order of Good Templars. By 1915, the SEL became an independent organization, coordinating public lectures in the Lake View area. The bylaws of the SEL stated that its object was "to promote self study among its members, chiefly in subjects dealing with Swedish and American culture and life," and that it would accomplish these goals "through study courses, lectures and by other means."[50]

The SEL represented an educational tradition brought from Sweden to serve a new purpose in America. Its founders were influenced by the movement for adult education in Sweden that stressed the importance of self-education and study, particularly among Sweden's laborers. As Sweden's society and government became more democratic in orientation, the importance of an educated public became crucial to their success. Henry Bengston, a noted socialist and active member of the SEL, observed that the group's "founders and early leaders had been trained in the famous study circles and lecture societies which grew up in practically every Swedish city and town during the early years of the century, and their arrival in America only emphasized the need of continuing their educational research."[51]

A clear example of this transatlantic continuity was SEL cofounder Gustaf L. Larson. Although by occupation Larson was a carpenter, Henry Bengston noted that he was "a scholar by inclination and choice."[52] While living in Göteborg, Sweden, Larson belonged to *Studenter och Arbetare*. This organization attempted to unite students and laborers for the purpose of improving communication between these two groups, and to further educational efforts among workers. This educational endeavor seemed even more important once workers found themselves living and working among so many other immigrant groups in Chicago.

The SEL was above all a lecture forum where a variety of ideas were presented. Organizers scheduled lectures for the second and fourth Fridays of each month from September through April. The editors of its publication *Swedish Educational League* described its program policies in the following manner: "While subjects dealing with politics, labor, and even religion often are discussed, this is done only in order to acquaint the audience with the current views and trends in

FIGURE 15. A portrait of the first officers of the Swedish Educational League, taken about 1915 when the group formally organized. Pictured standing, left to right: Carl Swanson, Nils Linnberg, Carl Person. Seated, left to right: Ludvig Holmstrom, Aksel G. S. Josephson, G. L. Larson, P. J. Berggren. Courtesy of Swedish-American Archives of Greater Chicago, North Park University, Chicago.

these fields. The organization as such never underwrites the opinion of its speakers. It limits itself to act as a clearing house for ideas of educational value."[53] As Bengston pointed out in a speech about the SEL, "We do not refuse to listen to a man because his views are radical, nor do we turn down a speaker because he is conservative."[54] In this manner, the SEL provided a unique forum in the Swedish community, uniting people who desired to expand their intellectual capabilities across the political spectrum. Because many Swedes were leery of socialism, however, the SEL had to walk a fine ideological line.

The steering committee's minutes reveal the behind-the-scenes maneuvering necessary to make this educational ideal happen. Yearly dues for the League were set at $1.00 for a single person and $1.50 for a married couple. Membership entitled individuals and couples to attend all lectures during a season without charge. Otherwise, the admission fee for each lecture was ten cents. The SEL sponsored musical concerts and Christmas parties to raise additional funds. It would sometimes organize a spring trip to the Indiana Dunes for its members once the lecture series was complete. Lectures generally attracted thirty-five to fifty-five persons during the 1918–1919 season, although membership in 1919 numbered a total of 150. Overall, the steering committee acted in accordance with the objectives of the organization: it showed no signs of favoritism when selecting program material and discussing potential lecturers.

Suggestions for lecturers for the 1917–1918 season, its first as an independent organization, included C. G. Wallenius of the Swedish Methodist Seminary and David Nyvall of North Park College, as well as Professor Anton J. Carlson from the University of Chicago. In 1918, the steering committee gave free tickets for a musical festival to a variety of Swedish American publications including *Svenska Socialisten*, the Swedish Socialist paper; *Sändebudet, Missions-Vännen*, and *Augustana*, published by the Swedish Methodist, Covenant, and Lutheran churches, respectively; and the liberal newspapers *Svenska Tribunen-Nyheter* and *Svenska Amerikanaren*. The leaders of the SEL respected and upheld the original purposes of the group, namely, that no one particular ideological point of view dominate the character of the organization.[55]

The variety of speakers and subjects actually covered on the seasonal programs continued this tradition of inclusiveness. The 1917–1918 season featured a series of lectures on "the progress of modern science" by Alderman John C. Kennedy, a professor from the University of Chicago; "How we talk and write" and "Social tendencies in Swedish literature" by C. G. Wallenius; and "A Swedish philosophy of War" by Axel G. S. Josephson, librarian at the John Crerar Library. A number of other professors from the University of Chicago and Northwestern University, engineers, and lawyers also lectured to the group during its initial years.

Early in the League's existence, speakers lectured in either Swedish or English, but soon the group preferred that English be used as the primary language to give the meetings a wider appeal and to attract non-Swedish-speaking lecturers. Anton J. Carlson was one of the League's favorite lecturers, who, according to Henry Bengston, "seldom if ever mingled with the social elite of the Swedish people, but only the most pressing official business could keep him from filling his annual speaking engagement on the Swedish Educational League program."[56] The SEL often called upon the North Park College Choir for musical programs, and the school's president David Nyvall frequented the lecture podium. To round out the program, the group also invited such speakers as John Keracher, secretary of the Proletarian Party, who specialized in history and Marxian philosophy. The 1919–1920 series featured a lecture by Clarence Darrow, the Chicago attorney famous for his work in issues of Progressive reform and who later defended John Scopes when he came under attack by William Jennings Bryan for teaching evolution in his high school classroom. These lectures presented to SEL members a variety of subjects and ideologies, opening their minds to new thoughts, and encouraging them to further their own knowledge.[57]

The SEL believed that through self-improvement and self-education, Swedish immigrants could enhance their chances of achieving success in America. The move to use English at meetings encouraged participants to become fully bilingual and exposed them to issues outside the Swedish community. Immigrants were not expected to leave their past behind, but to build on their Swedish traditions in order to improve their American future. One active SEL member stated this underlying duality of purpose as follows:

> The work we are doing among ourselves and for our own benefit might well be regarded as a part of the work of Americanization. You will never be able to reach the immigrants in this country with the view of making them true Americans except through the medium of their own native culture. Therefore, it is necessary that they should retain touch with their cultural past. The object of the Swedish Study League is to reach out in both directions.[58]

Although stressing a worker-oriented agenda, the SEL resembled other elite organizations in its attempt to forge a Swedish American consciousness.

A shortcoming of the Swedish Educational League—and other organizations that attempted to unify the Swedish community in Chicago—was that it never reached the majority of Swedes living in the city. While intellectually oriented religious professors such as Wallenius and Nyvall participated in the League's lectures, other pastors and church leaders were not highly visible in its activities and programs. Likewise, the educational program did not appeal to the greatest number of lodge members. Henry Bengston lamented that "Although the Swedish Educational League is widely known in adult education circles and has been pointed to as a model lecture forum, it has never won the wholehearted recognition as one of the outstanding Swedish organizations by the Swedish people themselves."[59]

Furthermore, any conservative Swedes and Americans were suspicious of the League, especially of the more radical lecturers it allowed to speak.[60] A pro-socialist reputation undoubtedly haunted the League—especially during these particularly sensitive years following the Russian Revolution and World War One, when the fear of communism was running rampant in the United States. Nevertheless, the SEL established a program of lectures that continued uninterrupted until 1955. In a speech about the impact of the SEL, Bengston believed that its longevity proved "that we always have held high the ideals planted in our hearts back in Sweden more than a quarter of a century ago. If we in turn are able to transplant them in the hearts of those who will carry on after us, then I think we have filled our mission well."[61]

While many of these centralizing and unifying organizations brought together leaders in the Swedish community—people such as Myhrman, Wallenius, Nyvall, Carlson, and Bengston—they did not succeed in providing a single forum for all strands of the Swedish community. Nevertheless, these associations managed to establish lines of communication and a sense of mutual respect between many of the leaders within the Swedish community, a feat highly unlikely in the more emotionally charged decades of the 1880s and 1890s when leaders were more concerned with organizing and establishing their own separate churches, schools, lodges, and newspapers. The centralizing societies created a citywide network of Swedish leaders who were firmly connected to one or more localized secular or religious organizations. Cooperation among intellectual leadership hardly filtered down to all levels of membership, but it did signal that the boundaries between many of the community's organizations were not completely impenetrable. Furthermore, these overarching organizations—like the neighborhood-based associations—built an ethnic identity that drew on their founders' experiences in Sweden and their perceived needs for Swedish community identity in Chicago. This Swedish American identity and how it should be legitimately expressed came under fire during the volatile ethnic dynamics generated by the First World War.

TEACHING SWEDISH IN CHICAGO'S PUBLIC SCHOOLS

One of the best ways for an immigrant's child to advance was through education, and the public schools of Chicago became a vehicle through which Swedish immigrant children could learn English and hopefully improve their lives. The public schools in Chicago were a forum in which many agendas intersected— the desire of many natives to see immigrant children Americanized into good model citizens; the attempt of many immigrant children to fit in with the other American children; and the hope of many parents to see their children succeed in their new land while not losing sight of their traditional heritage. In most cases, Swedish immigrants surrendered control over education to the American experts. But at the peak of their strength in Chicago, the Swedes chose to wage a battle for Swedish language in the public schools.[62]

The campaign by the Swedish community in Chicago to introduce Swedish language classes in the public high schools, which began in 1911, provides a perfect example of the tension between the preservation of ethnic identity on the one hand and the desire to succeed in America on the other. This tension undoubtedly was experienced not only by Swedes, but by all immigrants who established themselves in Chicago and in other American cities. The way in which the Swedish community leaders campaigned vigorously for Swedish in the schools in 1911 and 1912, then backed away from their demands in 1917 when the nation was at war, reflected the divided loyalty of a people with a Swedish and an American identity. The war itself marked the emergence of a new generation whose feet were firmly planted on the American side of the Atlantic.

In the late nineteenth and early twentieth centuries, Germans were the largest ethnic group in the city of Chicago. Because of the size of the German community, German organizations effectively lobbied the Chicago Board of Education and convinced the board to introduce German as an elective subject in the public schools in 1865.[63] The number of children studying German grew dramatically in subsequent years. In 1870, eight German teachers taught 2,597 pupils; by 1892 these numbers had grown to 242 teachers teaching 34,547 pupils, nearly one-fourth of all the children enrolled in Chicago's schools.[64] The public schools also began to offer French as an optional modern language and continued to offer and support German language instruction until the dynamics of World War One led them to reconsider their position.[65]

The Board of Education gradually added more language classes to the school curriculum. Spanish was accepted as a course in the public high schools at the September 6, 1899, Board of Education meeting. At that same meeting, Polish leaders petitioned the Board to provide instruction in the Polish language upon the same basis that German was being taught.[66] The Board did not accept their petition, even though the Poles were the third largest ethnic group in the city, behind the Germans and the Irish. Not until March 8, 1911, more than a decade later, did the Polish National Alliance successfully pressure the Board of Education into allowing Polish to be taught in the high schools. The Chicago school superintendent, Dr. Ella Flagg Young, recommended such action, giving the opinion that "any foreign language which is the medium of a great literature should be offered in the public high schools where the public interest is sufficiently great to make it likely that use will be made of the courses to be offered."[67] This action turned out to be extremely important to the Swedish community, as it paved the way for Swedish to be taught in the schools and gave community leaders the incentive to launch a major campaign to see that Swedish was adopted in the public school curriculum.[68] According to accounts in the Swedish press and the records of the Board of Education, Swedish was in fact offered as an elective subject in the Chicago public high schools from the fall of 1912 through the spring of 1917.

The introduction of Swedish into the public high schools of Chicago was achieved only through a carefully designed and orchestrated campaign led by elite members of the Swedish community.[69] Henry Henschen, a Chicago Swede who was cashier of the State Bank of Chicago as well as acting consul of Sweden, took the lead role in the campaign for Swedish in the Chicago schools. The Swedish newspaper *Svenska Amerikanaren* reported that Henschen called a meeting regarding Swedish in the schools for members of the Swedish American press, churches, and organizations. Those who attended the meeting approved a resolution calling for Swedish to be taught in Chicago's public schools.[70] From then on, a steering committee made up of Henschen, Harry Olson, Pastor C. E. Hoffsten, Professor Anton J. Carlson, Olof Nelson, and C. F. Erickson conducted the campaign for Swedish in the schools. They presented a petition to the Chicago Board of Education in April 1911, requesting that Swedish language instruction be offered in Chicago's public schools.

The most influential person in the decision-making process was Chicago public school superintendent Young, to whom the Board referred the entire Swedish language issue. Indeed, Young was not easily influenced, and as the Swedish American press reported at the beginning of June, she decided to postpone the introduction of Swedish in the schools until there was some result shown from the "experiment with the Polish language," which would be introduced in the schools the following fall.[71] The Swedes were not pleased that the opportunity to teach Swedish in the public schools depended upon the success of the Polish language experiment. The decision seemed to give preference to Poles over Swedes. Henschen pointed out that, although there were twenty thousand more Poles living in Chicago than Swedes, because the Poles were largely Catholic, a large proportion of them went to parochial schools. The Swedes, by contrast, sent most of their children to the public schools, and therefore they should be able to exert more influence over the schools than the Poles. "The Swedish children in the public schools," wrote Henschen, "are without a doubt much more numerous than the Polish, just as the Swedish nation in the city, both in reputation and in age, is more than equal to the Polish."[72]

Henschen also acknowledged the other, perhaps more significant challenge faced by the leaders in the Swedish community—convincing their children that they should indeed want to study the Swedish language. He wrote that:

> To introduce the Swedish language among Swedish American children in America is a Herculean task—how big, only those who have long lived in this country can understand. . . . Remember that the Americans only look up to 2 classes of foreigners—those who are rich and those who are lions. The Swedes in America most

often are neither one nor the other. Therefore their children seek to quickly become Americans. . . . They don't want anything to do with the mother tongue. But times are changing: when they have achieved success, they often turn with love toward their father's tongue and seek to imbue their children with reverence and love for Swedish culture.[73]

Henschen kept the language issue alive in the Swedish community. In November he called another meeting of the steering committee and in December, an "Appeal to the Swedes in Chicago" was announced in the Swedish American press.[74] The Swedish American newspapers reported that petitions to the Board of Education were being circulated widely in Swedish churches and clubs. Since Polish had been successfully introduced in the public schools that fall, it was time for the Swedish community to take action so that Swedish classes could begin in the schools the following academic year. The Swedish newspapers emphasized that Swedish instruction in the schools was a most important issue for the expression of the community's Swedish identity and for the future of the Swedish youth.[75] Norwegian community leaders also circulated petitions regarding Norwegian language instruction in the schools, paralleling the Swedes' activities.

A delegation of Swedish and Norwegian representatives brought their petitions to Dr. J. B. McFatrick, the Board of Education president, in January 1912. The delegation suggested that Swedish be introduced in Lake View and Englewood High Schools and the Norwegian language in Carl Schurz and Tuley High Schools. McFatrick raised no objection to their request, but referred them once again to school superintendent Young, and the delegation subsequently presented their petitions to her. She did not reach a decision immediately, and the following May, the board passed a general policy statement regarding foreign language instruction in the schools: "The superintendent of schools reports that many petitions have been received from societies and individuals requesting the addition of different modern languages to the list of optional studies in the high schools, and . . . recommends . . . that any modern language be offered in the public high schools of Chicago when, the number of pupils applying for a course in the language is sufficient to warrant the assignment of a teacher who is competent to teach that foreign language." The Swedish American newspapers interpreted this action as a direct approval of Swedish courses being introduced in the schools the following fall.[76]

Thus the initiative was back in the hands of the Swedish leaders in Chicago. As long as enough students registered to take Swedish, the Board of Education would introduce it in select public high schools. In July, the Swedish leaders' efforts were helped when Charles F. Erickson, a member of Henschen's Swedish steering committee, was appointed to the Board of Education. Erickson was publisher of the

Swedish language newspaper *Svenska Tribunen-Nyheter*, and had been involved with the press since immigrating from Sweden in 1887. "We're sure our country- man shall do as well as any other on the board," reported *Svenska Amerikanaren*.[77]

In August 1912, one month away from the beginning of school, the campaign began in earnest. *Svenska Amerikanaren* praised the hard work of those who led the fight for Swedish in the schools. But in reality, only the first battle had been won. Now the Swedish parents had to convince their American children actually to sign up for Swedish class. A minimum of twenty-five students needed to enroll at a particular school in order for the board to hire a teacher. The papers urged students to register for Swedish so that this golden opportunity would not be lost. To make it easy to enroll, *Svenska Amerikanaren* printed a form which the stu- dents, their parents, or guardians could fill out with their name, address, and high school, and send in to the newspaper. The newspaper staff would collect the forms and submit them to the Chicago Board of Education. *Svenska Amerikanaren* noted, "It is of utmost importance that the question of Swedish language studies in the high schools is embraced with great interest among our countrymen here in the city."[78] In America, where there were so many different nationalities, Swedes should encourage their children to study Swedish, one of the "oldest and richest cultural languages."[79]

Svenska Amerikanaren and other Swedish papers in Chicago continued the campaign in subsequent issues and reprinted the application form, maintaining pressure upon the Swedish community. By August 22, the editors of the paper seemed concerned that the goal would not be reached. They had not yet received the necessary twenty-five applications to begin Swedish instruction in even one city high school. School would begin on September 3, and some advance warning was necessary to organize a class. The good news was that a Swedish teacher had already been engaged at Lake View High School on Chicago's North Side. C. O. Sundstrom, formerly a professor of modern languages at Monmouth College in Illinois, was hired to teach Swedish and German.[80] The Swedish youth were not easily influenced, however, and by August 29, the paper's editors seemed desper- ate. Not only had they not received enough applications, but the school superin- tendent had raised the minimum number of students from twenty-five to thirty. Only twenty-one students had signed up at Lake View High School, as well as five at Englewood, two at Lane Technical, and one at each of four other high schools. With only one week left, the future of Swedish in the public schools looked grim.[81]

Apparently the newspaper's final push paid off, however, and on September 5 it reported "a beautiful result" regarding Swedish in the public schools.[82] Over one hundred students had enrolled in Swedish classes at the various high schools, but only one teacher, Sundstrom, had been hired to teach the single class formed at Lake View High School. The paper reported that another class would begin in the spring, most likely at Englewood or Farragut High School. The paper was disappointed that the response was not greater, but it remained optimistic. "[Swedish instruction] has begun on a small scale, but once it has begun, the registration will be bigger for spring term."[83] Ultimately, thirty-two students preregistered for Swedish at Lake View High School, and nine additional students enrolled after the first day of class. The interest continued to grow, and by the end of September, another Swedish class was added, so that each class had an enrollment of about thirty students. Sundstrom also helped to charter a Swedish Club at Lake View High School in October of 1912. The school's student newspaper, *Red and White*, informed its readers that the group planned nine meetings and two parties every year, and that the program was largely conducted in Swedish. It further reported that "All of [the members] understand Swedish to some extent."[84]

Leaders in the Swedish community undoubtedly were encouraged that their efforts had paid off. Swedish classes continued their success at Lake View and also were added to the curriculum at Englewood High School. What is surprising, however, is how comparatively few Swedish American students actually were persuaded to enroll in Swedish classes. The number of students taking Swedish each year at the two high schools was at the most two hundred. According to the school census of May 2, 1912, there were 1,413 Swedish-born minors living in Chicago, along with 44,673 minors who were American-born but whose fathers were Swedish. Thus, since this number does not include children whose mothers were Swedish and whose fathers were another nationality, a conservative estimate of first- and second-generation Swedish children in Chicago is 46,086. Assuming two hundred students enrolled in Swedish classes during each year it was offered in the high schools, only about 3 percent of the total number of Swedish American high-schoolers signed up for Swedish class during the entire period Swedish was offered in the schools.[85] Some of these students undoubtedly attended high schools where Swedish was not offered. The statistics do, however, give powerful testimony to the fact that despite all the valiant efforts of the Swedish leaders in Chicago, the vast majority of Swedish American high school students could not be persuaded that the study of the Swedish language was desirable or useful.

Lake View and Englewood High Schools continued to offer Swedish classes until the pressures of World War One brought all foreign language instruction into question. Critics attacked German instruction with particular vehemence. In the public schools the emphasis shifted toward 100 percent Americanism: the schools needed to mold foreign youngsters into good American citizens.[86] During the summer and fall of 1917, the Board of Education vigorously debated the role of foreign language in the public schools. They were especially concerned with German language instruction in the elementary schools, an enterprise that cost nearly sixteen thousand dollars per year. The superintendent, by that time John

D. Shoop, noted in his report to the board that "in the first 6 years of experience of a child in the elementary schools, there should be no encroachment that would diminish in any measure his opportunities for acquiring mastery of the tools of intelligence, namely, reading, speaking, writing, and spelling of our own language."[87] He recommended that no foreign language be offered below grade seven; that only French, German, and Spanish be offered in junior high; and that the current policy of modern foreign language instruction be continued in the high schools. After much debate, the recommendation was passed by the Board of Education. Interestingly enough, the two Scandinavian members of the board, Hart Hanson and Charles Peterson, voted down a proposal that would allow for any foreign language to be taught in the public elementary schools, including Czech, Polish, Italian, Russian, Swedish, Norwegian, Danish, and Dutch. Peterson defended his position, claiming that "our school year is too short . . . that I for one felt we were trying to teach too many things."[88] Although technically Swedish could continue to be taught in the high schools, it was dropped from the curriculum by 1918.

What were the leaders in the Swedish community doing throughout this debate in the Chicago Board of Education about foreign languages? They were busy jumping on the 100 percent Americanism bandwagon, attempting to prove their loyalty to the United States as the nation went to war. Henry Henschen and Harry Olson, who had been instrumental in rallying the Swedish community behind the issue of adopting Swedish in the schools, were by 1917 organizing a major Swedish American patriotic demonstration. The meeting was held on September 30, 1917, at Chicago's Municipal Pier Auditorium, which they decorated with over one thousand American flags for the occasion. Harry Olson began the rally with a resounding speech, emphasizing the link between America and her Swedish sons and daughters:

> Chicago has 150,000 inhabitants of Swedish descent . . . and America need not entertain any anxiety concerning their loyalty. Their faithfulness to the land which has given them such rich opportunities is proven. For nearly 1000 years, since Leif Ericson landed on our coast, the Nordic men have always been completely welcome to America's soil.[89]

Olson remarked that the outbreak of world war had bound Swedish immigrants more closely to their new homeland. Those assembled at the meeting went on to pass a resolution declaring their loyalty to the American flag, and supporting the actions of President Wilson and Congress in conducting the war effort. The meeting ended in a short prayer, and the singing of *The Star-Spangled Banner* and *Stridsbön* (War Prayer) by the Swedish Song Choir.

The Swedish American press concentrated on war coverage—carefully documenting the Swedish American boys who went marching off to war, and those who never returned.[90] The language issue was no longer important in the lives of these young people, and it dropped out of sight in the newspapers. In September of 1918, editors of *Svenska Amerikanaren* offered their own explanation of this shift in attitude and priorities:

> Right before America's entering the war, there was great interest in Chicago and other places for instruction in foreign languages in our schools. In Chicago, where the German language has long had a prominent place among courses of instruction, instruction also began in Swedish, Spanish, French, Polish, and other languages, and language interest was rather strong among the youth. But last year a . . . war of extermination began, so that [now] people want to be against foreign languages, especially . . . the German and that is an easily explained argument . . . times change and we with them.[91]

The continuation of Swedish language instruction in the public high schools required a sustained effort by the Swedish elite in Chicago, with the support of the churches and other ethnic organizations. But times had indeed changed, and members of the Swedish community found it more politically wise to concentrate on supporting the war and proving their loyalty rather than pursuing the issue of Swedish in the schools and emphasizing their foreignness. Furthermore, many of the Swedish American young people were taking a direct role in the war effort—it was they who went off to fight the war or who, in the case of the young women, stayed behind and joined war-support organizations. Their lives were changed forever by this war, and as a result, their identity was even more closely linked to the United States. It was better, then, to leave ethnic expressions to the community itself—to speak and learn the Swedish language in the homes and in the churches and clubs—rather than in the public sphere of the city's schools where such action could be misinterpreted as anti-American. Although ethnic identity remained important to Swedes in Chicago, they paid greater attention—at least publicly—to fitting in with the American mainstream.

THE GROWTH OF SWEDISH PROVINCIALISM

After World War One, Swedish organizations in Chicago wrestled with forging a more politically acceptable type of Swedish American identity. Not all groups responded in the same fashion, however. The Swedish Cultural Society of America argued against wholesale conformity to American society by raising the banner

of Swedish cultural superiority. The various provincial societies that prolifer-
ated during the 1920s promoted Swedish regionalism and folk culture. And the
American Daughters of Sweden, founded in 1926, fostered the memory of Swedish
culture among a largely American-born generation.

The organization that concentrated most fully on the preservation of Swedish
cultural identity during this period began as the Society for the Preservation of
Swedish Culture in America (*Riksföreningen för svenskhetens bevarande i Amerika*).
Founded in 1910 in conjunction with the celebration of the fiftieth anniversary of
Augustana College in Rock Island, Illinois, the group formed a Chicago branch
in 1923 and shortly thereafter changed its name to the Swedish Cultural Society
of America.[92] The principal objective of this organization was "the preservation
among Americans of Swedish descent of the traditions of the homeland, of the
true Swedish spirit and civic ideals, which have brought glory and renown to the
Swedish name, and to keep living the legitimate love for the fatherland."[93] Among
the group's leaders were A. G. Witting, a high-ranking engineer in the steel industry in Gary, Indiana; and Carl Chindblom and C. G. Wallenius, both leaders in the
Swedish Historical Society in America.

The Swedish Cultural Society gained momentum in the years after World
War One, when its leaders attempted to walk the tightrope between American
patriotism and the preservation of Swedish culture. Above all, the group reacted
strongly against the nativist sentiment evident during the war. The 100 Per Cent
Americanism campaign, which historian John Higham characterized as being
made up of persons who "belligerently demanded universal conformity organized
through total national loyalty," was particularly distasteful to these Swedes.[94] The
Swedish Cultural Society argued that a person could at once be true to his Swedish
traditions and to his American citizenship.

> The Society recognizes that the Swedish-Americans must give undivided loyalty and
> their fullest devotion to their new country, and it does not countenance any foster-
> ing of a separatist Swedish sentiment. But on the other hand, it fully believes in the
> truism that: the better Swede, the better American, because the Swedish-American
> who is imbued by a legitimate pride in and love for the land of his fathers will nec-
> essarily feel it as a personal responsibility and a bounden duty that the good name
> of the Swedes is not sullied or lowered. He will by such sentiment be spurred on to
> do his very best both in private life and as an American citizen and thus increase his
> efforts to serve his adopted country and uphold its standards and ideals.[95]

Henry Bengston, a leader in the Swedish Educational League, noted that the work
of the Swedish Cultural Society was particularly justified "during the first world war
on the grounds of the prevailing aversion against foreign languages and customs."[96]

Another popular movement among Chicago's Swedes in the early twentieth century that gained momentum after World War One was the formation of provincial societies. These societies added to the already complex array of Swedish organizations in Chicago and built on nostalgic sentiments Swedes held not for their nation, but for their villages and provinces. Provincial clubs were referred to as *hembygdsföreningar* or *landskapsföreningar*. Some of these organizations, such as Stockholms Klubben, assembled people from one particular city in Sweden; others centered their membership on persons from a particular province or region in Sweden. As Barton points out, these provincial societies were not only a response to the pressures to Americanize, they were also a reaction against efforts by Swedish American leaders to promote a national Swedish culture. Barton writes that "the kind of general, national Swedish folk culture that steadily gained ground in Swedish America was not altogether satisfying for some immigrants who longed for a closer bond with the particular local cultures in which they had grown up."[97] Churches and lodges, as well as the national associations, all included members who came from a variety of areas around Sweden. *Hembygdsföreningar*, on the other hand, were the only organizations that attempted to differentiate the Swedes according to their regional homes. They conveyed a particularistic brand of nationalism, one based heavily on romantic notions of their lost Swedish childhood.

Momentum for the organization of provincial societies began slowly and grew in the 1910s, as the Swedish population in Chicago diminished and as pressure for Americanism increased. Jämtlands Gille, one of the earliest provincial societies, was formed in 1897 to "assemble Jämtland-born persons and their relatives for mutual benefit and enjoyment" and to strengthen interest in their home province.[98] Föreningen Bohus, founded in 1904, also attempted to provide death benefits to its members, but over time offered a different kind of assistance instead—gifts of cash to marrying couples and flowers to sick members.[99] On March 17, 1917, an informal meeting of "Dalarna People" at the Viking Temple in Lake View resulted in the formation of Club Dalarna. One man present, A. Friman, had helped organize such a society in Stockholm and he encouraged Chicago's Swedes to follow suit. Membership was open to every man or woman who was born or raised in Dalarna and their spouses, but the group noted that none "who would prefer intoxicating drinks will be taken in, nor [will liquor be] served at any of the society's meetings or parties."[100] Not all provincial societies followed a platform of temperance, but because each club was formed by only a handful of persons, specific ideological viewpoints could easily dominate a particular organization.

The overwhelming impulse behind the formation of Provincial Societies was the power of romantic memories of rural Sweden. These memories contrasted greatly with the reality of heavily populated Chicago. As Chicago became more urbanized and its people pushed back the prairie to even greater distances, the memory of Sweden's forests captured these immigrants' imaginations. Not only were the Swedes proud of their nationalistic culture, they also found a need to associate with those who could remember a particular village, who possibly shared memories of the same people, and who grew up with similar traditional crafts and customs. E. Einar Andersson, a leader in the provincial society movement and the Good Templars, summed up his feelings quite poetically:

> How often do we not think back to the long winter nights, when the magnificent Northern lights spread their brilliance over the snow covered surroundings and the big, deep forest sang nature's praise in a powerful, harmonious sigh. Our thoughts also often go to the time, when the place back home stood dressed in its fairest garb, when the sun stood high in the sky and the flowers filled the surroundings with their fragrance. Maybe our parents are sitting back home, rejoicing over every letter they get from us over here . . .
>
> We remember them and their exhortation—we remember home, brothers and sisters and friends. We remember the smiling lakes with their reflecting surfaces, the islands back home, the winding steps we wandered in the days of our childhood, the pastures we played in, yes everything—these are memories we shall never forget.
>
> With these memories, which we wish to protect, renew, and talk about, [we should] not be astonished that former childhood friends will come together and build . . . provincial associations.[101]

The number of provincial societies in Chicago grew after 1920 to reach at least twenty-three clubs by 1932, displaying among Swedes a need for reliving memories of their Swedish past and finding new ways to personalize the city. Despite their backward-looking tendencies, they helped connect Swedes in Chicago with other immigrants from similar regions in Sweden, creating even more specialized channels of connection within the Swedish community and aiding in the process of adaptation to urban life.

As the Swedish-born population in Chicago declined during the 1920s and the number of immigrant children increased, a new generation of Swedish Americans was anxious to promote its American as well as its Swedish identity. Instead of looking backward to rural Sweden, they valued their Swedish heritage but formed new ways of making connections in the city. For example, the American Daughters of Sweden (ADS) ushered in a new era of organization-building within the Swedish American community. The ADS was founded in 1926, and its charter indicated that its overriding purpose was to "encourage sociability and unite more closely those interested in Swedish history in America." The ADS also sought to "cultivate a knowledge of and seek to further the interest of the Swedish-American woman," and finally, to "advance such educational, social, charitable and civic movements and all interests that form a part of our national life." This hybrid, Swedish and American identity was further illustrated by the requirement that members be both American citizens and of Swedish birth or descent.[102]

The ADS attempted to unite Swedish American women across a number of potential barriers—philosophical, professional, and generational. As ADS member Hedwig Melinder remembered, this new club was intended to represent a broad spectrum of Swedish American women, noting the large "number of lodges, churches and welfare organizations," and also recognizing the "need of a club which would include all of these groups." As Melinder further observed, "an unusual characteristic of this club is that it includes as members women from all walks of life, such as business, professional, housewives, etc."[103] Othelia Myhrman, well known as a businesswoman, cofounder of the Swedish National Association, and avid leader in the Swedish American community, was selected as its first president. Within a decade, however, the ADS came to be dominated by an American-born generation. Members of the ADS attempted to connect young Swedish American women with their Swedish heritage, educate themselves about issues of the day, and create a close group of friends in the process. To these ends, the most rewarding program supported by the ADS was to offer scholarships to young women of Swedish descent to the University of Chicago, and later to North Park College in Chicago and Augustana College in Rock Island, Illinois.

THE LIMITS OF ORGANIZATIONAL UNITY

Beginning in the 1890s, Swedes living in Chicago organized groups for the purpose of celebrating the virtues of Swedish culture and the noble character of the Swedish people. Infused with nationalistic spirit carried with them from Sweden, Swedes wanted to portray themselves as a group that would make positive contributions to their new homeland. This agenda was in large part a reaction to the growing presence of new immigrant groups in Chicago and to the increasing criticism of immigration by the American public. Centralized Swedish associations attempted to unify the variety of Swedish clubs and organizations in the city, hoping to counteract the geographic dispersal of the Swedish population and organizations into outlying neighborhoods in the city. They attempted to link Swedish institutions throughout the city, to move beyond neighborhood-based associations, and in the process, to create a unified Swedish presence in Chicago.

The Swedish community, however, could not be completely unified. The nature and sheer quantity of organizations created by Swedes in Chicago reflected a widespread, deeply ingrained diversity. Centralizing organizations succeeded in unifying individuals at the uppermost echelons of leadership, but they never took on the grassroots character of many of the churches and fraternal lodges. Furthermore, Swedish Americans showed a great deal of skepticism toward self-appointed leaders.[104] In 1920, Chicago's Swedish community included a large array of organizations that appealed to workingmen and professionals, men and women, religious and nonreligious persons, temperance advocates and hearty drinkers, and the educated and the uneducated. The boundaries between these organizations were not always clear-cut, but they all represented creative ways to make associations between Swedes with similar interests and ideological viewpoints. From the immigrants' perspective, they became ways of coping with a life very different from the one into which they had been born.

Overarching organizations founded by Swedes in Chicago built on and gave expression to a new kind of Swedish identity that reflected specifically American needs and pressures. Similar organizations did not exist in Sweden, for it was only in a big, heterogeneous location like Chicago that such associations were even necessary. Although nationalism was strong in Sweden, Swedes in many ways became more clearly and self-consciously Swedish in their American environment than many of them had been in their homeland. Even so, the celebration of their Swedish cultural heritage was always done within the context of their new life in Chicago; Swedes grafted memories of their Swedish past to their hopes for a successful future in America. The result was a new, distinctly Swedish American identity. Thus, while these overarching organizations drew on a pool of ideas and enthusiasm that linked Swedes in Chicago with their Swedish heritage, their particular shapes and histories were clearly and directly related to the pattern of Swedish settlement and the evolution of the Swedish community in Chicago in the late nineteenth and early twentieth centuries.

EPILOGUE

This war has bound us all together. Several years ago there existed Americans and hyphenated Americans of all kinds. Now all are completely Americans.

—Harry Olson, September 30, 1917, in a speech at a patriotic demonstration of Chicago's Swedes at the Municipal Pier Auditorium

Swedish immigrants living in and arriving at Chicago between 1880 and 1920 found the social, economic, and geographic environment dynamic, flexible, and malleable relative to their experience in Sweden. This aspect of living in a new American city allowed Swedes to be creative, molding their living conditions and religious and social affiliations to fit their own needs. Although many areas of Sweden had experienced unprecedented transitions by the end of the nineteenth century, Chicago was characterized by even more explosive growth and enormous change. Swedes found opportunities in such an environment to create their own community affiliations. They did not need merely to conform to Chicago life as they found it, but were in many ways able to transform aspects of the urban environment to meet the demands of their own lives. Within their own community, Swedish immigrants could create facets of their lives over which they had complete control.

During these same years, the burgeoning Swedish population in Chicago moved to scattered neighborhoods. Swedes responded to the dynamic nature of an expanding urban environment by bringing existing affiliations with them to these new areas, creating an extensive network of ethnic organizations throughout the city. The diverse pattern of association evident in the older, more centralized Swedish enclaves was replicated and expanded as Swedes moved out into new areas of the city. Furthermore, the very nature of the organizations themselves changed during these years, evolving from centralized enclave-based institutions to complex denominational and lodge configurations. These expanded structures allowed for branches to be established in new neighborhoods without jeopardizing the integrity of their original organizational purpose. These Swedish institutions complemented familial affiliations and added an important ethnic dimension to the Swedes' experience in Chicago. They contributed a measure of security to an often uncertain existence in an unfamiliar city. Through these organizations, Swedes created and expanded their community even as they suburbanized.

It is important to note, however, that some degree of intimacy was lost as Swedes moved away from older enclaves. While these immigrants made aspects of their new neighborhoods Swedish through new networks of affiliation, contacts became more formal. Attending a club meeting or church service was qualitatively very different from having casual conversations between neighbors. Certainly informal connections continued to some degree in new subdivisions. But by 1920 the context had changed from the earliest days of the Swedish settlement in the city. Chicago was bigger and more spread out, and its people were more numerous and ethnically diverse. Likewise, as the Swedish population in Chicago grew, it became more varied in terms of age, times of arrival, and ideological viewpoints, and hence, Swedes' connections with each other became ever more complex.[1]

Chicago continued to play an essential role in Swedish America. By the early twentieth century its Swedish population was larger than that of any other American city, and second in the world only to Stockholm. Its network of railroads spreading to points further west continued to make it the gateway though which immigrants moved to more distant farms and cities throughout the Midwest. Other Swedes migrated in the opposite direction as Chicago's robust economy drew them to the city from areas in rural America. Overall, this meant that even more Swedes experienced Chicago than actually lived there. Chicago also served as a nerve center for a significant portion of Swedish institutional life. The Independent Order of Vikings and the Independent Order of Svithiod, both founded in Chicago, were two of the three largest secular Swedish organizations in the United States. Swedish newspapers and books, many of which were published in Chicago, spread news about the city and its community throughout Swedish America and even back to Sweden.[2] In addition, strong Swedish congregations in Chicago influenced denominational decisions nationwide.

In terms of influencing the affairs of Chicago as a whole, however, Swedes faced a great deal of competition from other groups. As the sixth largest ethnic group in the city in 1910, Swedes could not dominate the larger cultural or political milieu. The Germans and the Irish had long outnumbered the Swedes. By 1910, the Polish and Russian communities were larger than the Swedish, and by 1920, so too was the Italian. In addition, by 1920 the city felt the impact of the Great Migration of African Americans from the rural South to Chicago and other destinations in the urban, industrial North. In contrast, in Minneapolis and St. Paul, Minnesota, Scandinavians as a whole and Swedes in particular dominated the Twin Cities' demographic composition. As Philip J. Anderson and Dag Blanck point out, "By 1920 the Swedes were the largest immigrant group in both Minneapolis and St. Paul, ahead of both the Norwegians and the Germans; they made up 30 percent of the immigrant population in Minneapolis and 20 percent in St. Paul."[3] This allowed the Swedes to create a strong cultural presence there and an ethnic consciousness that persists to this day, something they were not able to do to the same degree in Chicago, despite their large numbers.

The creation and maintenance of a vital Swedish organizational life in Chicago between 1880 and 1920 provides an important key in understanding how Swedes as an immigrant group adapted to life in Chicago. Voluntary associations forged webs of communication and linkages between members that transcended the purely territorial aspects of community life. Through these ethnic organizations, Swedes created a "middle ground" that combined aspects of their experiences in Sweden and America and formed a new, Swedish American identity. Swedish immigrants in Chicago were anxious to shelter and preserve their own traditions and beliefs, yet they were innovative in taking advantage of American circumstances to create new types of ethnic affiliation.

The new Swedish churches were strong, thriving organizations, supporting such institutions as colleges, hospitals, and homes for the aged for their members. Both churches and secular organizations combined aspects of the old traditions with the new conditions of living in Chicago. Meetings of the fraternal orders celebrated the members' Viking heritage while providing mutual support in times of sickness and death. Furthermore, the large network of churches and secular associations that extended throughout the city perpetuated the ethnic dimension of settlement in the new subdivisions. Elite organizations attempted to unify the various strands of the community but in fact added to the diversity. No single forum could unite Swedes in Chicago, although leaders of both secular and religious groups displayed an increased willingness to work together, especially for purposes of educating the Swedish immigrant population and for preserving the heritage of the new Swedish Americans. Ultimately, the resulting community was a complex array of organizational interests and philosophical points of view.

The story told here about Swedish community-building might be unique to Swedes in the particular details, but it follows patterns evident in other ethnic groups.[4] Religious impulses united and at times divided Germans, Jews, Poles,

Greeks, and other groups. The growth of fraternal orders, political associations, and sports and music clubs added diversity to all ethnic communities. Foreign-language newspapers and ethnic businesses of all kinds flourished in Chicago. First-generation immigrants struggled over the role the mother tongue would play in communal institutions as their increasingly Americanized children embraced English. Neighborhoods evolved as various groups transitioned through them. Dominic A. Pacyga observes that groups followed a general pattern whereby "middle class Chicagoans of every economic and ethnic background" flowed out from the center of the city to newly developing neighborhoods and suburbs.[5] All groups faced difficulties adjusting to Chicago, and none more so than African Americans, most of whom came from rural areas of the South. They faced the difficulty of transitioning to urban life while coping with racist attitudes of both native and foreign-born Chicagoans.

Change was inevitable for all groups, however, and after 1910, a number of factors converged to move the Swedish community toward gradual Americanization. The following decade marked the first time since Swedes set foot in Chicago that their numbers in the city actually declined. The large wave of Swedes who arrived in the 1880s while in the prime of life was aging, and immigrants were losing influence to their American-born children and grandchildren.[6] The new generations valued their Swedish heritage but viewed themselves as more American than Swedish. These pressures pushed many Swedish churches to adopt English as their official language in the 1920s, and even though many Swedish secular organizations continued to use the Swedish language, membership in such organizations often peaked by the late 1920s or 1930s.

Factors external to the Swedish community also led to a more guarded expression of Swedish ethnicity. The arrival of large numbers of non-Protestant immigrants from southern and eastern Europe and the ensuing alarm of many Americans initially encouraged Swedes to extol the virtues of their own particular culture. However, the eruption of World War One and the resulting escalation in the campaign for 100 percent Americanism caused Swedish leaders to mute their foreignness—at least in public forums. The outbreak of war also stopped the flow of all immigrants to America, and growing postwar concerns over a flood of refugees arriving on American shores led to the first restrictive laws on immigration. Swedish immigration resumed in the 1920s, but never again took on the massive proportions of earlier decades as Sweden itself modernized and conditions there improved. Without the influx of large numbers of Swedish-born newcomers, the infusion of new ideas and trends from Sweden diminished, and the community's view of Sweden itself became more romanticized and distant. Swedish suburbanization in Chicago—a trend that began as early as the 1880s—long preceded the push toward Americanization in the Swedish community. It was not suburbanization itself that diminished Swedish ethnicity, but rather demographic and generational trends among the Swedish population and the external pressures toward patriotism and conformity that nudged Swedish immigrants—and especially their children—toward identifying more closely with the American part of their hyphenated, Swedish American identity.

NOTES

Notes To Introduction

1. H. Arnold Barton notes that Swedish immigrants often needed to justify their emigration to the Swedes they left behind. Barton refers to the Swedish people as a "Folk Divided" between Sweden and America. As opinions against immigration increased on both sides of the Atlantic after 1890, immigrants in America felt pressured to "examine, explain, and justify their own community," and this process led to "intense introspection and . . . self-vindication." H. Arnold Barton, *A Folk Divided: Homeland Swedes and Swedish Americans, 1840–1940* (Carbondale and Edwardsville: Southern Illinois University Press, 1994), 114.

2. Josef J. Barton, *Peasants and Strangers: Italians, Rumanians, and Slovaks in an American City: 1890–1950.* (Cambridge, MA: Harvard University Press, 1975), 6.

3. Kathleen Neils Conzen, *Immigrant Milwaukee 1836–1860: Accommodation and Community in a Frontier City* (Cambridge, MA: Harvard University Press, 1976).

4. Dino Cinel, *From Italy to San Francisco: The Immigrant Experience* (Stanford, CA: Stanford University Press, 1982), 261.

5. Jon Gjerde, *From Peasants to Farmers: The Migration from Balestrand, Norway to the Upper Middle West* (Cambridge: Cambridge University Press, 1985), 9.

6. John Bodnar, *The Transplanted: A History of Immigrants in Urban America* (Bloomington: Indiana University Press, 1985).

7. Peter Kivisto, ed., *The Ethnic Enigma: The Salience of Ethnicity for European-Origin Groups* (Philadelphia: The Balch Institute Press, 1989), 16.

8. Verner Sollors, ed., *The Invention of Ethnicity* (New York: Oxford University Press, 1989), xiv.

9. Kathleen Neils Conzen, David A. Gerber, Ewa Morawska, George E. Pozzetta, and Rudolph J. Vecoli, "The Invention of Ethnicity in the United States," in *Major Problems in American Immigration and Ethnic History*, ed. Jon Gjerde (Boston and New York: Houghton Mifflin, 1998), 23. This article originally appeared as "The Invention of Ethnicity: A Perspective from the USA," *Journal of American Ethnic History* 12 (1992).

10. I borrow from Richard White's conception of a middle ground in Native American relations with white settlers in his book *The Middle Ground: Indians, Empires, and Republics in the Great Lakes Region, 1650–1815* (Cambridge and New York: Cambridge University Press, 1991). I further develop these comparisons in chapter 2 of this book.

11. Ulf Beijbom, *Swedes in Chicago: A Demographic and Social Study of the 1846–1880 Immigration* (Stockholm, Sweden: Läromedelsförlagen, 1971).

12. Philip J. Anderson and Dag Blanck, eds., *Swedish-American Life in Chicago: Cultural and Urban Aspects of an Immigrant People, 1850–1930* (Urbana and Chicago: University of Illinois Press, 1992).

13. Per Nordahl, *Weaving the Ethnic Fabric: Social Networks among Swedish-American Radicals in Chicago 1890–1940* (Umeå: Acta Universitatis Umensis, 1994), 212.

14. See Robert E. Park, Ernest W. Burgess, and Roderick D. McKenzie, *The City* (Chicago: University of Chicago Press, 1967), and Louis Wirth, "Urbanism as a Way of Life," in *Cities and Society: The Revised Reader in Urban Sociology,* ed. Paul K. Hatt and Albert J. Reiss Jr. (Glencoe, IL: The Free Press, 1957).

15. While Oscar Handlin's seminal work, *The Uprooted: The Epic Story of the Great Migration That Made the American People* (Boston: Little, Brown, 1951) has drawn criticism regarding its conclusions, its publication in many ways launched a modern era of immigration scholarship.

16. See Gerald D. Suttles, *The Social Construction of Communities* (Chicago: University of Chicago Press, 1972), and Jessie Bernard, *The Sociology of Community* (Glenview, IL: Scott, Foresman, 1973).

17. Thomas Bender, *Community and Social Change in America* (New Brunswick, NJ: Rutgers University Press, 1978), 7.

18. See Dag Blanck, *Becoming Swedish-American: The Construction of an Ethnic Identity in the Augustana Synod, 1860–1917* (Uppsala: Acta Universitatis Upsaliensis, 1997), 17–19.

19. Raymond Breton, "Collective Dimensions of the Cultural Transformation of Ethnic Communities and the Larger Society," in *Migration and the Transformation of Cultures,* ed. Jean Burnet et al. (North York, Ontario, Canada: Multicultural History Society of Ontario, 1992), 3.

20. Blanck, *Becoming Swedish-American,* 16. Also see Dag Blanck, "Constructing an Ethnic Identity: The Case of the Swedish-Americans," in *The Ethnic Enigma,* ed. Kivisto, 134–52.

21. See William M. Tuttle Jr., *Race Riot: Chicago in the Red Summer of 1919* (New York: Atheneum, 1985).

22. David R. Roediger, *The Wages of Whiteness: Race and the Making of the American Working Class* (London and New York: Verso, 1991), 8.

23. Matthew Frye Jacobson, *Whiteness of a Different Color: European Immigrants and the Alchemy of Race* (Cambridge, MA: Harvard University Press, 1998), 9.

24. Dag Blanck, "'A Mixture of People with Different Roots': Swedish Immigrants in the American Ethno-Racial Hierarchies," *Journal of American Ethnic History* 33, no. 3 (2014): 38.

25. Unless otherwise noted, all translation from the Swedish was made by the author.

Notes to Chapter 1

1. Lars Ljungmark, *Swedish Exodus* (Carbondale: Southern Illinois University Press, 1979), 10–12; Sten Carlsson, "Why Did They Leave?" in *Perspectives on Swedish Immigration,* ed. Nils Hasselmo (Duluth: University of Minnesota Press, 1978), 25–26.

2. Information compiled from Austin Covenant Church membership records, and from recollections of Carl Olson (1883–1969), the author's paternal grandfather, handwritten and undated. This book is an adaptation of the author's doctoral dissertation: Anita Ruth Olson, "Swedish Chicago: The Extension and Transformation of an Urban Immigrant Community, 1880–1920" (PhD diss., Northwestern University, 1990).

3. Household Examination Rolls, Regna Parish, Östergötland County, Sweden.

4. Carlo M. Cipolla, *Literacy and Development in the West* (Baltimore: Harmondsworth-Penguin, 1969), as discussed in H. Arnold Barton, "CLIO and Swedish America: Historians, Organizations and Publications" in *Perspectives on Swedish Immigration,* ed. Hasselmo.

5. For more information about the followers of Erik Jansson who remained in Chicago, see Beijbom, *Swedes in Chicago,* 44–48. For more about Jansson's colony in Bishop Hill, Illinois, see Ljungmark, *Swedish Exodus,* 18–21.

6. Sten Carlsson, "Why Did They Leave?" in *Perspectives on Swedish Immigration,* ed. Hasselmo; and Sten Carlsson, "Chronology and Composition of Swedish Emigration to America," in *From*

Sweden to America: A History of the Migration, ed. Harald Runblom and Hans Norman (Minneapolis: University of Minnesota Press, 1976), 114–29; also see Per Nordahl, *De sålde sina penslar: om några svenska målare som emigrerade till USA* (Stockholm: Svenska Målareförbundet, 1987).

7. Carlsson, "Chronology and Composition of Swedish Emigration," 131, 146–48.

8. Lars-Göran Tedebrand, "Those Who Returned: Remigration From America to Sweden," in *Perspectives on Swedish Immigration*, ed. Hasselmo, 88.

9. Ljungmark, *Swedish Exodus*, 76, 77.

10. Ljungmark, *Swedish Exodus*, 71. Also see p. 72 for more information about the role of the subagents.

11. Hilma Svensson, "Day Journal," September 1901. The Swedish Emigrant Institute in Växjö, Sweden [hereafter SEI].

12. Hilda Svensson, "Journal of Trip to America," April 14, 1895. SEI.

13. E. E. F. Frost to his parents, August 14, 1906. SEI.

14. Hilma Svensson, "Day Journal," September 21, 1901. SEI.

15. Svensson, "Day Journal," September 21, 1901.

16. Lars Ljungmark notes that many immigrants complained about ship food and about having to travel with Irish immigrants. The Swedish press criticized English shipping companies for conditions on their ships. See Ljungmark, *Swedish Exodus*, 77–80. For another interesting account of the immigrant journey, see Walter Johnson with Ruth Ingeborg Johnson, "Beda Erickson's Journey to Chicago, 1902," *The Swedish Pioneer Historical Quarterly* 32, no. 1 (1981): 7–19.

17. Hanna Carlson to her sister Hildur Carlson, July 1, 1912. Personal family collection.

18. Anders Gustaf Gustafsson and Maria Christina Gustafsson to Johannes Jansson and family, February 29, 1880. SEI.

19. H. Arnold Barton refers to this phenomenon as the "Stock Effect." Personal correspondence, March 1, 2006.

20. See Gjerde, *From Peasants to Farmers*.

21. For these samples, names, birthdates, and places of birth were derived from the membership register of the Austin Covenant Church (Covenant Archives Manuscript Collection). This information was then compared with Swedish parish records, including birth records and household examination rolls. From Swedish church records, the following can be ascertained: full name at birth; date of birth; parents' full names, ages, and occupations; parish and county; location of home; date the individual and his/her family members left their home and their intended destination. Swedish parish records were accessed on microfiche at Svensk arkivinformation in Ramsele, Sweden [hereafter SVAR] and also at the Family History Library in Salt Lake City, Utah. Although this specific data reflects the lives of Covenant church members, the information is very typical for families from the rural areas of southern Sweden. Church members were slightly more likely, however, to come from established farm families than were Swedes who joined fraternal associations. The latter group had a greater representation among families involved with the trades. See chapter 4 of this book for more details.

22. Anders Gustaf Johnson and Ada Lundgren: Membership Register, Austin Covenant Church; Birth Records and Household Examination Rolls, Rydaholm Parish, Jönköping County and Brevik Parish, Skaraborg County, SVAR.

23. Ernst Carlstrom: Membership Register, Austin Covenant Church; Birth Records and Household Examination Rolls, Askeryd Parish, Jönköping County, SVAR. Carlstrom was born to Karl August Andersson and Johanna Maria Kristina Petersdotter. His brother moved to America in 1892 and his sister in 1896.

24. Esther Dorothea Edwards: Membership Register, Austin Covenant Church; Birth Records and Household Examination Rolls, Askeryd Parish, Jönköping County, SVAR.

25. Lars Andersson, Kajsa Andersdotter, Emma Christina Johnson, Brita Lena (Helen) Carlberg, Annette Sophie Lundquist: Membership Register, Austin Covenant Church; Birth Records and Household Examination Rolls, Hultesta Parish, Kalmar County, SVAR. Emma Christina was born in 1863, lived in America from 1882 to 1884, then moved there permanently in 1888. Brita Lena was

born in 1865 and lived in the United States from 1882 to 1883, moving back to Chicago in 1887. A son died in Sweden when he was twenty years old, as did a daughter who died in infancy.

26. Although Agnes Teresia Nelson had no siblings to pave the way for her journey, she did not make the decision to leave by herself nor did she make the trip alone. Agnes was born in 1879 in Hultesta Parish, Kalmar County, to Anna Christina Nilsdotter, an unmarried maid. Given her circumstances, she faced few prospects for a secure future in Sweden. She emigrated to America when she was eighteen with a friend from the area, Emelia Christina Nelson (no apparent relation), and they both joined the Austin Covenant Church shortly after arriving in the Chicago area. In this case, companions from the same town forged a life-long friendship based upon childhood memories, the experience of migration, and the decision to join an ethnic church in their new American home, Chicago. Agnes Teresia Nelson: Membership Register, Austin Covenant Church; Birth Records and Household Examination Rolls, Hultesta Parish, Kalmar County, SVAR.

27. Charlotta Anderson: Membership Register, Austin Covenant Church; Birth Records and Household Examination Rolls, Vireda Parish, Jönköping County, SVAR. Charlotta was born to Carl Johan Jonsson and Lovisa Augusta Lund.

28. Hulda Rosell: Membership Register, Austin Covenant Church; Birth Records and Household Examination Rolls, Bottnaryd Parish, Jönköping County, SVAR. Hulda was born to Charlotta Jansdotter and Klas Otto Johannesson Rosell, who was a soldier. According to parish records, the couple married after the birth of their first child, and Klas committed suicide by slitting his throat with a knife after the birth of their sixth child.

29. See Beijbom, *Swedes in Chicago*, 39–51.

30. *The People of Chicago: Who We Are and Where We Have Been* (Chicago: Department of Development and Planning, 1970), 11, 14.

31. See Beijbom, *Swedes in Chicago*. The squatter and enclave periods, the main focus of Beijbom's study, roughly correspond to Carlsson's first two phases of Swedish emigration. The suburban period begins during the initial years of Sweden's largest population exodus, Carlsson's third stage of Swedish emigration.

32. Gustav Unonius, Eric Norelius, E. Johnson and C. F. Peterson, as quoted in Beijbom, *Swedes in Chicago*, 61, 62.

33. Statistics drawn from *The People of Chicago; Historic City: Settlement of Chicago* (Chicago: Department of Development and Planning, 1976); *Residential Chicago: Chicago Land Use Survey* (Chicago: Chicago Planning Commission, Works Progress Administration, 1942), 3. Some material in this chapter is based on my article: Anita R. Olson, "The Community Created: Chicago Swedes, 1880–1920," in *Swedish-American Life in Chicago*, ed. Anderson and Blanck, 49–59; and Anita R. Olson, "A Community Created: Chicago Swedes, 1880–1950," in *Ethnic Chicago: A Multicultural Portrait*, 4th edition, ed. Melvin G. Holli and Peter d'A. Jones (Grand Rapids, MI: William B. Eerdmans Publishing, 1995), 110–21.

34. Statistical data derived from *The People of Chicago*.

35. Walter Nugent, "Demography," in *The Encyclopedia of Chicago*, ed. James R. Grossman, Ann Durkin Keating, and Janice L. Reiff (Chicago and London: University of Chicago Press, 2004), 233–37.

36. *The People of Chicago; Residential Chicago*, 5; "From Intramural to L," Chicago Historical Society Pamphlet Collection, 1923. For a fascinating look at the problems and possibilities introduced by the Chicago World's Fair, see Eric Larson, *The Devil in the White City: Murder, Magic, and Madness at the Fair That Changed America* (New York: Vintage Books, 2003).

37. *Residential Chicago*, 6.

38. See *The People of Chicago*.

39. *Report of the School Census, City of Chicago* (Chicago: Board of Education, 1884). The neighborhood boundaries were determined by sociologists at the University of Chicago in the 1930s and published in Ernest W. Burgess, ed., *Community Factbook* (Chicago: Chicago Recreation Commission, 1938). The 1884 census lists the "Nationality of White Persons by Wards"; therefore, African Americans and Asians are not included in these population figures. The census categorizes

"Americans" as a separate ethnic group, and thus includes native whites only. Nationalities are not given for inmates of orphan asylums, hospitals, "Homes for the Friendless," and penal institutions, but these people are included in total population figures.

40. All population figures are drawn from the *Report of the School Census of May 2, 1910.* This census lists minor residents of Chicago by ward only, making detailed analysis of residential patterns impossible but allowing us to glimpse the settlement pattern of first and second-generation Swedish children. The census is admittedly biased toward family settlement but is useful in providing points of reference for tracking Swedes in the city. For a good 1910 Chicago ward map, see *The 36th Annual Report of the Department of Public Works* (Chicago, 1911).

41. All 1920 census data extracted from Ernest W. Burgess and Charles Newcomb, eds., *Census Data of the City of Chicago, 1920* (Chicago: University of Chicago Press, 1931). In this census study, American-born are considered separately, and thus ethnic groups reflect only the foreign-born. Americans dominated nearly all the census tracts.

42. Beijbom, *Swedes in Chicago,* 105.

43. See chapter 4 of this book for a more detailed discussion of the timing of organizational developments in Swedish neighborhoods.

44. Church addresses and listings derived from Tom Hutchinson, comp., *The Lakeside Annual Directory of Chicago* (Chicago: Chicago Directory Company, 1880, 1889, 1899, 1910, 1915, 1917). Statistics and locations of Lutheran churches derived from *Protokoll hållet vid Skandinaviska Evangeliska Lutherska Synodens årsmöte* (1880–94); *Referat öfver Evangelisk Lutherska Augustana-Synodens årsmöte* (1895–1920); *Almanack* (Rock Island, IL: Augustana Book Concern, 1920). For Covenant Church statistics, see *Protokoll: Svenska Evangeliska Missions-Förbundet i Amerika* (Chicago, 1885–1920); *Baptist information: Årsbok för Svenska Baptist-församlingarna inom Amerika* (Chicago, 1908, 1909). For Methodist churches: *Protokoll öfver förhandlingarna vid Nordvestra Svenska årskonferensen* (1877–93); *Protokoll fördt vid första årliga sammanträdet af Metodist Episkopal Kyrkans Svenska Central Konferens* (1894–1920). Free Church information is found in *De första tjugo åren eller begynnelsen till Svenska Evangeliska Frikyrkan i Nord Amerikas Förenade Stater enligt protokoll införda i Chicago Bladet* (1883–1903); *Protokoll öfver Svenska Evangeliska Fria Missionens årsmöte* (1904–20).

45. Ulf Beijbom, "Swedish-American Organizational Life," in *Scandinavia Overseas,* ed. Harald Runblom and Dag Blanck (Uppsala: Centre for Multiethnic Research, 1986), 57–58.

46. State of Illinois, *Charter,* The Svea Society, October 29, 1862.

47. C. George Ericson, "Bland Svenskar i Chicago" (1962), unpublished overview of Swedish people and organizations in Chicago, Swedish American Archives of Greater Chicago, North Park University [hereafter SAAGC].

48. The major exception to gender-based membership before the turn of the century occurred in the International Order of Good Templars, a temperance organization that, from its establishment in 1882, welcomed women and men as both members and leaders. See *I.O.G.T. efter 25 år, 1882–1907* (Chicago: IOGT, 1907); and *Good Templary Through Hundred Years* (Ringsted, Denmark: Folkbladets Bogtrykkeri, 1951).

49. Axel Hulten, ed., "Swedish-American Participation in 'A Century of Progress'" (Chicago: A.V.S.S. Festcommittee, 1933), SAAGC; *Runristningar: Independent Order of Vikings, 1890–1915* (Chicago: Martensons Tryckeri, 1915); *Historical Review of Activities During the First Thirty-five Years of the District Lodge Illinois No. 8 Vasa Order of America 1908–1943* (Chicago, 1943); *Historik öfver Vasa Orden af Amerika 25-åriga verksamhet 1896–1921* (1921); Enoch Leafgren, *Scandinavian Fraternity of America: historisk utveckling af Skandinaviska Brödraförbundet af Amerika* (Jamestown, NY, 1915); Svithiod Singing Club, *Seventy-five Years of Progress 1882–1957* (Chicago, 1957); State of Illinois, *Charter,* The Swedish Club, February 8, 1892.

50. The largest new organizational movement among Swedes in Chicago in the 1920s was the establishment of provincial-based clubs, reflecting a sense of Swedish regionalism and romanticism rare in earlier organizations. See chapter 5 of this book for more information.

51. For more about generational change among Swedish immigrants, see Harald Runblom, "Chicago Compared: Swedes and Other Ethnic Groups in American Cities," in *Swedish-American Life in Chicago*, ed. Anderson and Blanck, 68–88.

52. Sture Lindmark, *Swedish America, 1914–1932: Studies in Ethnicity with Emphasis on Illinois and Minnesota* (Stockholm: Läromedelsförlagen, 1971).

53. Palmer, vol. 6, part 1, doc. 9e.

54. *Community Fact Book*.

55. *Protokoll* from the Lutheran, Covenant, and Methodist denominations.

56. Palmer, vol. 3, part 2, doc. 18.

57. Palmer, doc. 21.

58. Palmer, doc. 22.

59. Palmer, doc. 23. Interview made by Mr. Zorbaugh, 1923.

60. *Residential Chicago*; Stephen Bedel Clark and Patrick Butler, *The Lake View Saga: 1837–1985* (Chicago: Lakeview Trust and Savings Bank, 1985).

61. Palmer, vol. 3, part 1, doc. 10.

62. Palmer, vol. 2, part 1, doc. 19, 1.

63. Palmer, vol. 2, part 1, doc. 28, 1. Interview with Reverend Silas Meckel.

64. Palmer, doc. 6, 4. Interview with Walter H. Baxter.

65. *Protokoll* from the Lutheran, Mission Covenant, and Methodist denominations; all information about secular societies derived from archival sources and anniversary booklets; for more on North Park history, see Anita Olson Gustafson, "North Park: Building a Swedish Community in Chicago," *Journal of American Ethnic History* 22, no. 2 (Winter 2003): 31–49.

Notes to Chapter 2

1. Richard White uses the concept of a "middle ground" when discussing the intermediary period when Native Americans tried to shape and control aspects of their interactions with white explorers, traders, and settlers to preserve their own way of life as much as possible. Although the middle ground was different from Pre-Columbian Native American life, it was not a complete capitulation to white culture and domination. I find this concept of a middle ground very useful in describing Swedish settlers forging a culture in Chicago that was neither completely Swedish nor completely American, but rather involved a new, negotiated identity that synthesized aspects of each. See Richard White, *The Middle Ground: Indians, Empires, and Republics in the Great Lakes Region, 1650–1815* (Cambridge and New York: Cambridge University Press, 1991).

2. Ellen Winblad's letters are part of a sample of twenty-five letters and five journals used in this study. The letters were written by Swedish immigrants in Chicago to family and friends in Sweden between the years 1880 and 1926. The letters and journals are found in the collection of the Swedish Emigrant Institute (SEI) in Växjö, Sweden.

3. Ellen Winblad to her parents, March 13, 1892; and Ellen Winblad to her parents, August 8, 1893.

4. Ellen Winblad to her parents, May 11, 1892. Also, Ellen Winblad to her parents, March 15, 1892 and March 1897.

5. Ellen Winblad to her parents, April 16, 1892.

6. Ellen Winblad to her parents, March 1892.

7. Ellen Winblad to her parents, July 28, 1897.

8. Ellen Winblad to her parents, June 12, 1895.

9. Ellen Winblad to her parents, August 19, 1896.

10. Ellen Winblad to her parents, August 19, 1896.

11. Ellen Winblad to her parents, February 14, 1899.

12. Hilma Svensson, "Day Journal," September 1901. SEI.

13. Hilda Svensson, "Dagbok," April 14, 1895. SEI.

14. E. E. F. Frost to his parents, August 14, 1906. SEI.

15. E. E. F. Frost to his parents, August 14, 1906.

16. Herman Olson to Ivar Olsson, November 15, 1923. SEI.

17. Peter A. Coclanis, "Business of Chicago," in *The Encyclopedia of Chicago*, 110–15.

18. Mark R. Wilson, "Construction," in *The Encyclopedia of Chicago*, 200–2.

19. Henry Bengston, "Chicago's Belmont and Clark: A Corner of Memories," *The Swedish Pioneer Historical Quarterly* 13, no. 4 (1962): 157.

20. See Edward E. Osberg, "Englewood Memories: Swedish Businessmen on Chicago's 59th Street," *The Swedish Pioneer Historical Quarterly* 28, no. 1 (1977): 57–61; and Edward E. Osberg, "Reminiscences of Chicago and Englewood," *The Swedish Pioneer Historical Quarterly* 36, no. 3 (1985): 200–7.

21. See Lilly Setterdahl, ed., *Swedish-American Newspapers: A Guide to the Microfilms Held by Swenson Swedish Immigration Research Center* (Rock Island, IL: Augustana College Library, 1981); and Ulf Beijbom, "The Printed Word in a Nineteenth Century Immigrant Colony: The Role of the Ethnic Press in Chicago's Swede Town," *The Swedish Pioneer Historical Quarterly* 28, no. 2 (1977): 82–96.

22. Anders Gustaf Gustafsson to Johannes Jansson, December 5, 1880. SEI.

23. Anders Gustaf Gustafsson to J. Jansson and children, May 6, 1883. SEI.

24. See Joy K. Lintelman, "'On My Own': Single, Swedish, and Female in Turn-of-the-Century Chicago," in *Swedish-American Life in Chicago*, eds. Anderson and Blanck, (Urbana and Chicago: University of Illinois Press, 1992), 89-99; and Joy K. Lintelman, *I Go to America: Swedish American Women and the Life of Mina Anderson* (St. Paul, MN: Minnesota Historical Society Press, 2009).

25. Anders Gustaf Gustafsson to his relatives, February 22, 1885. SEI.

26. Betty Johnsson to her parents, August 4, 1882. SEI.

27. Hanna Carlson to her sister Hildur Carlson, July 1, 1912. Personal Family Collection.

28. L. J. Peterson to his brother-in-law and relatives, December 6, 1891. SEI. The letter reads as follows:

Some of the poor here are lucky, and become rich. It is clear that it's easier for a poor person to get along here, even if they must (as I) remain poor for as long as they live. Even so, I have never yet lacked daily bread for myself and my family. I was not allowed to hold the position I had while you were here for more than 6 weeks. For a week now, or since the first of December, I've had a job as a clerk at the County Clerk's office, [it's] about the same as having a job with a Swedish *härad* clerk, and pays $100 a month. But a political job here is always tentative since one political party after another is always coming to power. The people's government here is not as constant and certain as the government [in Sweden]. The common people have just as heavy a tax burden here as at home in Sweden, but they are taxed in a somewhat different way. This is why I believe that those who are very well off there will by all means stay there, even though they might be able to do quite well here, too, basically because they would probably run into more difficulties here in America than one could imagine.

It is true that your sons are in good straits here; but it is also true that they probably would have done just as well at home [in Sweden], if not better, if they had worked equally as hard as they have here. A comfortably established farmer at home there would probably not want to trade places with a poor priest here, or with a shopkeeper, who no matter how well off he might seem is always in less certain circumstances than the solid farmer. This should not scare anyone, but it should be taken as a small word of caution! The matter of leaving the certain good of the homeland for an uncertain good here is worth consideration that much is sure. We would, of course, be very happy to see Noak come here, for we have not seen him yet. He could probably get a good job with his half-brothers or others, and avoid much of the despair that so many newcomers must go through here—but he would probably have a calmer life and fewer worries at home. Having the experience I now have, it would never occur to me to leave my old home in Hå and travel to America to stay. Just taking a trip here is a different thing.

29. Herman Olson to his brother Ivar Olsson, November 15, 1923. SEI.

30. Herman Olson to Ivar Olsson, January 1, 1924. SEI.

31. Herman Olson to his sister Jenny Olsson, February 4, 1924. SEI.

32. Hanna Gustafson to her cousin, December 7, 1908. SEI.

33. Anders Gustaf Gustafsson to Johannes Jansson, February 29, 1880; December 5, 1880; and May 6, 1883. SEI.

34. Walter Nugent, "Epidemics," in *The Encyclopedia of Chicago*, 279–80. For more on immigrants and disease, see Alan M. Kraut, *Silent Travelers: Germs, Genes, and the Immigrant Menace* (Baltimore and London: Johns Hopkins University Press, 1994).

35. Anders Gustaf Gustafsson to his relatives, February 22, 1885. SEI.

36. Anders Gustaf Gustafsson and Maria Chistina Gustafsson to his brother-in-Law Johannes Jansson and family, February 29, 1880. SEI.

37. Anders Gustaf Gustafsson to Johannes Jansson, July 13, 1880, and to Johannes Jansson and Family, December 5, 1880. SEI.

38. Anders Gustaf Gustafsson and his daughter Hanna to his relative Gustaf Engberg, March 11, 1907. SEI.

39. Hanna Gustafson to her cousin, December 7, 1908. SEI.

40. Charles G. Sundell to his parents and siblings, October 3, 1880. SEI.

41. L. J. Peterson to his brother-in-law and relatives, December 6, 1891. SEI.

42. Betty Johnsson to her parents and siblings, August 4, 1882. SEI.

43. Betty Johnsson to her parents and siblings, August 4, 1882.

44. Betty Johnsson to her parents, the John Jönsson Family, March 5, 1885. SEI.

45. The law was passed in 1734 and estate inventories were noted in parish records called "Bouppteckning," or "Estate Inventories."

46. O. H. Peterson to John Jönsson, November 8, 1886. SEI.

47. O. H. Peterson to John Jönsson, November 8, 1886.

48. O. H. Peterson to John Jönsson, November 8, 1886..

49. O. H. Peterson to J. Jönsson and family, December 12, 1886. SEI.

50. Charles G. Sundell to his parents and siblings, October 3, 1880. SEI.

51. Hanna Carlson to her sister Hildur Carlson, July 1, 1912. Personal Family Collection.

52. Herman Olson to Ivar Olsson, June 4, 1924. SEI.

53. Anders Gustaf Gustafsson to J. Jansson and children, May 6, 1883. SEI.

54. Anders Gustaf Gustafsson to his dear relatives, February 22, 1885. SEI.

55. Betty Johnsson to her parents, August 4, 1882. SEI.

56. Herman Olson to the Ola Johnsson family, April 8, 1926 (?). SEI.

57. Sven Stubbe, "Bilder från Clark Street" (1924?). SEI.

58. Frida and Herman Olson to Ola Johnsson, August 9, 1927. SEI.

Notes to Chapter 3

1. Reprinted from the minutes of the first congregational organizational meeting, January 26, 1883, in *Minnes-skrift: Svenska Evangeliska Lutherska Trefaldighetsförsamlingen i Chicago, Illinois.* (Rock Island, IL: Augustana Book Concern, 1908). Johan Enander was a journalist with *Hemlandet* and an active leader in the Swedish American community of Chicago. An earlier version of this chapter appears as Anita R. Olson, "Church Growth in Swedish Chicago: Extension and Transition in an Immigrant Community," in *Swedish Life in American Cities, ed. Dag Blanck and Harald Runblom* (Uppsala: Uppsala University, 1991), 72–94.

2. Blanck, *Becoming Swedish-American,* 36.

3. Breton, "Collective Dimensions of the Cultural Transformation."

4. See Blanck, *Becoming Swedish-American,* 119–22.

5. As pointed out by Scott E. Erickson, the free church movement in nineteenth-century Sweden also gave nonconforming Swedes experience with creating, joining, and supporting their own church structures. See Scott E. Erickson, *David Nyvall and the Shape of an Immigrant Church: Ethnic, Denominational, and Educational Priorities among Swedes in America* (Uppsala: Acta Universitatis Upsaliensis, 1996), 23.

6. For an account of how historians of American Christianity have incorporated immigration into their writing, see Jay P. Dolan, "Immigration and American Christianity: A History of Their Histories," in *A Century of Church History: The Legacy of Philip Schaff*, ed. Henry W. Bowden (Carbondale: Southern Illinois University Press, 1988), 119–47.

7. See Handlin, *The Uprooted*.

8. Timothy L. Smith, "Religion and Ethnicity in America," *American Historical Review* 83 (1978): 1178. Also see Timothy L. Smith, "Religious Denominations as Ethnic Communities: A Regional Case Study," *Church History* 35 (1966): 207–26. In Jay P. Dolan, "The Immigrants and Their Gods: A New Perspective in American Religious History," *Church History* 57 (1988): 61–72, Dolan argues that immigrants of a variety of ethnic and religious backgrounds experienced a very personal God. John Bodnar stresses religious divisions within immigrant groups in his book *The Transplanted*.

9. Erickson, *David Nyvall and the Shape of an Immigrant Church*, 21.

10. "Chicago, the Culmination of the Religious Movement of the Nineteenth Century," *Chicago Tribune*, December 12, 1897, 41. Also see Herbert L. Witsee, "Religious Developments in Chicago, 1893–1915" (unpublished MA thesis, University of Chicago, 1953).

11. A 1916 study of religious groups in the United States claimed that 132 of the 200 denominations studied reported that all or part of their congregations used a foreign language. Nationally, a total of forty-two languages were used in American churches. See Dolan, "Immigration and American Christianity," 125.

12. Statistics derived from the *Protokoll* for the Augustana Lutheran, Swedish Baptist, Swedish Methodist, and Covenant Churches. Free Church statistics are not available for this period. Chicago population figures drawn from *The People of Chicago*.

13. Smith, "Religion and Ethnicity in America," 1178.

14. For a more complete discussion of Swedish theological developments and debates, see Karl A. Olsson, *By One Spirit* (Chicago: Covenant Press, 1962), 1–174. Also see Franklin D. Scott, *Sweden: The Nation's History* (Minneapolis: University of Minnesota Press, 1977), and Erickson, *David Nyvall and the Shape of an Immigrant Church*, 37–44.

15. Olsson, *By One Spirit*, 84. For more about the founding of Methodism in Sweden and Swedish America, see Henry C. Whyman, *The Hedstroms and the Bethel Ship Saga: Methodist Influence on Swedish Religious Life* (Carbondale and Edwardsville: Southern Illinois University Press, 1992).

16. Olsson, *By One Spirit*, 120. For a comprehensive discussion of the forces behind the founding of the Swedish Mission Covenant Church, see 78–120; also see Erickson, *David Nyvall and the Shape of an Immigrant Church*, 37–44.

17. Torkel Jansson, *Adertonhundratalets associationer: Forskning och problem kring ett spräng-fullt tomrum eller sammanslutningsprinciper och föreningsformer mellan två samhällsformationer c:a 1800–1870* (Uppsala: Acta Universitatis Upsaliensis, 1985), 270.

18. Sven Lundquist, *Folkrörelserna i det svenska samhället: 1850–1920* (Stockholm: Sober förlag, 1977), 226, 227.

19. George M. Stephenson, *The Religious Aspects of Swedish Immigration: A Study of Immigrant Churches* (Minneapolis: University of Minnesota Press, 1932), 149, 150, 151, 163. The Augsburg Confession was the foundational document of the Church of Sweden. Adopted in 1593, it remained an important part of the Swedish Lutheran doctrine and tradition. See Erickson, *David Nyvall and the Shape of an Immigrant Church*, 40. For an overview of the formation of the Augustana Lutheran Synod, see G. Everett Arden, *Augustana Heritage: A History of the Augustana Lutheran Church* (Rock Island, IL: Augustana Press, 1963); Oscar N. Olson, *The Augustana Lutheran Church in America: Pioneer*

Period 1846-1860 (Rock Island, IL: Augustana Book Concern, 1950); and Emory Lindquist, *Shepherd of an Immigrant People: The Story of Erland Carlsson* (Rock Island: Augustana Historical Society, 1978).

20. Stephenson, *The Religious Aspects of Swedish Immigration*, 176-77.

21. See Nils William Olsson, "St. Ansgarius and the Immigrant Community," in *Swedish-American Life in Chicago*, ed. Anderson and Blanck, 39-48; Beijbom, *Swedes in Chicago*, 51-52; and Stephenson, *The Religious Aspects of Swedish Immigration*, 210-22.

22. See Stephenson, *The Religious Aspects of Swedish Immigration*, 246-63.

23. For a comprehensive study of the formation of the Evangelical Covenant Church in America, see Olsson, *By One Spirit*, and Erickson, *David Nyvall and the Shape of an Immigrant Church*. Also see David Nyvall, *The Swedish Covenanters: A History* (Chicago: Covenant Book Concern, 1930); Stephenson, *The Religious Aspects of Swedish Immigration*, 264-92; Dale Weaver, "*Evangelical Covenant Church of America: Some Sociological Aspects of a Swedish Emigrant Denomination 1885-1984*" (Lund University, Sweden, 1985); and Philip J. Anderson, "David Nyvall and Swedish-American Education," in *Swedish-American Life in Chicago*, ed. Anderson and Blanck, 327-42.

24. Princell wrote extensively in the Swedish religious newspaper *Chicago Bladet*, edited by John Martenson. In it, Princell castigated the formation of the Covenant denomination as "spiritual adultery" and "spiritual communism," expressions relating more to protecting congregational independence than to any Marxist ideology. His comments led the delegates at the Covenant's organizational meeting to ban Princell from addressing the group. See the Covenant yearbook *Protokoll, Svenska Evangeliska Missions-Förbundet* (1885); translations by Fred O. Jansson available in the Covenant Archives for the 1885-1889 yearbooks. Also see Olsson, *By One Spirit*, 314-15; Karl A. Olsson, *Into One Body . . . By the Cross* (Chicago: Covenant Press, 1985), 3-81; Erickson, *David Nyvall and the Shape of an Immigrant Church*, 150-54; and Frederick A. Hale, *Trans-Atlantic Conservative Protestantism in the Evangelical Free and Mission Covenant Traditions* (New York: Arno Press, 1979).

25. The history of the Scandinavian Salvation Army is a story unto itself. See Edward O. Nelson, "Recollections of the Salvation Army's Scandinavian Corps," *The Swedish Pioneer Historical Quarterly*, 39, no. 4 (October 1978): 257-76.

26. See Conrad Bergendoff, *The Augustana Ministerium; A Study of the Careers of the 2,504 Pastors of the Augustana Evangelical Lutheran Synod/Church, 1850-1862* (Rock Island, IL: Augustana Historical Society, 1980). Further information about Augustana Lutheran pastors found in the pastoral registers in Augustana Lutheran *Protokoll* (1855, 1890); and *Referat öfver Evangelisk Lutherska Augustana Synodens årsmöte* (Rock Island, IL, 1900, 1910, 1920). George Stephenson argues that in comparison to education in the Church of Sweden, education among Augustana pastors was sorely lacking. He also stresses the shortcomings of the Swedish educational institutions in America. Even assuming some of the doctorates were bestowed honorarily, however, the level of education among these pastors was remarkable. See Stephenson, *The Religious Aspects of Swedish Immigration*, 384-96. For a comparison with the background of Augustana Lutheran and Covenant pastors, see Anita Ruth Olson, "Swedish Chicago," 353-59.

27. See Olsson, *By One Spirit*, 227-339, 352, 372-73, 510-15, 519.

28. Regional and socioeconomic backgrounds of immigrants can be determined by examining membership records of Swedish churches in Chicago and tracing a sample group of members back to their Swedish birth records. Church records of Swedish churches in Chicago indicate the Swedish parish in which an immigrant was born, as well as his or her date of birth. From this information, Swedish birth records can be located. These records, administered by Swedish parish churches, clearly indicate the occupation of an immigrant's parents, and further investigation in household examination rolls reveals the number of children born into a family, a child's birth order, and the destination of family members if they left the parish. For these samples, names, birth dates, and places of birth were derived from the membership register of the Austin Covenant Church (Covenant Archives) and the Messiah Lutheran Church (Swenson Center). Both churches were located in the Austin neighborhood on Chicago's West Side. Occupations of the immigrants' parents were found by comparing this

information with the Swedish parish records at SVAR and the Swedish Civil Registration records at the Family History Library in Salt Lake City, Utah.

29. Farm owners represented 42.4 percent of the sample from the Covenant Church and tenant farmers numbered 9.1 percent. Of the Augustana Lutheran Church sample, 31.2 percent of members' fathers were farm owners and 22.6 percent were tenant farmers.

30. Crofters and farmhands accounted for 13 percent of the Covenant sample group and 12 percent of the Lutheran sample.

31. In 1892, 1,510 people belonged to the Immanuel Lutheran Church; by 1900, the number had decreased to 1,319. By 1917 membership at Immanuel had dropped to 986, 63 percent of its all-time high in 1887. Membership statistics and church activity documented in Augustana Lutheran *Protokoll* (1893–1894); Augustana Lutheran *Referat* (1895–1920); and *Abounding in Thanksgiving: Immanuel Lutheran Church, A Member of the Illinois Synod Lutheran Church in America* (Chicago: Printed in commemoration of the 125th Anniversary, 1853–1978), 14. For the best treatment of the early history of the Immanuel Lutheran Church, see Lindquist, *Shepherd of an Immigrant People*.

32. *Abounding in Thanksgiving, Protokoll,* and *Referat.*

33. See Philip J. Anderson, "'Once Few and Poor . . .': A Brief History of the Early North Side Chicago Covenant Churches," in *North Side Centennial Celebration, 1885–1985* (Chicago, 1985), 4–12; *Diamond Jubilee Book, First Mission Covenant Church of Chicago* (Chicago, 1944); and Oscar Theodore Backlund, "Survival Factors of Mission Covenant Churches in Chicago" (unpublished MA thesis, University of Chicago, 1935).

34. *The One Hundred Years,* Anniversary Booklet, First Covenant Church (Chicago, 1968).

35. *The One Hundred Years.*

36. Statistics from Covenant *Protokoll* (1885–1920).

37. Augustana Lutheran *Protokoll* (1881); and *The People of Chicago.*

38. The exception to this would be those Swedes who helped establish free churches in Sweden. In the United States, however, every Swedish church had to be built by its members.

39. *Abounding in Thanksgiving,* 11–12; Augustana Lutheran *Protokoll* (1882–1894); Augustana Lutheran *Referat* (1895–1921).

40. As recounted in *Bethlehem, 1875–1950* (Chicago, 1950), 10.

41. *Bethlehem, 1875–1950,* 10.

42. Augustana Lutheran *Protokoll* (1881–1894); Augustana Lutheran *Referat* (1895–1921).

43. Statistics compiled from Covenant *Protokoll* (1885–1920). For more about the leadership and internal dynamics of the Tabernacle church, see Karl A. Olsson, "Dwight L. Moody and Some Chicago Swedes," in *Swedish-American Life in Chicago,* ed. Anderson and Blanck, 305–26.

44. See *The Evangelical Covenant Church of South Chicago 75th Anniversary Services* (Chicago, 1958), and *The Evangelical Covenant Church of South Chicago, 90th Anniversary* (Chicago, 1973).

45. *Sixty-seven Years of Yesterdays and Dedication: Mission Covenant Church, Blue Island, Illinois* (Chicago, 1961); and *The Golden Jubilee of the Mission Covenant Church, Blue Island, Illinois* (Chicago, 1944).

46. *Seventy-fifth Anniversary Booklet: Lake View Mission Covenant Church* (Chicago, 1961).

47. *Calvary Covenant Church: Fiftieth Anniversary* (Chicago, 1956).

48. *Grace Covenant Church Fifteenth Anniversary* (Chicago, 1976). This church was created by the merger of Irving Park and Maplewood Mission Covenant Churches.

49. *Protokoll-bok öfver Svenska Evangeliska Missions-församlingen i Moreland, Illinois* (Chicago, July 25, 1890).

50. Augustana Lutheran *Protokoll* (1880–1894); Augustana Lutheran *Referat* (1895–1921); and Augustana Lutheran *Referat Illinois-Konferensen* (1921–1930).

51. Augustana Lutheran *Protokoll* (1880–1894); Augustana Lutheran *Referat* (1895–1921); and Augustana Lutheran *Referat Illinois-Konferensens* (1921–1930).

52. *Nebo Evangelical Lutheran Church: 75 Years of Worship, Fellowship and Service* (Chicago, 1976), 3. See also Blanck, *Becoming Swedish-American,* 61–62, and Karl A. Olsson, *By One Spirit,* 147.

53. For further information on the founding of the North Park community, see Gustafson, "North Park," 31–49.

54. Augustana Lutheran *Referat* (1895–1921); Augustana Lutheran *Referat Illinois Konferensen* (1921–1931).

55. *The One Hundred Years.*

56. My conclusions are based upon a sample of 143 "Certificates of Membership Transfer" to the Mission Covenant Church in Edgewater, 1909–1921, found in the Manuscript Collection of the Covenant Archives. These certificates indicate a member's name, gender, birth date, birthplace, date of immigration, marital status, and the church that issued the transfer certificate.

57. Trinity Lutheran Church was the eighth Swedish Lutheran church designed by Erick G. Petterson. During his career as an architect, he built a total of fifteen churches, all of them Swedish Lutheran churches in the Midwest and seven of them in Chicago. He also built the following charitable institutions: Augustana Children's Home and Salem Home for the Aged in Joliet, and an addition to Augustana Hospital in Chicago. Born in Sweden, Petterson's training was as a carpenter and a blacksmith. He moved to Chicago in 1871 and joined the forces of carpenters who rebuilt the city after the Great Fire. Three years later, he became a building contractor, and at night he taught himself architecture. He designed his first building, the Swedish Evangelical Lutheran Bethlehem Church of Chicago, in 1876. For more information, see *A History of the Swedish Evangelical Lutheran Bethany Church of South Chicago, Illinois* (Chicago, 1968). Also see Augustana Lutheran *Protokoll* (1886–1894); *Referat* (1893–1911); and *Minnes-skrift.*

58. See Anne M. Boylan, *Sunday School: The Formation of an American Institution 1790–1880* (New Haven, CT: Yale University Press, 1988).

59. In the case of North Park Covenant Church, for example, minutes from the Sunday school and Young People's Society were recorded in English as early as 1898, and sporadically through the next decade. Worship services and church business meetings were held primarily in Swedish until the 1930s, even though the denomination made English its official language in 1928. For the immigrant generation, to allow the English language into the Sunday schools meant that many of them might lose their control over Sunday school education. A. V. Julin, Sunday school teacher at the North Side Mission Church, believed that "to hasten the use of English meant the training of our children in the Sunday school in a language in which we could not care for them in our churches, at least not for many years to come." David Nyvall, president of North Park College, noted in 1899 that Swedish was already diminishing in importance and many young people could not understand a Swedish sermon. See Karl A. Olsson, *By One Spirit,* and Erickson, *David Nyvall and the Shape of an Immigrant Church.*

60. *Minnes-skrift.*

61. *The Evangelical Covenant Church of South Chicago, 75th Anniversary* (Chicago, 1958).

62. *Sixty Years for Christ, 1877–1937: Douglas Park Covenant Church* (Chicago, 1937).

63. "Protokoll vid Svenska Ev. Missionsföreningen i Morelands Undgdomsmöte," January 14, 1899, through December 12, 1913.

64. "North Park, Church, College and Community," Interview of Sarah Swanson by Charles Strom, October 1, 1985. For more about the issue of the Swedish language and the Swedish American identity in the Augustana churches, see Dag Blanck, "Teaching Swedes in America to Be Swedish: Educational Endeavors in the Augustana Synod," in *Scandinavian Immigrants and Education in North America,* 38–49.

65. "North Park, Church, College, and Community," Interview of Walter Enstrom by Dorothy Vann, October 12, 1982.

66. Augustana Lutheran *Referat* (1909), 148; (1915), 32, 34.

67. *Minnes-skrift,* 39–44, 56. For every married man who belonged to the Covenant Church in Edgewater, there were 1.2 women who belonged. For more about the role of women's religious and secular organizations in the Swedish community, see Anita Olson Gustafson, "'We Hope to Be Able to Do Some Good': Swedish-American Women's Organizations in Chicago," *The Swedish-American Historical Quarterly* 59, no. 4 (2008): 178–201.

68. *Abounding in Thanksgiving,* 14.

69. Dag Blanck, *Becoming Swedish-American,* 28–29. See also Erickson, *David Nyvall and the Shape of an Immigrant Church,* 22.

70. While religious Swedes projected middle-class values, this does not suggest that they were not working-class people. Chapter 4 deals with secular organizations whose members held opinions very different from churchgoing Swedes. Many secular organizations often projected values that would be at odds with those of Protestant religious groups. Also, Per Nordahl addressed the trade union movement, certainly a perceived threat to the Protestant mainstream, in *Weaving the Ethnic Fabric.*

71. Augustana Lutheran *Protokoll* (1880), 63.

72. Covenant *Protokoll* (1887).

73. Augustana Lutheran *Protokoll* (1884), 50–51.

74. Augustana Lutheran *Referat* (1911), 226.

75. Augustana Lutheran *Referat* (1902), 46.

76. Raymond Breton, "Institutional Completeness of Ethnic Communities and the Personal Relations of Immigrants," *American Journal of Sociology* 70 (September 1964): 193–205. See also Erickson, *David Nyvall and the Shape of an Immigrant Church,* 24; and Blanck, *Becoming Swedish-American.*

77. Augustana Lutheran *Protokoll* (1885), 50–69; Covenant *Protokoll* (1885); and Gustafson, "'We Hope to Be Able to Do Some Good.'" Swedish Methodists and Baptists also established institutions that created a sense of "institutional completeness" suggested by Breton. See also Lintelman, "'On My Own': Single, Swedish, and Female, 89–99.

78. Augustana Lutheran *Protokoll* (1885); *Referat* (1897), 89; *Referat* (1914), 162.

79. Augustana Lutheran *Referat* (1885), 81.

80. Augustana Lutheran *Referat* (1908), 147.

81. See John J. Rumbarger, *Profits, Power, and Prohibition: Alcohol Reform and the Industrializing of America, 1800–1930* (Albany: State University of New York Press, 1989). See chapter 4 of this book for more about the Swedish temperance movement.

82. Augustana Lutheran *Protokoll* (1880), 82–83, in a letter to the Women's Christian Temperance Union of Iowa, June 24, 1880.

83. Temperance issues were addressed in the following church documents: Augustana Lutheran *Protokoll* (1882), 79, and *Referat* (1916), 59; Covenant *Protokoll* (1887), 142; (1906), 114; (1910), 123; (1914), 137–38; (1915), 126; (1917), 123; (1919), 121; (1920), 117.

84. Augustana Lutheran *Referat* (1898), 101. The denomination further resolved that "We as citizens of the United States and as a church body, many of whose members have come as emigrants from Sweden and found homes in this great Republic, rejoice that in the person of the Chief Executive of the United States we have a sincere and true lover of humanity, liberty and justice, and an able statesman and ruler; and that we hereby express our unqualified confidence in his integrity and uprightness of purpose, and in his wisdom and ability to guide the affairs of this nation in the present crisis."

85. Covenant *Protokoll* (1916), 141. For more about the tensions of ethnicity during World War One, see chapter 5 of this book.

86. Augustana *Referat* (1919), 29.

87. For more about suspicion and hostility aimed at Scandinavian-Americans during World War One, see Carl H. Chislock, *Ethnicity Challenged: The Upper Midwest Norwegian-American Experience in World War I* (Northfield, MN: Norwegian-American Historical Association, 1981).

88. *Minnesskrift öfver Svenska E. Lutherska Missions-församlingen vid Humboldt Park* (Chicago, 1909), 11–12.

89. The Illinois Conference of the Augustana Lutheran Synod adopted English as their official language in 1921; the Covenant Church adopted English in 1929. Most churches continued to offer at least one Swedish language service per month.

90. For more about these transitions, see Stephenson, *The Religious Aspect of Swedish Immigration*, 458–456; Sture Lindmark, *Swedish America, 1914–1932: Studies in Ethnicity with Emphasis on Illinois and Minnesota* (Stockholm: Läromedelsförlagen, 1971); Philip J. Anderson, "The Covenant and the American Challenge: Restoring a Dynamic View of Identity and Pluralism," in Philip J. Anderson, ed., *Amicus Dei: Essays on Faith and Friendship Presented to Karl A. Olsson On His 75th Birthday*, Covenant Quarterly 46 (1988): 109–147; John E. Kullberg, "Age Distribution in the Covenant," *Covenant Quarterly* 1 (1941): 33–37; and Lorraine R. Oblom, "Determining Factors in the Growth of the Evangelical Mission Covenant Church of America," *Covenant Quarterly* 3 (1943): 25–33; and Erickson, *David Nyvall and the Shape of an Immigrant Church.*

Notes to Chapter 4

1. For more about the symbolic importance of voluntary associations, see Vernon L. Lidtke, *The Alternative Culture: Socialist Labor in Imperial Germany* (New York: Oxford University Press, 1985). Christen T. Jonassen discusses the deliberate movement of Norwegian immigrants in New York City and its relationship to ethnic identity in "Cultural Variables in the Ecology of an Ethnic Group," *American Sociological Review* 14 (February 1949): 32–41. Mark C. Carnes argues for the importance of ritual in attracting men to fraternal lodges in *Secret Ritual and Manhood in Victorian America* (New Haven, CT: Yale University Press, 1989).

2. Per Nordahl, *Weaving the Ethnic Fabric*, 13–14. Nordahl also correctly points out that until his study was published, organized labor within the Swedish ethnic community had not been adequately examined. While my own study focuses on religious developments and more traditional fraternal lodges, Nordahl's work helps provide a broader view of the Swedish ethnic community.

3. Orvoel R. Gallagher, "Voluntary Associations in France," *Social Forces* 36 (December 1957): 153–60.

4. See Richard Oestreicher, "Industrialization, Class, and Competing Cultural Systems: Detroit Workers, 1875–1900," in *German Workers in Industrial Chicago, 1850–1910: A Comparative Perspective*, ed. Hartmut Keil and John B. Jentz (DeKalb: Northern Illinois University Press, 1983). Oestreicher further argues that ethnic identification hindered the organization of workers, due to both interethnic antagonism and the ability of ethnic associations to address workers' problems.

5. Roy Rosenzweig, *Eight Hours for What We Will: Workers and Leisure in an Industrial City, 1870–1920* (New York: Cambridge University Press, 1983), 27.

6. Arnold M. Rose, *Theory and Method*, as quoted in Gallagher, "Voluntary Associations," 153. In Arthur P. Jacoby and Nicholas Babchuk, "Instrumental and Expressive Voluntary Associations," *Sociology and Social Research* 47 (July 1963): 461–71, the authors argue that persons who have similar interests in a highly industrialized urban society will deliberately affiliate with each other in order to act out their interests. Charles K. Warriner and Jane Emery Prather put forth a system that classifies voluntary associations according to the collective values of the members and the designated set of group activities in their article, "Four Types of Voluntary Associations," *Sociological Inquiry* 35 (Spring 1965): 138–48.

7. Richard Oestreicher defines a cultural system as a "mutually reinforcing set of values, informal personal associations, and formal institutions" in "Industrialization, Class, and Competing Cultural Systems," 61. He argues that ethnic cultural systems among Detroit workers hindered the formation of a working-class subculture of opposition.

8. Nordahl, *Weaving the Ethnic Fabric*, 153.

9. Jansson, *Adertonhundratalets associationer*, 271.

10. Jansson, *Adertonhundratalets associationer*, 274.

11. For more on the American temperance movement, see John J. Rumbarger, *Profits, Power, and Prohibition: Alcohol Reform and the Industrializing of America 1800–1930* (Albany: State University of New York Press, 1989).

12. Oskar Petersson, *Godtemplarordens i Sverige historia* (Stockholm: Svenska nykterhetsförlaget, 1903), 24; Nordahl, *Weaving the Ethnic Fabric,* 120, 126; Franklin D. Scott, *Sweden: The Nation's History.*

13. *Göteborgs distriktloge af I.O.G.T.: ett tioårsminne och ett tjugoårsjubileum : 1879-1889-1899* (Göteborg: Wald Zachrissons Boktryckeri, 1899). Membership figures in 1899 for the largest districts in Sweden are as follows: Skåne, 10,600; Östergötland, 7,450; Östersund, 5,837; and Dalarna, 5,479. In Jönköping, where the free church movement was particularly strong, membership in Templars was limited to 1,125.

14. Werner Johanson, *Nykterhetsrörelsen i Halland : några anteckningar ur dess historia* (Halmstad, Sweden: Nykterhetsfolkets länsarkiv, 1983); Nordahl, *Weaving the Ethnic Fabric,* 120-22.

15. See Rumbarger, *Profits, Power, and Prohibition.*

16. See *Göteborgs distriktloge af I.O.G.T.*

17. *International Order of Odd Fellows: Gustaf II Adolf, 1895-1920* (Göteborg, Sweden: Oscar Usacssibs Boktryckeri, 1920). See also Carnes, *Secret Ritual and Manhood,* 25, 26.

18. *International Order of Odd Fellows,* 33-41. For details about the occupations held by members of the Gustaf II Adolf lodge, see Olson, "Swedish Chicago" 310-11.

19. Bylaws found in "Logen N:r 452 Göteborg av Vasa Orden av Amerika," Medlemsmatrickel (Göteborg, 1933).

20. *Protokoll,* Vasa Orden av Amerika Logen "Göteborg," September 4, 1924. Manuscript Collection, Stadsarkivet, Göteborg, Sweden.

21. Nordahl, *Weaving the Ethnic Fabric,* 122.

22. The issue of women's lodges and auxiliaries will be examined later in this chapter. H. Arnold Barton provides interesting analysis of children's groups associated with Vasa lodges in New York in "'The Last Chieftains: Johannes and Helga Hoving," *Swedish-American Historical Quarterly* 48 (1997): 5-25. The entire issue of children's lodges in Chicago would provide an interesting window into how fraternal lodge members cultivated Swedish ethnic sentiments in the next generation, and it merits further research.

23. *The People of Chicago,* 14.

24. Beijbom, *Swedes in Chicago,* 286. For more about conflicts within the early Swedish community, see George M. Stephenson, "The Stormy Years of the Swedish Colony in Chicago before the Great Fire," *Transactions of the Illinois State Historical Society* (1929): 166-84.

25. See Odd S. Lovoll, "A Scandinavian Melting Pot," in *Swedish-American Life in Chicago,* ed. Anderson and Blanck, 62; John R. Jenswold, "The Rise and Fall of Pan-Scandinavianism in Urban America," in *Scandinavians and Other Immigrants in Urban America: The Proceedings of a Research Conference, October 26-27,. 1984* (Northfield, MN, 1985), 159-70; and H. Arnold Barton, "Partners and Rivals: Norwegian and Swedish Emigration and Immigrants," *Swedish American Historical Quarterly* 54 (2003): 83-110. In 1880, 12,930 Swedes lived in Chicago as did 9,783 Norwegians. By 1890, Chicago's Swedish population numbered 43,032, compared to 21,835 Norwegians. See *The People of Chicago,* 18, 21.

26. For more details about membership statistics for each of the Svithiod and Viking lodges, see Olson, "Swedish Chicago," 321-22.

27. *Swedish-American Athletic Association 40th Anniversary Booklet* (Chicago, 1954). For a listing of Swedish athletic clubs in Chicago, see Olson, "Swedish Chicago," 312.

28. State of Illinois, *Charter,* Swedish American Athletic Association, July 17, 1914. Although the profile of early members is difficult to determine, a survey of membership applications from 1938-1940 indicates that 86 percent of the members were skilled, blue collar workers, 9.3 percent held white collar positions, and the remainder were undeclared. See "Membership Applications," The Swedish-American Athletic Association, SAAGC.

29. "Short History of Swedish American Recreation Club of Chicago," *Sixtieth Anniversary Program,* 1974.

30. For further discussion of the invention of ethnic identity, see Dag Blanck, *Becoming Swedish American,* 22-29, as well as chapter 3 of this book. A complete listing of Swedish Music and Social Clubs in Chicago can be found in Olson, "Swedish Chicago," 313-14.

31. A significant exception to all-male choruses was the mixed chorus called The Swedish Choral Club of Chicago, formed in 1915 by members of the Swedish church choirs in Chicago. This group performed such works as Handel's "Messiah" and Verdi's "Requiem" and had both women and men as officers. See Hulten, ed., "Swedish-American Participation in 'A Century of Progress.'" The Chicago members of IOGT formed two separate choirs, "Godtemplarbröderna" for the men and "IOGT Damkör" for the women. See "Nykterhets- och folkbildningsarbetet bland Chicagos svenskar," *Allsvensk Samling*, no. 8–9–10, May 1933, Göteborg, 45, 46.

32. State of Illinois, *Charter*, Svithiod Singing Club, February 23, 1893. (The club was organized before it formally incorporated.) Also see Gunnar A. Bloom, *Seventy-Five Years of Progress: 1882–1957* (Chicago: Svithiod Singing Group, 1957), 33. An important part of the Svithiod Singing Club's social activities surrounded alcohol consumption. When prohibition became federal law, the club's historian reminisced that "The shadows of prohibition descended slowly after the war and by July, 1919, had engulfed the land. On June 28th a Farewell Party for John Barleycorn was held with a filled clubhouse . . . it is only fair to assume that many of Bacchus' disciples lingered at the Club until the cock had crowed for the third time." See Bloom, 35.

33. State of Illinois, *Charter*, The Swedish Singers Union of Chicago, June 27, 1911; State of Illinois, *Charter*, the American Union of Swedish Singers, June 5, 1894.

34. The Swedish Club of Chicago was founded as part of the male chorus movement, but soon distanced itself from that particular agenda and evolved to become one of the most important social clubs in the Swedish community. See "The Swedish Club History," pamphlet in the manuscript collection of the SAAGC.

35. *Souvenir Programme*, Quadrennial National Song and Music Festival of the American Union of Swedish Singers in New York, New York, May 28–31, 1910; and "The Svithiod Singing Club Chorus 90th Anniversary Concert, May 12, 1972." See also *Konstitution för The Swedish Singers Union of Chicago* (Chicago, 1912); and Gunnar A. Bloom, "Seventy-five Years of Chorus Singing: Svithiod Singing Club of Chicago, Illinois in Diamond Jubilee" (Chicago: unpublished paper, 1957), SAAGC.

36. H. Arnold Barton, "Cultural Interplay between Sweden and Swedish America," in *Swedes in America: Intercultural and Interethnic Perspectives on Contemporary Research*, ed. Ulf Beijbom (Växjö, Sweden: The Swedish Emigrant Institute Series 6, 1993), 135. This article also appears in *Swedish American Historical Quarterly* 43 (1992): 5–18.

37. Henriette C. K. Naeseth, *The Swedish Theatre of Chicago 1868–1950* (Rock Island, IL: Augustana Historical Society, 1951), 10.

38. Naeseth dates the first Swedish theatrical production in Chicago to 1868. Lars Furuland has more recently claimed that the first such production was given in the fall of 1866 in German Hall. See Lars Furuland, "From *Vermländingarne* to *Slavarna på Molokstorp*: Swedish-American Ethnic Theater in Chicago," in *Swedish-American Life in Chicago*, ed. Anderson and Blanck, 133–34.

39. Naeseth, *The Swedish Theatre of Chicago*, 6–8; Furuland, "From *Vermländingarne* to *Slavarna på Molokstorp*," 140, 144.

40. Furuland, "From *Vermländingarne* to *Slavarna på Molokstorp*," 140.

41. Ann-Charlotte Harvey and Richard H. Hulan, "'Teater, Visafton, och Bal': The Swedish-American Road Show in its Heydey," *Swedish-American Historical Quarterly* 37 (1986): 126–41.

42. *Good Templary Through One Hundred Years* (Denmark: Folkbladets Bogtrykkeri, 1951), 5. For a list of Swedish Temperance Organizations in Chicago, see Olson, "Swedish Chicago," 315.

43. Information about the American temperance movement derived from Rumbarger, *Profits, Power, and Prohibition*. Per Nordahl examines the strong ties between the temperance and Swedish labor movements in his article "Swedish-American Labor in Chicago," in *Swedish-American Life in Chicago*, ed. Anderson and Blanck, 211–25, as well as in his book, *Weaving the Ethnic Fabric*.

44. In 1951, the IOGT's 100-year anniversary publication noted that the majority of American members were of Scandinavian origin. For more about the IOGT, see *Good Templary Through Hundred Years*; "Nykterhets och folkbildningsarbetet bland Chicagos svenskar," *Allsvensk Samling*, no. 8–9–10,

May 1933, Göteborg; "Swedish-American Participation in 'A Century of Progress'"; and *IOGT efter 25 år: Revy öfver den Svenska God Templarverksamheten i Chicago, 1882–1907* (Chicago, 1907). For more about the concept of institutional completeness, see Raymond Breton, "Institutional Completeness," 193–205.

45. See Nordahl, *Weaving the Ethnic Fabric,* 153, 213.

46. *IOGT Efter 25 år,* 33. For a statistical analysis of the prior lodge affiliation for Chicago IOGT leadership, see Olson, "Swedish Chicago," 324.

47. See Beijbom, "Swedish-American Organizational Life."

48. Hulten, ed., "Swedish-American Participation in 'A Century of Progress,'" 72.

49. Membership statistics and historical overview found in Enoch Leafgren, *Historisk Utveckling af Skandinaviska Brödraförbundet af Amerika* (Jamestown, NY, c. 1915).

50. See Hulten, ed., "Swedish-American Participation in 'A Century of Progress,'" 68, 70; *Historik öfver Vasa Orden af Amerika 25-åriga verksamhet 1896–1921* (1921); and *Historical Review of Activities During the First Thirty-five Years of the District Lodge Illinois No. 8 Vasa Order of America, 1908–1943* (Chicago, 1943).

51. Byron J. Nordstrom, "*Trasdockan*: The Yearbook of the Swedish Engineers Society of Chicago," in *Swedish-American Life in Chicago,* ed. Anderson and Blanck, 181–92.

52. Henry Nyberg, *History and Bylaws: Swedish Engineers of Chicago* (1949), Swedish American Archives of Greater Chicago.

53. Carnes, *Secret Ritual and Manhood,* 1. Also see Mary Ann Clawson, *Constructing Brotherhood: Class, Gender and Fraternity* (Princeton, NJ: Princeton University Press, 1989), 135–44.

54. Carnes, *Secret Ritual and* Manhood, 2.

55. Carnes, *Secret Ritual and* Manhood, 14.

56. Clawson, *Constructing Brotherhood,* 131.

57. For a complete listing of Swedish fraternal organizations in Chicago, see Olson, "Swedish Chicago," 316–20, 341–44.

58. State of Illinois, *Charter,* The Independent Order of Svithjod of Chicago, Illinois, September 2, 1881. The document was signed by John Lundin, John A. Sahlstrom, Carl Lundström, S. Hallberg, P. Sundquist, Gus Williams, L. Carlson, John Johnson, Ben Bloom, and Sven J. Nelson. Note that the charter spelled the club's name as "Svithjod," but the common spelling soon became "Svithiod."

59. State of Illinois, *Charter.* The charter also stated as its fourth point of purpose, "That the number of Trustees of said order shall consist of three and that the names of the first trustees for the first year after its certificate of organization shall have been issued are as follows. Viz: John Lunden, John A. Salstrom, and Charles Lundstrum which trustees shall continue for the first year of its existence and S. Hallberg, P. Lundquist, Gus Williams, L. Carlson, John Johnson, Ben Bloom, Sven J. Nilson as members."

60. For more about the foundation of this organization, see Timothy J. Johnson, "The Independent Order of Svithiod: A Swedish-American Lodge in Chicago," in *Swedish-American Life in Chicago,* ed. Anderson and Blanck, 343–63; *Golden Jubilee Program, 1880–1930* (Chicago, June 29, 1930); *Golden Jubilee of Independent Order of Svithiod at Lyceum Theater* (Minneapolis, December 9, 1930); Hulten, ed., "*Swedish-American Participation in 'A Century of Progress'*"; and *Svithiod Journal* .49 (November 1950): 11.

61. State of Illinois, *Charter,* January 7, 1891, Vikingarne.

62. This working-class background also differed significantly from that of the Swedish Engineers Society, an affiliation of Swedes involved in technical professions who were more affluent than members of the early fraternal lodges. For more information about Swedish engineers, see Sten Carlsson, "Swedish Engineers in Chicago," in *Swedish-American Life in Chicago,* ed. Anderson and Blanck, 181–92, and Byron J. Nordstrom, "*Trasdockan*," 193–212. Mary Ann Clawson also points out that working-class men were well represented in many American fraternal orders, but the cross-class nature of these affiliations "undercut class as a category." See Clawson, *Constructing Brotherhood,* 107.

63. Timothy Johnson, "The Independent Order of Svithiod," 8, 22, 23. Johnson notes that 18 percent of incoming Svithiod members from 1916–1920 were machinists and 10 percent were carpenters.

64. Independent Order of Viking Lodge No. 8 Odin, membership records 1900–1907, and membership applications 1910, 1915. Applications found at the Swenson Center.

65. For these samples, the names, birthdates, and places of birth were derived from the membership registers of the Austin Messiah Lutheran Church (Lutheran Archives) and the Austin Covenant Church (Covenant Archives), and from membership applications for the Independent Order of Vikings Lodge #8 Odin (Swenson Center). This information was compared with Swedish parish records, including birth recordings, civil registration, and household examination rolls (SVAR and Salt Lake City). Records reveal that 69 percent of the membership sample from Austin Messiah Lutheran Church came from Sweden's agricultural sector, as did 65 percent of the Austin Covenant Church sample and 56 percent of the sample from the Viking Lodge Odin. Compared to the church families, the Viking members' families were less likely to own their own farms. Out of all the groups, the Covenanters most often came from farm-owning families. For further statistical details, see Olson, "Swedish Chicago," 326–33. A comparison of membership records of these three organizations reveals only minimal overlapping membership. Johannes Andersson and Ellis Hjalmar Wickum belonged to both the Lutheran church and the Viking lodge. Church records do not reflect a specific conflict of interest for these two men; after joining the church they remained members in good standing of both the church and the lodge. It is remarkable, however, that more cases of overlapping membership could not be distinguished, and in some cases tension between the two groups was evident. Carl Olson, mentioned at the outset of chapter 1, belonged to the Austin Covenant Church for nearly fifty years. His younger brother Eric joined the Viking Lodge Odin, and throughout these brothers' long lives, they never saw eye to eye on issues of alcohol consumption and lodge membership.

66. *Runristningar*, 41.

67. *History Viking Brage #2*, 45.

68. *Runristningar*, 5.

69. Breton, "Institutional Completeness," 193–205.

70. *Ritual of the Independent Order of Svithiod* (Chicago, 1892), 54.

71. The treasury was $6,544 in 1890, $8,452 in 1900, $18,027 in 1910, and $24,098 in 1920. These figures derived from an early handwritten history of the first Svithiod Lodge: A. P., "Historik över Svithiod Loge #1 I.O.S." SAAGC.

72. *Bi-Lagar*, Independent Order of Svithiod, c. 1881. See also Timothy Johnson, "The Independent Order of Svithiod."

73. *Protokoll*, Independent Order of Svithiod, December 10, 1881 through May 16, 1891.

74. Information derived from membership applications for the Independent Order of Vikings Lodge #8 Odin at the Swenson Center and Civil Registration records of the various Swedish parishes found at the Family History Library, Salt Lake City, Utah.

75. John Bodnar has concluded that among most immigrant groups, fraternal associations preceded the formation of churches. See Bodnar, *The Transplanted*, 123. My observations indicate that Swedes were an exception to Bodnar's rule, contradicting Timothy J. Johnson's concurrence with Bodnar in "The Independent Order of Svithiod," 343.

76. *History of Verdandi Lodge No. 3 I.O.S.* (Chicago, 1930).

77. Brage was the name of the Viking god of poetry, song, and eloquence, and was often pictured playing a harp. Brage was one of the greatest gods in Valhalla—the hall of the most important god, Odin, and the place where Viking souls were received.

78. For more on the history of the Independent Order of Vikings, see *Runristningar*; Hulten, ed., "Swedish-American Participation in 'A Century of Progress,'" 66–67, 72; *Program*, 54th Grand Lodge Convention in Chicago, Illinois, June 11, 12–13, 1959; and *History, Viking Brage Lodge No. 2* (Chicago, 1942).

79. "Address Book: 1880–1892," Svithiod Lodge #1, Manuscript Collection, SAAGC. A total of seventeen members died during the 1880–1892 period, and thirteen others were stricken from the membership.

80. State of Illinois, *Charter*, Vikings' Valhalla Association, June 17, 1909.

81. See *History of Viking Brage Lodge #2.*

82. *Ritual*, Independent Order of Vikings, 21.

83. Carnes, *Secret Ritual and Manhood*, 22. Carnes also argues that American fraternal orders utilized ancient symbols derived from Old Testament, Egyptian, and Native American sources as an escape from the context of Evangelical Christianity.

84. *By laws for Unity Lodge No. 44*, Independent Order of Svithiod, Chicago, Illinois, established April 19, 1911; *Ritual for the Independent Order of Svithiod (IOS)* (Chicago, c. 1923), 50–51. Although this English-language ritual was formally adopted in 1923, it was based on the older, Swedish ceremony, *Ritual of the Independent Order of Svithiod* (Chicago, 1892).

85. *Ritual for the Independent Order of Svithiod (IOS)*, 44–45. The *History of Verdandi Lodge #3* notes that "'The old ceremony was an elaborate affair with costumes and paraphernalia galore, and was rather lengthy. At times, when only a few candidates were to be admitted, the ceremony was considerably shortened in order to save time. This acted as a damper on the interest of the members of the [initiation] Staff who dropped out one by one until finally the Staff was practically dissolved. . . . On October 2, 1924, the [new initiation] staff made its first appearance and won a well deserved acclamation. . . . This Staff, although well organized and capable, performs the ceremony in the Swedish language only, and as the lodge was adding new, young blood to its membership—the sons of members and their friends—it became apparent that an English speaking staff was needed in order to give the American born the true understanding of his obligation."

86. *Ritual of the IOS*, 78.

87. "Begravnings-Ceremoni" in *Ritual, Independent Order of Vikings* (undated).

88. *History, Viking Brage Lodge #2*, 26, 27.

89. See Carnes, *Secret Ritual and Manhood*, and Clawson, *Constructing Brotherhood*, 178–210. Also see *Ritual, Independent Order of Vikings*, and *Ritual for the Independent Order of Svithiod* (Chicago, c. 1923) as examples, SAAGC. For an expanded examination of gender in the Swedish community of Chicago, see Gustafson, "'We Hope to Be Able to Do Some Good,': Swedish-American Women's Organizations in Chicago," *The Swedish-American Historical Quarterly* 59, no. 4 (2008): 178–201.

90. Membership applications, Ingeborg Society Records, Swedish-American Archives of Greater Chicago. Applications include name, occupation, birthplace, and year of birth.

91. The exchange between these two groups is recorded in Gunnar A. Bloom, *Seventy-Five Years of Progress* (Chicago: Svithiod Singing Club, 1957), 23.

92. *History of the Viking Lodge Brage*, 19–30.

93. "Bylaws, Valkyria Loge No. 1," Independent Order Ladies of Vikings (1928).

94. See *A.U.S.S. Festskrift*, Ladies Independent Order of Svithiod (1933), 70.

95. A women's Vasa Lodge, Ladies Victoria Vasa #182, was formed in 1910 as the first women's lodge in Chicago within the Vasa Order of America. The Scandinavian Fraternity of America admitted women from the time it first arrived in Chicago in 1905.

96. *The Swedish Blue Book*, 91–92.

97. Otto Hanson, "A Brief History of The Independent Order of Svithiod," *Souvenir Program of the Golden Jubilee of the Independent Order of Svithiod at Lyceum Theater* (Minneapolis, December 9, 1930), 9.

98. See *The Svithiod Journal* 11 (November 1950): 1–14.

99. *Ritual for the Independent Order of Svithiod.* (Chicago, 1920s), 51.

100. *Ritual for the Independent Order of Svithiod*, 61.

101. For a discussion about the spectrum of ethnic affiliation, see chapter 3 of this book, as well as Blanck, *Becoming Swedish-American*, 28–29.

102. *Ritual I.O.S.* (1923), 50–51, 53–54.

103. *Ritual I.O.S.* (1923), 60–61.

104. *Runristningar*, 5–6.

105. See Timothy J. Johnson, "The Independent Order of Svithiod," 9, 10, 15.

Notes to Chapter 5

1. Jacobson, *Whiteness of a Different Color*, 8. Also see Blanck, "A Mixture of People with Different Roots."

2. Blanck, *Becoming Swedish-American*, 16.

3. For a good introduction to Swedish cultural influences, see G. Everett Arden, *The School of the Prophets: The Background and History of Augustana Theological Seminary 1860–1960* (Rock Island, IL: Augustana Book Concern, 1960), 27–33, and H. Arnold Barton, *Sweden and Visions of Norway: Politics and Culture 1814–1905* (Carbondale and Edwardsville: Southern Illinois University Press, 2003), 87–117. For more about Tegnér and his influence upon American authors, see Ulf Beijbom, "Tegnér and America," in *Scandinavians in Old and New Lands: Essays in Honor of H. Arnold Barton*, ed. Philip J. Anderson, Dag Blanck, and Byron J. Nordstrom (Chicago: The Swedish-American Historical Society, 2004), 185–94.

4. Scott, *Sweden: The Nation's History*, 326.

5. Barton, *Sweden and Visions of Norway*, 118–58; Scott, 549–53.

6. Barton, "Cultural Interplay," 132.

7. Barton, "Cultural Interplay," 133.

8. Barton, "Cultural Interplay," 132–41.

9. For more about immigrants and their relation to Swedes back in Sweden as well as the increased pressure in 1890 to "examine, explain, and justify their own community," see Barton, *A Folk Divided*, xii, 59, 114–18. In this book, Barton also comments on the dynamic nature of the Swedish community in the early twentieth century by writing that "In [the Swedish American community], more generations of immigrants and their descendants mingled than at any other time. There were still those living who had been among the earliest Swedish pioneers in the 1840s and 1850s, those who had just gotten off the boat, and those that had arrived at every stage in between. With continued immigration, Swedish America remained a relatively young community with the vitality and hopefulness of youth. . . . It was borne up by its far-flung network of churches, organizations, colleges, and publications." (237).

10. See Bodnar, *The Transplanted*. Bodnar argues that historians need to move beyond the "old" and "new" immigrant categories to examine the commonalities of the immigrant experience. (xvii). The purpose here is to stress contemporary perceptions of the shift in immigration patterns as a context for the actions of Swedes in Chicago. Oscar Handlin points out that the Dillingham Commission took for granted that which it was supposed to prove: "that the new immigration was essentially different from the old and less capable of being Americanized." See Oscar Handlin, *Race and Nationality in American Life* (New York: Doubleday, 1957), 80, 81. A good overview of anti-immigrant legislation is presented in Roger Daniels, *Guarding the Golden Door: American Immigration Policy and Immigrants Since 1882* (New York: Hill and Wang, 2004).

11. Eric Johannesson, "The Flower King in the American Republic: The Linnaeus Statue in Chicago, 1891," in *Swedish-American Life in Chicago*, ed. Anderson and Blanck, 267–82. Johannesson notes that by 1914, eight ethnic groups in Chicago had erected twelve monuments. In addition to the Swedes, monument-builders included the Germans, Danes, Italians, Norwegians, Poles, Scots, and Czechs. The only significant immigrant group to refrain from erecting a monument was the Irish.

12. See Dag Blanck, "Swedish Americans and the Columbian Exposition," in *Swedish-American Life in Chicago*, ed. Anderson and Blanck, 283–95, and Odd S. Lovoll, "Swedes, Norwegians, and the Columbian Exposition of 1893," in *Swedes in America*, ed. Beijbom, 185–94.

13. Adam Hjorthén examines festivals in the 1930s celebrating the Swedish identity in border-crossing commemorations in which both Swedes and Swedish Americans planned and participated. See his *Border-Crossing Commemorations: Entangled Histories of Swedish Settling in America* (PhD diss., Stockholm University, 2015).

14. "Prominent Swedes," *Chicago Times*, July 12, 1891, vol. 36, 14.

15. "Swedes Celebrate Their Settlement in Illinois," *Chicago Tribune*, October 20, 1895, 38.

16. State of Illinois, *Charter, The American Union of Swedish Singers, June 5, 1894; Souvenir Programme*, Quadrennial National Song and Music Festival (Sångerfest) of the American Union of Swedish Singers in New York, New York, May 28–31, 1910.

17. See Hjalmar Nilsson, *Ett triumftåg genom svenska bygder: axplockning från svensk-amerikanska elitkörens Sverigeturné 22 juni–24 juli 1910* (Svenska sångareförbundet i Amerika, 1910).

18. *Souvenir Programme*, 89. Also see Hulten, ed., "Swedish-American Participation in 'A Century of Progress,'" 26.

19. State of Illinois, *Charter*, Svenska Föreningarnes Central Förbund, August 17, 1894.

20. State of Illinois *Amendment to Charter*, The Swedish Societies' Old People's Home Association, February 13, 1908, and April 28, 1909.

21. See C. G. Wallenius, "Sex svenska ålderdomshem i Chicago: Ett frivillighetens barmhärtighetsverk," *Allsvensk Samling*, no. 8–9–10 (Göteborg, May 1933), 29–31. Other "Old People's Homes" in Chicago were run by the Augustana Lutheran Church, the Covenant Church, the Swedish Methodists, the Swedish Baptists, and the Viking Order.

22. State of Illinois, *Charter*, Swedish National Association, May 25, 1894.

23. *Runristningar,* 89.

24. J. Thelin, Secretary, Swedish National Association, to Swedish Organizations, November 8, 1895. Correspondence of Verdandi Lodge #3, Independent Order of Svithiod Manuscript Collection, SAAGC.

25. State of Illinois, *Amendment to Charter*, Swedish National Association, December 31, 1896.

26. Anita Olson Gustafson, "Othelia Mörk Myhrman," in *Women Building Chicago: A Biographical Dictionary*, ed. Adele Hast and Rima Lunin Schultz (Bloomington and Indianapolis: Indiana University Press, 2001), 615–17. The number of people served by this agency is far greater than the number of Swedish-born residents in Chicago who were noted in the census records. This likely meant that second-generation Swedes were included in this statistic, as well as Swedes who may have been in the city looking for work on a temporary basis. It is also possible that individuals were counted more than once if the agency placed them in more than one position.

27. "Free Swedish Employment Bureau," *Chicago Tribune*, January 20, 1896, vol. 55, no. 20, 7.

28. Barton, *A Folk Divided*, 211.

29. H. Arnold Barton examines the selective nature of Swedish American identity, its anti-elitist bias, and its emphasis on the peasant tradition in "Swedish Americans and the Genteel Tradition," in *Swedish-American Historical Quarterly* 57 (2006): 14–32.

30. *Bylaws*; "Membership Book," Linnea Aid Society manuscript collection, SAAGC. See also "'We Hope to Be Able to Do Some Good,'" 178–201.

31. State of Illinois, *Charter*, The Swedish Singers Union of Chicago, June 27, 1911; *Konstitution för The Swedish Singers Union of Chicago*, Antagen i Januari, 1912, Swedish Singers Union of Chicago Manuscript Collection, SAAGC.

32. *Bylaws*, The Swedish-American Athletic Association, 3–4, Manuscript Collection, SAAGC.

33. State of Illinois, *Charter*, The Swedish National Society of Chicago, December 15, 1913.

34. Rudolph Hallberg, "En tjugofemårsrevy," *25th Year Jubilee Festival* (Chicago, 1938), 4, 11; *Stadgar för Svenska Nationalförbundet i Chicago*, The Swedish National Society manuscript collection, SAAGC.

35. *Amendment to Charter*, State of Illinois, Cook County, Swedish National Association, November 14, 1916.

36. See "En tjugofemårsrevy" 4. In 1915, Josef Hillström was condemned to death in the "Mormon state of Utah." Known to Americans as Joe Hill, this Swede wrote labor songs in English and was active in the International Workers of the World. The Swedish National Society of Chicago sent a telegram to Utah's governor requesting him to pardon Hillström due to insufficient evidence. This immediate action was taken "despite Hillström's possible diametrically opposite social philosophy and political views to the majority of members," in an effort to avert the tragedy. Hillström was executed

despite protests from President Woodrow Wilson, Jane Addams, and Helen Keller. Thirty thousand people took part in his funeral procession in Chicago.

37. See *Svensk National-Dag: anordnar Svenska National-förbundet i Chicago* (June 9, 1929), pamphlet in the Swedish National Society Manuscript Collection, SAAGC. The organizations represented included the Independent Orders of Svithiod, Ladies of Svithiod, Vikings, Ladies of Vikings, Good Templars, Vasa Order of America, Scandinavian Fraternity of America, Nordstjärnan Singing Club, Svithiod Singing Club, Ladies Society Ingeborg, Viking Staff Association, Society Sirius, Ingeborg, Ladies of Brage, Smålandsförbundet, and Värmlands Nation, among others.

38. *Yearbook of the Swedish-American Historical Society*, vol. 1, 1905–1907 (Chicago, 1907), 3.

39. The first Swedish-American Historical Society was chartered in 1888, following the 250th anniversary of the New Sweden colony on the Delaware. Thereafter, nothing further was heard from it. See Roy Swanson, "Our Predecessors," *The Swedish Pioneer Historical Quarterly* 1 (1950): 12–21.

40. Swanson, "Our Predecessors," 12–21.

41. *Yearbook of the Swedish-American Historical Society*. Vol. 2, 1908. David Nyvall also spoke about the immigrants' hybrid Swedish American identity. See Erickson, *David Nyvall and the Shape of an Immigrant Church*, 95–96.

42. For more on this move, see Byron J. Nordstrom, "The Swedish Historical Society of America: The Minnesota Years," in *Swedes in the Twin Cities: Immigrant Life and Minnesota's Urban Frontier*, ed. Philip J. Anderson and Dag Blanck (St. Paul: Minnesota Historical Society Press, 2001), 104–16. Also see Swanson, "Our Predecessors."

43. Per Nordahl devotes one of his chapters to the Cooperative Temperance Café Idrott in *Weaving the Ethnic Fabric*, 114–55.

44. Vivien M. Palmer, *Documents*. vol. 3, part 1, doc. 18.

45. Palmer, *Documents*. vol. 3, part 1, doc. 18. For a list of reading materials at the Café Idrott, see Nordahl, *Weaving the Ethnic Fabric*, 225.

46. State of Illinois, *Charter*, Co-operative Temperance Café Idrott, March 23, 1917.

47. August Olson, Secretary of the Cooperative Temperance Café Idrott, "Brev till Svenska föreningar och loger in Lake View och omnejd," November 11, 1919; and Rudolph Ahlstrand, Chair of the Swedish Educational League, "Letter from the steering committee to the Cooperative Temperance Café Idrott's members," undated. The Swedish Educational League Manuscript Collection, SAAGC.

48. See E. Einar Andersson, "Pigg och populär tjugoåring i Svensk-Amerikas huvudstad. Kafé Idrott—ett svenskt kooperativt företag som haft framgång," *Allsvensk Samling* (Göteborg, 1933), no. 8–9–10, 35. See also Nordahl, *Weaving the Ethnic Fabric*, 114–55.

49. The organization was first called the *Svenska Studieförbundet*, or the Swedish Study Society. In 1925, it joined forces with Society Verdandi and the Literature Committee of the Cooperative Café Idrott, and changed its name to the Swedish Educational League.

50. *Bylaws* as quoted in a speech written by A. G. Josephson in 1917 or 1918. Swedish Educational League Manuscript Collection, SAAGC. For more about the Swedish Educational League, see Nordahl, *Weaving the Ethnic Fabric*, 137–45.

51. Henry Bengston, "Men and Ideas Behind the Swedish Educational League," *Swedish Educational League: An Adult Education Experiment in Scandinavian Tradition* (Chicago, 1946), 19.

52. Bengston, "Men and Ideas Behind the Swedish Educational League," 19. Also see Nordahl, *Weaving the Ethnic Fabric*, 95.

53. Henry Bengston, Gunnar Adolfsson, and Martin Sundstrom, eds., "Swedish Educational League," Swedish Educational League Manuscript Collection, SAAGC.

54. Henry Bengston, speech delivered over W. C. and L. Radio, October 13, 1935; Swedish Educational League Manuscript Collection., SAAGC.

55. *Protokoll: Svenska Studieförbundets styrelse*, May 16, 1917 through July 30, 1920; Swedish Educational League Manuscript Collection, SAAGC.

56. Bengston, "Men and Ideas Behind the Swedish Educational League," 23.

57. See Henry Bengston, "A Fiftieth Anniversary in Adult Education," *Midsummer News*, 1966, 22–24; *Swedish Educational League Programs*: 1917, 1917–1918, 1926–1927, 1927–1928; and *I.O.G.T. Jupiters Studieförbund, Medlemskort, 1916–1917*.

58. Letter to Mr. A. L. Stevenson from an unidentified member of SEL, March 18, 1919, Swedish Educational League Manuscript Collection, SAAGC.

59. Bengston, "Men and Ideas Behind the Swedish Educational League," 37. In this same essay, written in the 1940s, Bengston complained that a major reason so few Swedes involved themselves with the SEL lectures was that "listening to a lecture and getting benefit from what is heard requires a certain amount of concentrated thinking, and most people are unwilling to make the necessary effort. Motion pictures and other forms of light entertainment seem adequately to fill the recreational demands of the general run of the people."

60. In 1918, for example, the Open Court Publishing Company denied the SEL's request to publish a collection of essays—written versions of the lectures delivered at the League. The letter incorrectly referred to the SEL as the Swedish Socialist Society and mentioned that the publishing company wished to avoid "possible conflict with the government," as noted in Open Court Publishing's letter to the Swedish Socialist Society, May 2, 1918. In his reply, Axel G. S. Josephson emphatically stated that

> The character of this organization has been entirely misinterpreted to you. It is not a socialist society. It was formed as an outgrowth of a reading circle formed by members of a number of Goodtemplar lodges . . . quite a number of the members of the circle were socialists, very many were not, and among the members of the present organization are to be found persons who are neither socialists nor good-templars. . . . None of [these lectures] had anything to do with present [political] problems, with [one] possible exception. . . . In none of the others could there possibly be room for anything in any way seditious; nor would the governing board of the Study-League have countenanced anything of the kind.

See Axel Josephson to the Open Court Publishing Company, May 5, 1918. Two days later, the publisher once again rejected the manuscript, "for reasons . . . it may be difficult to explain." Open Court Publishing Company to Axel G. S. Josephson, May 7, 1918, Swedish Educational League Manuscript Collection. SAAGC.

61. Henry Bengston, notes from a speech delivered c. 1942, Swedish Educational League Manuscript Collection, SAAGC.

62. A version of the language debate appeared in Anita Olson Gustafson, "Ethnic Preservation and Americanization: The Issue of Swedish Language Instruction in Chicago's Public Schools," in *Scandinavian Immigrants and Education in North America*, ed. Philip J. Anderson, Dag Blanck, and Peter Kivisto (Chicago: Swedish-American Historical Society, 1995), 62–75.

63. Prior to that time, the public schools taught only the classic languages of Greek and Latin. The Germans hoped instruction in the German language would help their children learn about their ethnic heritage. For their part, the Board of Education hoped that German instruction would make public education attractive to German immigrants in the city and increase the likelihood that they would send their children to the public schools, which would in turn increase the opportunities for the school system to Americanize these foreigners. See Hannah Clark, "The Public Schools of Chicago: A Sociological Study" (unpublished Ph.D. diss., University of Chicago, 1897), 72. See also Mary J. Herrick, *The Chicago Schools: A Social and Political History* (Beverly Hills, CA: Sage Publications, 1971). Julia Wrigley notes that during the 1890s the philosophy of the Chicago schools changed from "an elite training center to that of mass agents of education for hundreds of thousands of children, many of whom spoke little or no English." In Wrigley, *Class Politics and Public Schools: Chicago 1900–1950* (New Brunswick, NJ: Rutgers University Press, 1982), 49.

64. Statistics drawn from Herrick, *The Chicago Schools*, 60.

65. See *Proceedings of the Board of Education of the City of Chicago* (July 12, 1899–June 27, 1900 and July 10, 1901–June 15, 1902).

66. *Proceedings of the Board of Education of the City of Chicago* (September 6, 1899), 53, 76.

67. *Proceedings of the Board of Education of the City of Chicago* (March 8, 1911), 724–25.

68. Between 1900 and 1911, the Board of Education did not receive a single petition from Chicago's Swedish community for any type of recognition or special action. The Norwegians, however, began in 1905 to lobby the board to excuse Norwegian students to celebrate their independence from Sweden on the May 17.

69.Two days before the Chicago Board of Education approved the introduction of Polish into the public schools and less than one year after Minneapolis introduced Swedish into the public schools, Ernst W. Olson of Chicago began to inquire about how the Minneapolis Swedes' successes could be duplicated in his city. Olson, the secretary of the Swedish Historical Society of America, wrote Dr. A. A. Stomberg, the professor of Scandinavian at the University of Minnesota and a leader of the campaign for Swedish in the Minneapolis schools, to seek his advice. Olson wrote, "I believe it might be worth our while trying to do here what you people did in your city. Any tips as to your mode of procedure . . . would be welcome." Stomberg responded promptly to Olson's request for information, emphasizing that the key was to have the solid backing of the entire Swedish community in Chicago when approaching the school board about the issue. Stomberg commented that "I might say that members of the Minneapolis school board told us afterwards that no matter had ever been laid before them in so dignified and convincing a way as ours." Ernst W. Olson, Chicago, Illinois, to A. A. Stomberg, Minneapolis, Minnesota, March 6, 1911, Swedish Historical Society of America Collection, Minnesota Historical Society, St. Paul, Minnesota. For more about the campaign for Swedish in the schools in Minneapolis, see Anita Olson Gustafson, "Teaching Swedish in the Public Schools: Cultural Persistence in Minneapolis," in *Swedes in the Twin Cities: Immigrant Life and Minnesota's Urban Frontier*, ed. Anderson and Blanck, 223–39. Due to the dominant role Swedes played in Minneapolis, Swedish in the public schools persisted there until 1973.

70. The resolution read as follows:

WHEREAS, in the opinion of the Board of Education, any foreign language having a rich literature and possessing cultural value, should, where practicable, be taught in the public schools; and

WHEREAS, the Swedish language is the medium of a literature and culture the dignity of which is recognized by scholars the world over; and

WHEREAS, the Swedish-American citizens are virtually a unit in favor of educational courses affording access to the literary treasures of Sweden, as well as of other countries of a high state of civilization;

THEREFORE be it resolved that we, the undersigned, on behalf of a large number of citizens, respectfully ask that Swedish be added to the list of modern languages constituting elective studies in the curriculum of the public high schools of Chicago.

"Svenska språket i skolorna," *Svenska Amerikanaren*, March 30, 1911, 14.

71. *Svenska Kuriren*, June 3, 1911, as translated in the Foreign Language Press Survey, Section I.A.1.b. See also *Svenska Amerikanaren* June 1, 1911, 14.

72. Henry Henschen, "Skall svenska språket införas vid Chicagos skolor?" *Årsbok 1912: Utgifven af Riksföreningen för svenskhetens bevarande i utlandet* (Göteborg, 1912), 101.

73. Henschen, "Skall svenska språket införas vid Chicagos skolor?," 103.

74. "Svenska språket i högskolorna," *Svenska Amerikanaren*, November 16, 1911, 15.

75. "Appeal to the Swedes in Chicago," *Svenska Amerikanaren*, December 7, 1911, 13.

76. *Proceedings of the Board of Education of the City of Chicago* (May 1, 1912), 903. See also "Svenska språket i skolorna," *Svenska Amerikanaren*, May 9, 1912, 15.

77. *Svenska Amerikanaren*, July 25, 1912, 14.

78. "Svenska språket i högskolorna," *Svenska Amerikanaren*, August 8, 1912, 14.

79. "Svenska språket i högskolorna," *Svenska Amerikanaren*, August 15, 1912, 15.

80. *Svenska Amerikanaren*, August 22, 1912, 14.

81. *Svenska Amerikanaren*, August 29, 1912, 14.

82. "Ett vackert resultat," *Svenska Amerikanaren*, September 5, 1912, 15.

83. "Ett vackert resultat," *Svenska Amerikanaren*, September 5, 1912, 15.

84. *Red and White*, published by the pupils of Lake View High School, June 1913, 47. Also see *Svenska Amerikanaren*, September 12, 1912, 15; and September 26, 1912.

85. School census, May 2, 1912, as reported in *Proceedings of the Board of Education of the City of Chicago* (July 24, 1912), 55–63. This computation assumes that the age of Swedish American minors is evenly distributed between all ages twenty-one and under. Statistics of Swedes studying at Englewood High School appear in *Svenska Amerikanaren*, May 31, 1917, 15.

86. The pressure to conform was great, as reflected in the annual report of the Chicago Board of Education, which noted that "unfortunately, all too large a fraction of the population is still foreign, despite the heroic measures which have been taken to imbue them with American ideals and to instill in them a love for American institutions . . . without a knowledge of our language and an understanding of . . . our institutions, a thorough sympathy with American ideals is impossible on the part of those who have come to our shores. . . ." *64th Annual Report of the Board of Education* (Chicago: June 30, 1918), 38, 39.

87. *Proceedings of the Board of Education of the City of Chicago* (September 18, 1917), 436.

88. *Proceedings of the Board of Education of the City of Chicago* (October 17, 1917), 559.

89. "Swedish-American Demonstration—Meeting at Municipal Pier," *Svenska Amerikanaren*, October 4, 1917.

90. The Swedish Press—along with other foreign-language newspapers—came under suspicion during the war. As Kermit B. Westerberg points out in his article "Henry Bengston and Socialism" in *Swedish-American Life in Chicago*, ed. Anderson and Blanck, 226–40, the socialist press was particularly targeted for attack. The more conservative Swedish newspapers such as *Svenska Amerikanaren* undoubtedly felt pressure to prove their loyalty and to support the American war effort.

91. "Språket och skolorna," *Svenska Amerikanaren*, September 12, 1918, 14.

92. This organization was part of the "Riksföreningen för svenskhetens bevarande i utlandet" (The Association for the Preservation of Swedish Culture in Foreign Lands), formed in Sweden in 1908. Concerned about the exodus of so many Swedish citizens and influenced by the resurgence of Swedish nationalism, this association attempted to maintain contact between the Swedes who remained in the homeland and those who emigrated. Its American counterpart focused more exclusively on the preservation of Swedish culture in America. See Lennart Limberg, "Almost a Century's Work: Preserving Swedishness Outside of Sweden," in *Scandinavians in Old and New Lands*, 125–57.

93. A. G. Witting, *Meddelanden från Svenska Kulturförbundet i Amerika* (Chicago, 1933), 23. Also see *Stadgar för Chicagoavdelningen av föreningen för svenskhetens bevarande i Amerika* (1923); and *Stadgar för Svenska Kulturförbundet i Amerika* (1924).

94. John Higham, *Strangers in the Land: Patterns of American Nativism 1860–1925* (New York: Atheneum, 1974), 205.

95. Witting, *Meddelanden från Svenska Kulturförbundet i Amerika*, 23.

96. Henry Bengston, "Kulturarvet," *Bryggan* (Chicago, 1965), 54.

97. Barton, "Cultural Interplay between Sweden and Swedish America," 138.

98. E. Einar Andersson, ed., *Hembygden: historisk festskrift för Chicagos svenska hembygds-föreningar utställningsåret 1933* (Chicago, 1933), 40.

99. See *Stadgar för Föreningen Bohus*, Bohus Society of Chicago Manuscript Collection, SAAGC. Also Andersson, *Hembygden*, 10, 11.

100. *Protokoll*, Club Dalarna, March 17, 1917 through July 17, 1919; Chicago Dala Förbundet Manuscript Collection, SAAGC.

101. Andersson, *Hembygden*, 4.

102. Application for Charter, American Daughters of Sweden, Department of Public Welfare (Chicago, 1926).

184 NOTES TO EPILOGUE

103. Hedwig Melinder, untitled report on the activities of the American Daughters of Sweden (1941), 1.

104. See Barton, *A Folk Divided*, 222.

Notes to Epilogue

1. As H. Arnold Barton noted (February 6, 2006) in personal correspondence to the author, "The biggest problem here is that so little documentation on the informal, unstructured 'little world' of the ethnic neighborhood [exists] compared with the copious records of the ethnic organizational world, both religious and secular.".

2. Allan Kastrup, *The Swedish Heritage in America: The Swedish Element in America and Swedish-American Relations in Their Historical Perspective* (St. Paul, MN: Swedish Council of America, 1975), 195, 637–39. The third organization that ranked among the top three was the Vasa Order of America, founded in Connecticut but active in Chicago as well.

3. Philip J. Anderson and Dag Blanck, eds., *Immigrant Life and Minnesota's Urban Frontier*, 5; see also 11.

4. For a sampling of stories about other groups, see Holli and Jones, eds. *Ethnic Chicago: A Multicultural Portrait*.

5. Dominic A. Pacyga, "Chicago's Ethnic Neighborhoods: The Myth of Stability and the Reality of Change," in *Ethnic Chicago: A Multicultural Portrait* (1995), 615.

6. For a more detailed analysis of this generational transition, see Runblom, "Chicago Compared," 51; Barton, *A Folk Divided*, 253–64, 329.

SELECTED BIBLIOGRAPHY

Anders, John Olson. *The Origin and History of Swedish Religious Organizations in Minnesota, 1853–1885.* Rock Island, IL: Augustana Book Concern, 1932.

Anderson, Philip J. "'Once Few and Poor . . .': A Brief History of the Early North Side Chicago Covenant Churches." *North Side Centennial Celebration, 1885–1895.* Chicago: 1985.

———. "The Covenant and the American Challenge: Restoring a Dynamic View of Identity and Pluralism." In *Amicus Dei: Essays on Faith and Friendship Presented to Karl A. Olsson on His 75th Birthday,* edited by Philip J. Anderson. *Covenant Quarterly* 46 (1988): 109–47.

———. "David Nyvall and Swedish-American Education." In *Swedish-American Life in Chicago: Cultural and Urban Aspects of an Immigrant People, 1850–1930,* edited by Philip J. Anderson and Dag Blanck, 327–42. Urbana and Chicago: University of Illinois Press, 1993.

Anderson, Philip J., and Dag Blanck, eds. *Swedes in the Twin Cities: Immigrant Life and Minnesota's Urban Frontier.* St. Paul: Minnesota Historical Society Press, 2001.

———. eds. *Swedish-American Life in Chicago: Cultural and Urban Aspects of an Immigrant People, 1850–1930.* Chicago and Urbana: University of Illinois Press, 1992.

Anderson, Philip J., Dag Blanck, and Peter Kivisto, eds. *Scandinavian Immigrants and Education in North America.* Chicago: Swedish-American Historical Society, 1995.

Anderson, Philip J., Dag Blanck, and Byron J. Nordstrom, eds. *Scandinavians in Old and New Lands: Essays in Honor of H. Arnold Barton.* Chicago: The Swedish-American Historical Society, 2004.

Arden, G. Everett. *Augustana Heritage: A History of the Augustana Lutheran Church.* Rock Island, IL: Augustana Press, 1963.

———. *The School of the Prophets: The Background and History of Augustana Theological Seminary, 1860–1960.* Rock Island, IL: Augustana Book Concern, 1960.

Backlund, Oscar Theodore. "Survival Factors of Mission Covenant Churches in Chicago." MA thesis, University of Chicago, 1935.

Barton, H. Arnold. "CLIO and Swedish America: Historians, Organizations and Publications." In *Perspectives on Swedish Immigration,* edited by Nils Hasselmo. Duluth: University of Minnesota Press, 1978.

———. "Cultural Interplay between Sweden and Swedish America." In *Swedes in America: Intercultural and Interethnic Perspectives on Contemporary Research,* edited by Ulf Beijbom. Växjö, Sweden: The Swedish Emigrant Institute Series 6, 1993, 135. Also appears in *Swedish-American Historical Quarterly* 43 (1992): 5–18.

———. *A Folk Divided: Homeland Swedes and Swedish Americans, 1840–1940.* Carbondale and Edwardsville: Southern Illinois University Press, 1994.

———. "The Last Chieftains: Johannes and Helga Hoving." *Swedish-American Historical Quarterly* 48 (1997): 5–25.

———. "Partners and Rivals: Norwegian and Swedish Emigration and Immigrants." *Swedish-American Historical Quarterly* 54 (2003): 83–110.

———. "Stage Migration and Ethnic Maintenance." *The Swedish Pioneer Historical Quarterly* 30, no. 4 (1979): 231–33.

——. *Sweden and Visions of Norway: Politics and Culture 1814–1905*. Carbondale and Edwardsville: Southern Illinois University Press, 2003.

——. "Swedish Americans and the Genteel Tradition." *Swedish-American Historical Quarterly*. 57 (2006): 14–32.

Barton, Josef J. *Peasants and Strangers: Italians, Rumanians, and Slovaks in an American City, 1890–1950*. Cambridge, MA: Harvard University Press, 1975.

Beijbom, Ulf. "Anders Larsson, Immigrant Pioneer in Chicago." *The Swedish Pioneer Historical Quarterly* 16, no. 3 (1965): 155–70.

——. "Chicago's 'Swede Town'—Gone but Not Forgotten." *The Swedish Pioneer Historical Quarterly* 15, no. 4 (1964): 144–58.

——. "The Printed Word in a Nineteenth Century Immigrant Colony: The Role of the Ethnic Press in Chicago's Swede Town." *The Swedish Pioneer Historical Quarterly* 28, no. 2 (1977): 82–96.

——. "The Societies—A Worldly Alternative in the Chicago Colony." *The Swedish Pioneer Historical Quarterly* 23, no. 3 (1972): 135–50.

——. *Swedes in Chicago: A Demographic and Social Study of the 1846–1880 Immigration*. Stockholm: Läromedelsförlagen, 1971.

——. "Swedish-American Organizational Life." In *Scandinavia Overseas*, edited by Harald Runblom and Dag Blanck, 57–58. Uppsala: Centre for Multiethnic Research, 1986.

——. "Tegnér and America." In *Scandinavians in Old and New Lands: Essays in Honor of H. Arnold Barton*, edited by Philip J. Anderson, Dag Blanck, and Byron Nordstrom, 185–94. Chicago: The Swedish-American Historical Society, 2004.

Beijbom, Ulf, ed. *Swedes in America: Intercultural and Interethnic Perspectives on Contemporary Research*. Växjö, Sweden: The Swedish Emigrant Institute Series 6, 1993.

Bender, Thomas. *Community and Social Change in America*. New Brunswick, NJ: Rutgers University Press, 1978.

Bengston, Henry. "Chicago's Belmont and Clark: A Corner of Memories." *The Swedish Pioneer Historical Quarterly* 13, no. 4 (1962): 155–59.

Bergendoff, Conrad. "The Beginnings of Swedish Immigration into Illinois a Century Ago." *Journal of the Illinois State Historical Society* 41 (1948).

Bernard, Jessie. *The Sociology of Community*. Glenview, IL: Scott, Foresman, 1973.

Blanck, Dag. *Becoming Swedish-American: The Construction of an Ethnic Identity in the Augustana Synod, 1860–1917*. Uppsala: Acta Universitatis Upsaliensis, 1997.

——. "Constructing an Ethnic Identity: The Case of the Swedish-Americans." In *The Ethnic Enigma: The Salience of Ethnicity for Euro-Origin Groups*, edited by Peter Kivisto, 134–52. Philadelphia: The Balch Institute Press, 1989.

——. "History and Ethnicity: The Case of the Swedish Americans." *Swedish-American Historical Quarterly* 46, no. 1 (1995): 58–73.

——. "'A Mixture of People with Different Roots': Swedish Immigrants in the American Ethno-Racial Hierarchies." *Journal of American Ethnic History* 33, no. 3 (2014): 37–54.

——. "Swedish Americans and the Columbian Exposition." In *Swedish-American Life in Chicago: Cultural and Urban Aspects of an Immigrant People, 1850–1930*, edited by Philip J. Anderson and Dag Blanck, 283–95. Urbana and Chicago: University of Illinois Press, 1992.

——. "Teaching Swedes in America to Be Swedish: Educational Endeavors in the Augustana Synod." In *Scandinavian Immigrants and Education in North America*, edited by Philip J. Anderson, Dag Blanck, and Peter Kivisto, 38–49. Chicago: Swedish-American Historical Society, 1995.

Blumin, Stuart M. *The Urban Threshold: Growth and Change in a Nineteenth-Century American Community*. Chicago: University of Chicago Press, 1976.

Bodnar, John. *The Transplanted: A History of Immigrants in Urban America*. Bloomington: Indiana University Press, 1985.

Bowman, C. V. *Carl August Bjork, A Biography*. Translated by Eric G. Hawkinson. Chicago: Covenant Book Concern, 1934.

Boylan, Ann M. *Sunday School: The Formation of an American Institution 1790–1880*. New Haven, CT: Yale University Press, 1988.

Breton, Raymond. "Collective Dimensions of the Cultural Transformation of Ethnic Communities and the Larger Society." In *Migration and the Transformation of Cultures*, edited by Jean Burnet et. al. North York, Ontario, Canada: Multicultural History Society of Ontario, 1992.

———. "Institutional Completeness of Ethnic Communities and the Personal Relations of Immigrants." *American Journal of Sociology* 70 (September 1964): 193–205.

Carlson, Leland H. *A History of North Park College*. Chicago: North Park College, 1941.

Carlsson, Sten. "Chronology and Composition of Swedish Emigration to America." In *From Sweden to America: A History of the Migration*, edited by Harald Runblom and Hans Norman, 114–29. Minneapolis: University of Minnesota Press, 1976.

———. "Swedish Engineers in Chicago." In *Swedish-American Life in Chicago: Cultural and Urban Aspects of an Immigrant People*, 1850–1930, edited by Philip J. Anderson and Dag Blanck, 181–92. Urbana and Chicago: University of Illinois Press, 1992.

———. "Why Did They Leave?" In *Perspectives on Swedish Immigration*, edited by Nils Hasselmo. Duluth: University of Minnesota Press, 1978.

Carnes, Mark C. *Secret Ritual and Manhood in Victorian America*. New Haven, CT: Yale University Press, 1989.

Chislock, Carl H. *Ethnicity Challenged: The Upper Midwest Norwegian-American Experience in World War I*. Northfield, MN: Norwegian-American Historical Association, 1981.

Chudacoff, Howard P. "A New Look at Ethnic Neighborhoods: Residential Dispersion and the Concept of Visibility in a Medium-Sized City." *Journal of American History* 60 (1973): 76–93.

Cinel, Dino. *From Italy to San Francisco: The Immigrant Experience*. Stanford, CA: Stanford University Press, 1982.

Clark, Hannah. "The Public Schools of Chicago: A Sociological Study." PhD diss., University of Chicago, 1897.

Clawson, Mary Ann. *Constructing Brotherhood: Class, Gender and Fraternity*. Princeton, NJ: Princeton University Press, 1989.

Coclanis, Peter A. "Business of Chicago." In *The Encyclopedia of Chicago*, edited by James R. Grossman, Ann Durkin Keating, and Janice L. Reiff, 110–15. Chicago: University of Chicago Press, 2004.

Conzen, Kathleen Neils. *Immigrant Milwaukee 1836–1860: Accommodation and Community in a Frontier City*. Cambridge, MA: Harvard University Press, 1976.Conzen, Kathleen Neils, David A. Gerber, Ewa Morawska, George E. Pozzetta, and Rudolph J. Vecoli. "The Invention of Ethnicity in the United States." In *Major Problems in American Immigration and Ethnic History*, edited by Jon Gjerde, 22–28. Boston and New York: Houghton Mifflin, 1998.

Daniels, Roger. *Guarding the Golden Door: American Immigration Policy and Immigrants Since 1882*. New York: Hill and Wang, 2004.

Dolan, Jay P. "The Immigrants and Their Gods: A New Perspective in American Religious History." *Church History* 57 (1988): 61–72.

———. "Immigration and American Christianity: A History of Their Histories." In *A Century of Church History: The Legacy of Philip Schaff*, edited by Henry W. Bowden, 119–47. Carbondale: University of Southern Illinois Press, 1988.

Erickson, Scott E. *David Nyvall and the Shape of an Immigrant Church; Ethnic, Denominational, and Educational Priorities among Swedes in America*. Uppsala: Acta Universitatis Upsaliensis, 1996.

Frisch, Michael H. *Town into City: Springfield, Massachusetts and the Meaning of Community, 1840–1880*. Cambridge, MA: Harvard University Press, 1972.

Furuland, Lars. "From *Vermländingarne* to *Slavarna på Molokstorp*: Swedish-American Ethnic Theater in Chicago." In *Swedish-American Life in Chicago: Cultural and Urban Aspects of an Immigrant People*, 1850–1930, edited by Philip J. Anderson and Dag Blanck, 133–49. Urbana and Chicago: University of Illinois Press, 1992.

Gallagher, Orvoel R. "Voluntary Associations in France." *Social Forces* 36 (December 1957): 153–60.

Gjerde, Jon. *From Peasants to Farmers: The Migration from Balestrand, Norway to the Upper Middle West*. Cambridge: Cambridge University Press, 1985.

Gordon, C. Wayne, and Nicholas Babchuk. "A Typology of Voluntary Associations." *American Sociological Review* 24 (1959): 22–29.

Gordon, Milton M. *Assimilation in American Life: The Role of Race, Religion, and National Origin*. New York: Oxford University Press, 1964.

Grossman, James R., Ann Durkin Keating, and Janice L Reiff, eds. *The Encyclopedia of Chicago*. Chicago and London: University of Chicago Press, 2004.

Gustafson, Anita Olson. "Ethnic Preservation and Americanization: The Issue of Swedish Language Instruction in Chicago's Public Schools." In *Scandinavian Immigrants and Education in North America*, edited by Philip J. Anderson, Dag Blanck, and Peter Kivisto, 62–75. Chicago: Swedish-American Historical Society, 1995.

———. "North Park: Building a Swedish Community in Chicago." *Journal of American Ethnic History* 22, no. 2 (2003): 31–49.

———. "Othelia Mörk Myhrman." In *Women Building Chicago: A Biographical Dictionary*, edited by Adele Hast and Rima Lunin Schultz, 615–17. Bloomington and Indianapolis: Indiana University Press, 2001.

———. "Teaching Swedish in the Public Schools: Cultural Persistence in Minneapolis." In *Swedes in the Twin Cities: Immigrant Life and Minnesota's Urban Frontier*, edited by Philip J. Anderson and Dag Blanck, 223–39. St. Paul: Minnesota Historical Society Press, 2001.

———. "'We Hope to Be Able to Do Some Good': Swedish-American Women's Organizations in Chicago." *The Swedish-American Historical Quarterly*. 59, no. 4 (2008): 178–201.

Hale, Frederick A. *Trans-Atlantic Conservative Protestantism in the Evangelical Free and Mission Covenant Traditions*. New York: Arno Press, 1979.

Handlin, Oscar. *Race and Nationality in American Life*. New York: Doubleday, 1957.

———. *The Uprooted: The Epic Story of the Great Migration That Made the American People*. Boston: Little, Brown, 1951.

Harvey, Ann-Charlotte and Richard H. Hulan. "'Teater, Visafton, och Bal': The Swedish-American Road Show in its Heyday." *Swedish-American Historical Quarterly* 37 (1986): 126–41.

Hasselmo, Nils, ed. *Perspectives on Swedish Immigration*. Duluth: University of Minnesota Press, 1978.

Herrick, Mary J. *The Chicago Schools: A Social and Political History*. Beverly Hills, CA: Sage Publications, 1971.

Higham, John. *Strangers in the Land: Patterns of American Nativism 1860–1925*. New York: Atheneum, 1974.

Hjorthén, Adam. *Border-Crossing Commemorations: Entangled Histories of Swedish Settling in America*. Ph.D. diss., Stockholm University, 2015.

Holli, Melvin G., and Peter d'A. Jones, eds. *Ethnic Chicago: A Multicultural Portrait*. Grand Rapids, MI: William B. Eerdmans Publishing, 1995.

Jacobson, Matthew Frye. *Whiteness of a Different Color: European Immigrants and the Alchemy of Race*. Cambridge, MA: Harvard University Press, 1998.

Jacoby, Arthur P., and Nicholas Babchuk. "Instrumental and Expressive Voluntary Associations." *Sociology and Social Research* 47 (July 1963): 461–71.

Jansson, Torkel. *Adertonhundratalets associationer: Forskning och problem kring ett spängfullt tomrum eller sammanslutnings principer och föreningsformer mellan två samhällsformationer c:a 1800–1870*. Uppsala: Acta Universitatis Upsaliensis, 1985.

———. *Samhällsförändring och sammanslutningsformer: Det frivilliga föreninsväsendets uppkomst och spridning: Husby-Rekarne från omkring 1850 till 1930*. Uppsala: Acta Universitatis Upsaliensis, 1982.

Jenswold, John R. "The Rise and Fall of Pan-Scandinavianism in Urban America." In *Scandinavians and Other Immigrants in Urban America: The Proceedings of a Research Conference, October 26–27, 1984*, edited by Odd S. Lovoll, 159–70. Northfield, MN: St. Olaf College, 1985.

Johannesson, Eric. "The Flower King in the American Republic: The Linneaus Statue in Chicago, 1891." In *Swedish-American Life in Chicago: Cultural and Urban Aspects of an Immigrant People*, 1850–1930, edited by Philip J. Anderson and Dag Blanck, 267–82. Urbana and Chicago: University of Illinois Press, 1992.

Johnson, Gustav Elwood. "The Swedes of Chicago." PhD diss., University of Chicago, 1940.

Johnson, Timothy J. "The Independent Order of Svithiod: A Swedish-American Lodge in Chicago." In *Swedish-American Life in Chicago: Cultural and Urban Aspects of an Immigrant People*, 1850–1930, edited by Philip J. Anderson and Dag Blanck, 343–63. Urbana and Chicago: University of Illinois Press, 1992.

Johnson, Walter, ed. and trans., with Ruth Ingeborg Johnson. "Beda Erickson's Journey to Chicago, 1902." *The Swedish Pioneer Historical Quarterly* 32, no. 1 (1981): 7–19.

Jonassen, Christen T. "Cultural Variables in the Ecology of an Ethnic Group." *American Sociological Review* 14 (February 1949): 32–41.

Kastrup, Allan. *The Swedish Heritage in America: The Swedish Element in America and Swedish-American Relations in Their Historical Perspective*. St. Paul, MN: Swedish Council of America, 1975.

Keil, Hartmut. "The German Immigrant Working Class of Chicago, 1875–1890: Workers, Labor Leaders, and the Labor Movement." In *American Labor and Immigration History, 1877–1920s: Recent European Research*, edited by Dirk Hoerder, 156–75. Urbana: University of Illinois Press, 1983.

Keil, Hartmut, and John B. Jentz, eds. *German Workers in Industrial Chicago: 1850–1910: A Comparative Perspective*. DeKalb: Northern Illinois University Press, 1983.

Kivisto, Peter, ed. *The Ethnic Enigma: The Salience of Ethnicity for European-Origin Groups*. Philadelphia: The Balch Institute Press, 1989.

Kraut, Alan M. *Silent Travelers: Germs, Genes, and the Immigrant Menace*. Baltimore and London: Johns Hopkins University Press, 1994.

Kullberg, John E. "Age Distribution in the Covenant." *Covenant Quarterly* 1 (1941): 33–37.

Larson, Eric. *The Devil in the White City: Murder, Magic, and Madness at the Fair That Changed America*. New York: Vintage Books, 2003.

Lidtke, Vernon L. *The Alternative Culture: Socialist Labor in Imperial Germany*. New York: Oxford University Press, 1985.

Liljegren, N. M., N. O. Westergreen, and C. G. Wallenius. *Svenska Metodismen i America*. Chicago: Svenska M. E. Bokhandels-Föreningens Förlag, 1895.

Limberg, Lennart. "Almost a Century's Work: Preserving Swedishness Outside of Sweden." In *Scandinavians in Old and New Lands: Essays in Honor of H. Arnold Barton*, edited by Philip J. Anderson, Dag Blanck, and Byron Nordstrom, 125–27. Chicago: The Swedish-American Historical Society, 2004.

Lindmark, Sture. *Swedish America, 1914–1932: Studies in Ethnicity with Emphasis on Illinois and Minnesota*. Stockholm: Läromedelsförlagen, 1971.

Lindquist, Emory. *Shepherd of an Immigrant People: The Story of Erland Carlsson*. Rock Island, IL: Augustana Historical Society, 1978.

Lintelman, Joy K. *I Go to America: Swedish American Women and the Life of Mina Anderson*. St. Paul: Minnesota Historical Society Press, 2009.

———. "'On My Own': Single, Swedish, and Female in Turn-of-the-Century Chicago." In *Swedish-American Life in Chicago: Cultural and Urban Aspects of an Immigrant People*, 1850–1930, edited by Philip J. Anderson and Dag Blanck, 89–99. Urbana and Chicago: University of Illinois Press, 1992.

Ljungmark, Lars. *Swedish Exodus*. Translated by Kermit B. Westerberg. Carbondale: Southern Illinois University Press, 1979.

Lovoll, Odd S. "A Scandinavian Melting Pot." In *Swedish-American Life in Chicago: Cultural and Urban Aspects of an Immigrant People*, 1850–1930, edited by Philip J. Anderson and Dag Blanck, 60–67. Urbana and Chicago: University of Illinois Press, 1992.

———. "Swedes, Norwegians, and the Columbian Exposition of 1893." In *Swedes in America: Intercultural and Interethnic Perspectives on Contemporary Research*, edited by Ulf Beijbom, 185–94. Växjö, Sweden: The Swedish Emigrant Institute Series 6, 1993.

Lundquist, Sven. *Folkrörelserna i det svenska samhället: 1850–1920*. Stockholm: Sober förlag, 1977.

Naeseth, Henriette C. K. *The Swedish Theatre of Chicago: 1868–1950*. Rock Island, IL: Augustana Historical Society, 1951.

Nelli, Humbert S. *Italians in Chicago 1880–1939: A Study in Ethnic Mobility*. New York: Oxford University Press, 1970.

Nelson, Edward O. "Recollections of the Salvation Army's Scandinavian Corps." *The Swedish Pioneer Historical Quarterly* 39, no. 4 (October 1978): 257–76.

Nordahl, Per. *De sålde sina penslar: om några svenska målare som emigrerade till USA*. Stockholm: Svenska Målareförbundet, 1987.

———. "Swedish-American Labor in Chicago." In *Swedish-American Life in Chicago: Cultural and Urban Aspects of an Immigrant People*, 1850–1930, edited by Philip J. Anderson and Dag Blanck, 211–25. Urbana and Chicago: University of Illinois Press, 1992.

———. *Weaving the Ethnic Fabric: Social Networks among Swedish-American Radicals in Chicago 1890–1940*. Umeå: Acta Universitatis Umensis, 1994.

Nordstrom, Byron J. "The Swedish Historical Society of America: The Minnesota Years." In *Swedes in the Twin Cities: Immigrant Life and Minnesota's Urban Frontier*, edited by Philip J. Anderson and Dag Blanck, 104–16. St Paul: Minnesota Historical Society Press, 2001.

———. "*Trasdockan*: The Yearbook of the Swedish Engineers Society of Chicago." In *Swedish-American Life in Chicago: Cultural and Urban Aspects of an Immigrant People*, 1850–1930, edited by Philip J. Anderson and Dag Blanck, 181–92. Urbana and Chicago: University of Illinois Press, 1992.

Norman, Hans. *Från Bergslagen till Nordamerika: studier i migrationsmönster, social rörlighet och demografisk struktur med utgångspunkt från Örebro Län 1851–1915*. Uppsala: Sudia Historica Upsaliensia 62, 1974.

Norton, W. Wilbert, Olai Vrang, Roy A. Thompson, and Mel Larson. *The Diamond Jubilee Story of the Evangelical Free Church of America*. Minneapolis: Free Church Publications, 1959.

Nugent, Walter. "Demography." In *The Encyclopedia of Chicago*, edited by James R. Grossman, Ann Durkin Keating, and Janice L. Reiff, 233–37. Chicago and London: University of Chicago Press, 2004.

———. "Epidemics." In *The Encyclopedia of Chicago*, edited by James R. Grossman, Ann Durkin Keating, and Janice L. Reiff, 279–80. Chicago and London: University of Chicago Press, 2004.

Nyvall, David. *The Swedish Covenanters: A History*. Chicago: Covenant Book Concern, 1930.

Oblom, Lorraine R. "Determining Factors in the Growth of the Evangelical Mission Covenant Church of America." *Covenant Quarterly* 3 (1943): 25–33.

Oestreicher, Richard. "Industrialization, Class, and Competing Cultural Systems: Detroit Workers, 1875–1900." In *German Workers in Industrial Chicago, 1850–1910: A Comparative Perspective*, edited by Hartmut Keil and John B. Jentz. DeKalb: Northern Illinois University Press, 1983.

Olson, Anita R. "Church Growth in Swedish Chicago: Extension and Transition in an Immigrant Community." In *Swedish life in American Cities*, edited by Dag Blanck and Harald Runblom, 72–94. Uppsala: Uppsala University, 1991.

———. "The Community Created: Chicago Swedes, 1880–1920." In *Swedish-American Life in Chicago: Cultural and Urban Aspects of an Immigrant People, 1850–1930*, edited by Philip J. Anderson and Dag Blanck, 49–59. Urbana and Chicago: University of Illinois Press, 1992.

———. "The Community Created: Chicago Swedes, 1880–1950." In *Ethnic Chicago: A Multicultural Portrait*, 4th edition, edited by Melvin G. Holli and Peter d'A. Jones, 110–21. Grand Rapids, MI: William B. Eerdmans Publishing, 1995.

Olson, Anita Ruth. "Swedish Chicago: The Extension and Transformation of an Immigrant Community, 1880–1920." PhD diss., Northwestern University, 1990.

Olson, Oscar N. *The Augustana Lutheran Church in America: Pioneer Period 1846–1860*. Rock Island, IL: Augustana Book Concern, 1950.

Olsson, Karl A. *By One Spirit*. Chicago: Covenant Press, 1962.

———. "Dwight L. Moody and Some Chicago Swedes." In *Swedish-American Life in Chicago: Cultural and Urban Aspects of an Immigrant People, 1850–1930*, edited by Philip J. Anderson and Dag Blanck, 305–26. Urbana and Chicago: University of Illinois Press, 1992.

———. *Into One Body . . . By the Cross*. Chicago: Covenant Press, 1985.

Olsson, Nils William. "St. Ansgarius and the Immigrant Community." In *Swedish-American Life in Chicago: Cultural and Urban Aspects of an Immigrant People, 1850–1930*, edited by Philip J. Anderson and Dag Blanck, 39–48. Urbana and Chicago: University of Illinois Press, 1992.

Osberg, Edward E. "Englewood Memories: Swedish Businessmen on Chicago's 59th Street." *The Swedish Pioneer Historical Quarterly* 28, no. 1 (1977): 57–61.

———. "Reminiscences of Chicago and Englewood." *The Swedish Pioneer Historical Quarterly* 36, no. 3 (1985): 200–207.

Ostergren, Robert Clifford. *A Community Transplanted: The Trans-Atlantic Experience of a Swedish Immigrant Settlement in the Upper Middle West, 1835–1915*. Madison: University of Wisconsin Press, 1988.

Pacyga, Dominic A. "Chicago's Ethnic Neighborhoods: The Myth of Stability and the Reality of Change." In *Ethnic Chicago: A Multicultural Portrait*, edited by Melvin G. Holli and Peter d'A. Jones, 604–17. Grand Rapids, MI: William B. Eerdmans Publishing, 1995.

Palm, August. *Ögonblicksbilder från en tripp till Amerika*. Stockholm: Författarens Förlag, 1901.

Park, Robert E., Ernest W. Burgess, and Roderick McKenzie. *The City*. Chicago: University of Chicago Press, 1967. Roediger, David R. *The Wages of Whiteness: Race and the Making of the American Working Class*. London and New York: Verso, 1991.

Rosenzweig, Roy. *Eight Hours for What We Will: Workers and Leisure in an Industrial City, 1870–1920*. New York: Cambridge University Press, 1983.

Rumbarger, John J. *Profits, Power, and Prohibition: Alcohol Reform and the Industrializing of America, 1800–1930*. Albany: State University of New York Press, 1989.

Runblom, Harald. "Chicago Compared: Swedes and Other Ethnic Groups in American Cities." In *Swedish-American Life in Chicago: Cultural and Urban Aspects of an Immigrant People, 1850–1930*, edited by Philip J. Anderson and Dag Blanck, 68–88. Urbana and Chicago: University of Illinois Press, 1992.

Runblom, Harald, and Dag Blanck, eds. *Scandinavians Overseas*. Uppsala: Centre for Multiethnic Research, 1986.

Runblom, Harald, and Hans Norman, eds. *From Sweden to America: A History of the Migration*. Minneapolis: University of Minnesota Press, 1976.

Scott, Franklin D. *Sweden: The Nation's History*. Minneapolis: University of Minnesota Press, 1977.

Setterdahl, Lilly, ed. *Swedish-American Newspapers: A Guide to the Microfilms Held by Swenson Swedish Immigration Research Center*. Rock Island, IL: Augustana College Library, 1981.

Smith, Timothy L. "Religion and Ethnicity in America." *American Historical Review* 83 (1978): 1155–85.

———. "Religious Denominations as Ethnic Communities: A Regional Case Study." *Church History* 35 (1966): 207–26.

Sollors, Verner, ed. *The Invention of Ethnicity*. New York: Oxford University Press, 1989.

Stephenson, George M. *The Religious Aspects of Swedish Immigration: A Study of Immigrant Churches*. Minneapolis: University of Minnesota Press, 1932.

———. "The Stormy Years of the Swedish Colony in Chicago before the Great Fire." *Transactions of the Illinois State Historical Society*, 1929.

Suttles, Gerald D. *The Social Construction of Communities*. Chicago: University of Chicago Press, 1972.

———. *The Social Order of the Slum: Ethnicity and Territory in the Inner City*. Chicago: University of Chicago Press, 1969.

Swanson, Roy. "Our Predecessors." *The Swedish Pioneer Historical Quarterly* 1 (1950): 12–21.

Tedebrand, Lars-Göran. "Those Who Returned: Remigration from America to Sweden." In *Perspectives on Swedish Migration Immigration*, edited by Nils Hasselmo. Duluth: University of Minnesota Press, 1978.

———. *Västernorrland och Amerika, 1875–1913: Utvandring och återinvandring*. Uppsala: Läromedelsförlagen, 1972.

Telleen, Jane. "'Yours in the Master's Service': Emmy Evald and the Women's Missionary Society of the Augustana Lutheran Church, 1892–1942." *The Swedish Pioneer Historical Quarterly* 30, no. 3 (1979): 183–95.

Tuttle, William M. Jr. *Race Riot: Chicago in the Red Summer of 1919*. New York: Atheneum, 1985.

Wallenius, C. G., and E. D. Olson. *A Short Story of the Swedish Methodism in America*. Chicago: Swedish American Historical Society, 1931.

Warriner, Charles K., and Jane Emery Prather. "Four Types of Voluntary Associations." *Sociological Inquiry* 35 (1965): 138–48.

Weaver, Dale. "Evangelical Covenant Church of America: Some Sociological Aspects of a Swedish Emigrant Denomination, 1885–1984." PhD diss., Lund University, Sweden, 1985.

Westerberg, Kermit B. "Henry Bengston and Socialism." In *Swedish-American Life in Chicago: Cultural and Urban Aspects of an Immigrant People, 1850–1930*, edited by Philip J. Anderson and Dag Blanck, 226–40. Urbana and Chicago: University of Illinois Press, 1992.

White, Richard. *The Middle Ground: Indians, Empires, and Republics in the Great Lakes Region, 1650–1815*. Cambridge and New York: Cambridge University Press, 1991.

Whyman, Henry C. *The Hedstroms and the Bethel Ship Saga: Methodist Influence on Swedish Religious Life*. Carbondale and Edwardsville: Southern Illinois University Press, 1992.

Wilson, Mark R. "Construction." In *The Encyclopedia of Chicago*, edited by James R. Grossman, Ann Durkin Keating, and Janice L. Reiff, 200–202. Chicago: University of Chicago Press, 2004.

Wirth, Louis. "Urbanism as a Way of Life." In *Cities and Society: The Revised Reader in Urban Sociology*, edited by Paul K. Hatt and Albert J. Reiss Jr. Glencoe, IL: Free Press, 1957.

Wrigley, Julia. *Class, Politics and Public Schools: Chicago 1900–1950*. New Brunswick, NJ: Rutgers University Press, 1982.

ORIGINAL SOURCES: UNITED STATES

Chicago Historical Society, Chicago, Illinois

"Chicago, the Culmination of the Religious Movement of the Nineteenth Century." *Chicago Tribune*, December 12, 1897, 41.

The Chicago Plan Commission, "Forty-Four Cities in the City of Chicago." Chicago: April 1942.

Clark, Stephen Bedel, and Patrick Butler. *The Lake View Saga: 1837–1985*. Chicago: 1985.

"Fifty Years in Chicago: Swedish Residents to Celebrate the Semi-Centennial." *Chicago Tribune*, September 6, 1896, 14.

"Free Swedish Employment Bureau." *Chicago Tribune*, January 20, 1896, 7.

FRIHET: Skandinaviska Socialistförbundets Majskrift. Chicago: Scandinavian Workers Publishing Society, 1919.

Historical Review of Activities During the First Thirty-Five Years of the District Lodge Illinois No. 8 Vasa Order of America, 1908–1943. Chicago: District Lodge Illinois No. 8, Vasa Order of America, 1943.

Historik öfver Första Svenska Baptist Församlingens i Chicago, Illinois. Chicago: Fyrtioåriga Verksamhet, 1906.

History of . . . Communities, Chicago, Illinois. Documents research under the direction of Vivien M. Palmer, 6 volumes typescript, Chicago, Illinois, 1925–1930. Vol. 1: Rogers Park, W.

Rogers Park (West Ridge); vol. 2: Uptown, Ravenswood; vol. 3: North Center, Hamlin Park, Lake View, Lower North Side (Near North Side); vol. 4: Near South Side, Armour Square, Douglas, Oakland; vol. 5: Grand Boulevard, Washington Park, Woodlawn, Grand Crossing; vol. 6: west Englewood, Bridgeport, Canaryville (Fuller Park), Riverdale, East Side.

Leafgren, Enoch. *Historisk utveckling af Skandinaviska Brödraförbundet af Amerika.* Jamestown, NY: c. 1915.

Peterson, Charles S. "Chicago, 'U.S. Stockholm,' Home of 125,000 Swedes." *Chicago Herald and Examiner,* October 23–25, 1927.

Proceedings of the Board of Education of the City of Chicago. Chicago: 1899–1917.

"Prominent Swedes." *Chicago Times,* July 12, 1891, 14.

Red and White. Lake View High School Yearbook, Chicago: 1913.

Residential Chicago: Chicago Land Use Survey. Chicago: Chicago Plan Commission, conducted by the Works Progress Administration, 1942.

Runristningar: Independent Order of Vikings, 1890–1915. Chicago: Martensons Tryckeri, 1915.

Schersten, Albert. *The Relation of the Swedish-American Newspaper to the Assimilation of Swedish Immigrants.* Rock Island: Augustana Library Publications No. 15, 1935.

Schmidt, Emanuel. *Svenska Baptisternas i Amerika Teologiska Seminarium: 1871–1921.* Chicago: Conference Press, 1921.

"Swedes Celebrate Their Settlement in Illinois." *Chicago Tribune,* October 20, 1895, 38.

Swedish-American Societies, Miscellaneous Pamphlets, Chicago Historical Society Manuscript Collection.

Westin, Gunnar. *Emigranterna och kyrkan: brev från och till Svenskar i Amerika, 1849–1892.* Stockholm, Sweden: Bokförlag, 1932.

Witsee, Herbert. "Religious Developments in Chicago, 1893–1915." MA thesis, University of Chicago, 1953.

Yearbook of the Swedish-American Historical Society. Chicago: vol. 1, 1905–1907; vol. 2, 1908; vol. 3, 1909–1910; vol. 4, 1911–1913.

Årsbok för Svenska Baptistförsamlingarna inom Amerika. Chicago: The Swedish Baptist General Conference of America, 1907, 1908, 1909.

Covenant Archives, North Park University, Chicago, Illinois

Anderson, James A. "The Austin Evangelical Covenant Church: A Case Study of a Church in the Midst of Change." Unpublished paper, May 23, 1972.

Anniversary Booklets of the following Swedish Evangelical Mission Covenant Churches, Chicago, Illinois:

Austin—25 Years, 1894–1919.
Austin—60 Years, 1894–1954.
Bethany—30 Years, 1882–1912.
Bethany—40 Years, 1882–1922.
Bethany—50 Years, 1882–1932.
Beverly—100 Years, 1882–1982.
Blue Island—50 Years, 1894–1944.
Blue Island—67 Years, 1894–1961.
Calvary—50 Years, 1906–1956.
Douglas Park—40 Years, 1877–1917.
Douglas Park—60 Years, 1877–1937.
Douglas Park—100 Years, 1877–1977.
Englewood—25 Years, 1888–1913.

Englewood—50 Years, 1888–1938.
First—75 Years, 1868–1943.
First—100 Years, 1868–1968. *The One Hundred Years.*
Humboldt Park—25 Years, 1884–1909.
Humboldt Park—40 Years, 1884–1924.
Humboldt Park—50 Years, 1884–1934.
Irving Park—25 Years, 1898–1923.
Irving Park—50 Years, 1898–1948.
Lake View—75 Years, 1886–1961.
Maplewood—60 Years, 1892–1952.
North Park—25 Years, 1898–1923.
North Park—50 Years, 1898–1948.
North Park—60 Years, 1898–1958.
Oakdale—50 Years, 1902–1952.
Ravenswood—25 Years, 1887–1912.
Ravenswood—40 Years, 1887–1927.
Ravenswood—50 Years, 1887–1937.
Ravenswood—75 Years, 1887–1962.
South Chicago—75 Years, 1883–1958.
South Chicago—90 Years, 1882–1972.
Redeemer—75 Years, 1888–1963.
Roseland—50 Years, 1882–1932.
Austin Mission Covenant Church. *Membership Lists.* (*Församlingens-bok*). 1895–1903.
Bethany Mission Church. *Församlings Baneret.* Vol. 1, 1906–vol. 4, 1909.
Covenant Annual Meeting Minutes. (*Protokoll öfver Svenska Evangeliska Missions-förbundets i Amerika årsmöte*). From the organizational meeting in 1886, and each year through 1920.
Covenant Yearbooks, 1885–1889. Translated by Fred O. Jansson.
Cragin Mission Covenant Church. *Membership Lists.* (*Församlingens-bok*).
Edgewater Mission Covenant Church. *Membership Lists.* (*Församlingens-bok*). 1909–1921.
Englewood Mission Church. *Församlingsvännen.* Vol. 12, no. 6, July 1916; vol. 13, no. 7, July 1917; and vol. 13, no. 12, December 1917.
Humboldt Park Swedish Evangelical Lutheran Mission Church. *Address Book.* Young People's Society, May 1915.
Kristna Bröders Hjälpförening vid Humboldt Park. *Minutes.* 1891–1916, 1891–1921.
Lake View Swedish Mission Church. *Bible Class News.* Issued on the first of each month for Rev. Normann's Bible Class, 1915 and 1916.
Lindgren, James O. "The Struggle of a Church; a History of Maplewood Covenant Church, Chicago, Illinois, 1892–1960." Unpublished paper, May 31, 1967.
Linnea Society, Austin Mission Church. *Minutes.* January 21, 1915–July 1921.
"North Park, Church, College and Community." From interviews of Walter Enstrom by Dorothy Vann, October 12, 1982, and of Sarah Swanson by Charles Strom, October 1, 1985.
Ogden Park Mission Church. *Församlingens Bladet.* Vol. 4, no. 1, January 1913.
Protokoll vid Svenska Ev. Missionsföreningen i Morlands ungdomsmöte. January 14, 1899–December 12, 1913.
Protokoll-bok öfver Svenska Evangeliska Missions-församlingen i Moreland, Illinois. Chicago: July 25, 1890.
Svenska Evangeliska Missionsförsamlingen i Austin. *Protokolls bok.* (*Minutes*). May 12, 1894 to November 27, 1911.
Svenska Evangeliska Missionsförsamlingen i Moreland. *Protokolls bok.* (*Minutes*). July 25, 1890 to December 7, 1923. Three volumes.

Swedish Christian Radio. *Hymnbook: Hemlands-Toner.* Tillägnande den Svenska WIBO Församlingen, 1927.
Swedish Mission Church in Moreland. *Protokolls bok. (Minutes).* 1918.

LEGAL DOCUMENTATION

Organizations Chartered in the State of Illinois

American Union of Swedish Singers, June 5, 1894.
Brage Athletic Club, April 28, 1911. Dissolved May 21, 1937.
Chicago Swedish American Club, August 13, 1924. Dissolved May 24, 1937.
Co-operative Temperance Café Idrott, March 23, 1917, Certificate No. 111. Dissolved November 19, 1942, General No. 115411.
The Independent Order of Svithjod of Chicago, Illinois, September 2, 1881. Name changed to Independent Order of Svithiod, July 22, 1933. Change of purpose, July 23, 1977.
The Svea Society, October 29, 1862.
Svelhiods Singing Club, February 23, 1893. Corrected to Svithiod Singing Club, August 24, 1900. Change of Purpose, April 21, 1954.
Svenska Föreningarnes Central Förbund, August 17, 1894. Name changed to Swedish Societies' Old People's Association, February 13, 1908. Change of purpose, April 28, 1909.
Swedish American Athletic Association, July 17, 1914.
Swedish Club, February 8, 1892. Name changed to The Swedish Building Club, August 13, 1923.
The Swedish Engineers' Society of Chicago, Illinois, June 25, 1912. Dissolved November 1, 1986.
Swedish National Association, May 25, 1894. Amendment included temperance, December 31, 1896. Amendment excluded temperance, November 14, 1916.
Swedish National Society of Chicago, December 15, 1913. Dissolved May 1, 1981.
The Swedish Singers Union of Chicago, June 27, 1911.
Vikingarne, January 7, 1891. Name changed to Independent Order of Vikings No. 1, May 28, 1892. Dissolved June 1, 1937.
Vikings' Valhalla Association. June 17, 1909.

Methodist Archives, Garrett Theological Seminary, Evanston, Illinois

Anderson, Arlow. W. "Sändebudet and American Public Affairs: 1862–1872." *Augustana Quarterly.* (1945)
Central Northwest Conference Program. Elim Methodist Church, June 20–23, 1942.
Golden Jubilee: Fiftieth Anniversary Austin Trinity Methodist Church. 1893–1943.
Illustrerad Historik: Metodistkyrkans Svenska Teologiska Seminarium, 1870–1920. Chicago: Swedish Methodist Episcopal Book Concern, 1920.
Jubilee Album: Austin Swedish Methodist Episcopal Church. 25th Anniversary, June 11–17, 1929.
Protokoll fördt vid första årliga sammanstädet af Metodist Episcopal Kyrkans Svenska Central Konferensens . . . sammanträdde. 1894–1902.
Protokoll fördt vid Svenska Central Konferensens . . . sammanträdde. 1902–1920.
Protokoll öfver förhandlingarna vid Nordvestra Svenska årsconferensen. 1877–1893.
"Report of the Foreign Language Commission to the General Conference of the Methodist Episcopal Church." O. W. Auwan, Chairman, Springfield, Massachusetts, May 1924, with letter of response from the Methodist leadership.
Sändebudet 48, 49 (1910).
Svenska Metodist Episcopal Församlingen i Austin, Chicago, Illinois: membership, marriage, and baptismal records.

STATISTICAL SOURCES

Burgess, Ernest W., ed. *Community Factbook*. Chicago: Chicago Recreation Commission, 1938.
Burgess, Ernest W., and Charles Newcomb, eds. *Census Data of the City of Chicago, 1920*. Chicago: University of Chicago Press, 1931.
Historical Statistics of the United States: Colonial Times to 1970. Part I: U.S. Bureau of the Census, Washington, DC, 1975.
Historic City: The Settlement of Chicago. City of Chicago: Richard J. Daley, mayor, Department of Development and Planning, Lewis W. Hill, Commissioner, 1976.
The Lakeside Annual Directory of the City of Chicago. Chicago: The Chicago Directory Company, 1880, 1889, 1899, 1910, 1915, and 1917.
Local Community Fact Book: Chicago Metropolitan Area. Based on the 1970 and 1980 censuses. Chicago: The Board of Trustees of the University of Illinois, 1984.
The People of Chicago: Who We Are and Where We Have Been. City of Chicago Department of Development and Planning, 1970.
Report of the School Census, City of Chicago. Chicago: Board of Education, 1884, 1910, and 1914.
The 36th Annual Report of the Department of Public Works to the Mayor and City Council of the City of Chicago. Chicago: For the year ending December 1911, showing 1910 ward boundaries, 408.

SWEDISH-AMERICAN ARCHIVES OF GREATER CHICAGO (SAAGC), NORTH PARK UNIVERSITY

Allsvensk Samling. Göteborg, Sweden: No. 8, 9, and 10.
American Daughters of Sweden, Manuscript Collection.
The American-Scandinavian Foundation, Manuscript Collection.
Andersson, E. Einar. *Hembygden: historisk festskrift för Chicagos Svenska hembygdensföreningar utställningsåret, 1933*. Chicago: 1933.
Bengston, Henry. "Men and Ideas Behind the Swedish Educational League." *Swedish Educational League: An Adult Education Experiment in Scandinavian Tradition*. Chicago: 1946.
Bengston, Henry. Papers, 1915–1971, Manuscript Collection. Includes "Hembygden: historisk festskrift för Chicagos svenska hembygdsföreningar utställningsåret, 1933"; Swedish National Society, *Bulletin*, vol. 1, no. 1, Chicago: 1933; "50 Years of Christian Service in Lake View, 1889–1939," an anniversary booklet for the Lake View Swedish Baptist Church. Personal letter collection.
Bethlehem Lutheran Church. *Bethlehem, 1875–1950*.
Bloom, Gunnar A. *Seventy-Five Years of Progress 1882–1957*. Chicago: Svithiod Singing Club, 1957.
Bohus Society of Chicago, Manuscript Collection.
Club Dalarna of Chicago, or Chicago Dala Förbundet, Manuscript Collection.
Ericson, C. George. "Bland Svenskar i Chicago," 1962. Handwritten overview of Swedish people and organizations.
Erickson, Martin. *Centenary Glimpses: Baptist General Conference of America, 1852–1952*. Chicago: Baptist Conference Press, 1952.
First Evangelical Free Church 75th Anniversary Diamond Jubilee, 1880–1955. Chicago: 1909.
Första Svenska Metodist Kyrkans i Chicago, årsbok och kalendar år 1908–1909. Chicago: 1909.
Good Templary Through One Hundred Years. Ringsted, Denmark: Folkbladets Bogtrykkeri, 1951.
Gustavus Adolphus Lutheran Church. *Through 50 Years*. Historical Review, November 6, 1891–1941.
Hallberg, Rudolph. "En Tjugofemårsrevy." *25th Year Jubilee Festival*, Chicago, 1938.
Hanson, Earl, Compiler. *A Place for Midsummer: The Scandinavian Tradition of Good Templar Park*. 1975.
Hanson, Otto. "A Brief History of the Independent Order of Svithiod." *Souvenir Program of the Golden Jubilee of the Independent Order of Svithiod at Lyceum Theater*. Minneapolis: December 9, 1930, 9.

Henschen, Henry. "Skall svenska språket införas vid Chicagos skolor?" *Årsbok 1912: Utgifven af Riksföreningen för svenskhetens bevarande i utlandet.* Göteborg: 1912.

Historik öfver Vasa Orden af Amerika, 25 åriga verksamhet, 1896–1921. 1921.

History, Viking Brage Lodge No. 2. Chicago: 1942.

A History of the Swedish Evangelical Lutheran Bethany Church of South Chicago, Illinois. Chicago, 1968.

Hulten, Axel, ed. "Swedish-American Participation in 'A Century of Progress.'" Chicago: Official Program, AVSS Festcommittee, June 23–25, 1933.

Independent Order of Svithiod, Manuscript Collection.

Ingeborg Society, Manuscript Collection.

International Order of Good Templar (IOGT) efter 25 år: Revy öfver den Svenska God Templarverksamheten i Chicago, 1882–1907 (Chicago, 1907).

Linnea Aid Society, Manuscript Collection.

Lundqvist, Carl Hjalmar, Papers, Manuscript Collection.

Minnes-skrift från Illinois Konferensen sextiofjärde årsmöte. Chicago: Den Svenska Evangeliska Lutherska Elim Kyrkan, 1916.

Minnes-skrift: Svenska Evangeliska Lutherska Trefaldighetsförsamlingen i Chicago, Illinois. Rock Island, IL: Augustana Book Concern, 1908.

Nebo Evangelical Lutheran Church: 75 Years of Worship, Fellowship and Service. Chicago: 1976.

Nelson, Edward O. *Recollections of the Salvation Army's Scandinavian Corps.*

Nilsson, Hjalmar. *Ett triumftåg genom svenska bygder: axplockning från svensk-amerikanska elitkörens Sverigeturné 22 juni–24 juli 1910.* Svenska sångareförbundet i Amerika, 1910.

Nyberg, Henry. *History and Bylaws: Swedish Engineers of Chicago.* 1949.

Souvenir Programme. Quadrennial National Song and Music Festival (Sångerfest) of the American Union of Swedish Singers in New York, New York, May 28–31, 1910.

Stadgar för Chicagoavdelning af föreningen för svenkahetens bevarande i Amerika. 1923.

Stadgar för Svenska Kulturförbundet i Amerika. 1924.

Statistics: Fraternal Societies. Rochester, NY: Fraternal Monitor, 1933.

Svenska Amerikanaren, March 1911–September 1912; May 1917–September 1918.

Svenksa Kuriren, June 3, 1911, as translated in the Foreign Language Press Survey, Section I A. 1 b.

Svensk-Amerikanska Kalendern. Worcester, MA: Carl G. Fredin, 1911.

Svithiod Singing Club, Manuscript Collection.

Swedish American Athletic Association, Manuscript Collection.

The Swedish American Republican League of Illinois. *Proceedings.* 1895–1897.

Swedish Cultural Society, Manuscript Collection.

Swedish Educational League, Manuscript Collection, 1915–1956.

Swedish Engineers' Society, Manuscript Collection.

Swedish Journalist's Society of America, Chicago Chapter, Manuscript Collection.

Swedish National Society, Manuscript Collection.

The Swedish Typographical Union, Manuscript Collection.

Värmlands Nation, Manuscript Collection.

Witting, A. G. *Meddelanden från Svenska Kulturförbundet i Amerika.* Chicago: 1933.

Yearbook of the Swedish-American Historical Society. Vol. 1, 1905–1907. Chicago: 1907.

SWENSON SWEDISH IMMIGRATION RESEARCH CENTER, AUGUSTANA COLLEGE, ROCK ISLAND, ILLINOIS

Abounding in Thanksgiving. Chicago: printed in commemoration of the 125th anniversary of the Immanuel Lutheran Church, 1853–1978.

Addison Street Baptist Church. *Membership Lists.* 1866–1910.

Almanack. Rock Island: Augustana Book Concern, 1920.

Augustana Lutheran *Protokoll.* 1855–1920.

Augustana Lutheran *Referat.* 1880-1921.
Augustana Lutheran *Referat Illinois-Konferensen,* 1921-1931.
Bergendorf, Conrad. *The Augustana Ministerium: A Study of the Careers of the 2,504 Pastors of the Augustana Evangelical Lutheran Synod Church, 1850-1962.* Rock Island: Augustana Historical Society, 1980.
Bethany Evangelical Lutheran Church. *Membership Records.* 1880-1920.
Bethel Baptist Church. *Membership Records.* 1904-1920.
Bethel Free Church. *Membership Records.* 1907-1923.
Central Avenue Baptist Church. *The Golden Record: 1891-1941.* Chicago: 1941.
Central Avenue Baptist Church, formerly Austin Swedish Baptist Church. *Membership Records.* 1891.
Ebenezer Lutheran Church. *Membership Records.* 1892-1920.
Historik öfver Första Baptist Församlingen i Chicago, Illinois, 1866-1906. Chicago: 1906.
Holding forth the Word of Life. Sixtieth Anniversary, Bethel Free Church, 1907-1967.
IOGT District Lodge #14, Cook County, Illinois. *Minutes.*
IOGT Lodges in Sweden. *Transfer Certifications.*
I.O. Vikings Odin Lodge. *Membership Records.* 1900-1907.
Referat öfver Evangelisk Lutherska Augustana Synodens årsmöte. Rock Island, IL, 1895-1920.
Rosenberg, C. M. *Geografiskt—statistic handlexikon öfver Sverige.* Göteborg, Sweden: Faksmilutgåva, 1982.
St. Ansgarius Episcopal Church. *Register Book.* Communicant list with addresses, 1880; and marriages 1877-1879, 1882, and 1883.
Skandinaviska Evangeliska Lutherska Synodens årsmöte. *Protokoll.* 1880-1921.

TRINITY SEMINARY LIBRARY ARCHIVES, DEERFIELD, ILLINOIS

De första tjugo åren eller begynnelsen till Svenska Evangeliska Frikyrkan i Nord Amerikas Förenade Stater enligt protokoll införda i Chicago Bladet. 1883-1903.
Lindberg, Frank Theodor. *Looking Back 50 Years: Over the Rise and Progress of the Swedish Evangelical Free Church of America.* Minneapolis: Franklin Printing, 1935.
Minnesskrift utgiven med anledning af Svenska Evangeliska Frikyrkans i Amerika Trettioårsjubileum i Rockford, Illinois, 1884-1914. Minneapolis: Larson Printing, 1914.
Protokoll öfver Svenska Evangeliska Fria Missionens årsmöte. 1904-1920.

ORIGINAL SOURCES: SWEDEN, THE SWEDISH EMIGRANT INSTITUTE (SEI), VÄXJÖ

Beijbom, Ulf, Papers. "Impulspridningen från moderförsamlingarna i Swede Town."
"Berättelse om moderns resa från Finspång till Chicago, Illinois." July 25, 1889.
"In Memoriam Joe Hill murdered by the authorities of the State of Utah." Program. November 19, 1915.
Karlsson, John Anders. "Resegång." Dikt om överresan till USA med skeppet Oscar II, hösten, 1902.
Ljungren, Per Edvard Teodor. "Dagbook." Journal during his emigration to America, 1891-1894.
Miscellaneous letters written from immigrants in Chicago to relatives in Sweden.
Pamp, Frederick, translator. "Claes Frederick Pamp—Autobiographical Notes." 1960.
"Society Balder i Chicago." Typewritten article, author unknown, probably written 1952.
Svenska Emigrant Föreningen i Chicago. "Broschyr."
Svensson, Bernhard. Dikt om avresan från Chicago, May 1902.
Svensson, Hilda. "Dagbok." Journal about her trip to America beginning April 14, 1895.

Svensson, Hilma. "Day Journal." Journal during her trip from Jönköping to Chicago, August 14 to September 1901.

SVENSK ARKIVINFORMATION (SVAR), RAMSELE, SWEDEN

Birth records, death records, and household examination records from various parishes throughout Sweden.

SWEDISH DOCUMENTS, MISCELLANEOUS

80 år med blåbands rörelsen. Örebro, Sweden: Tryckcentralen, 1963.

Evangeliska Missionsföreningen i Göteborg. Göteborg, Sweden: Scheel and Sjögrens Tryckeri, 1860–1910.

Evangeliska Missionsföreningarna i Göteborg. *Minnes-skrift 1860–1935.* Göteborg, Sweden: C. R. Holmqvists Boktryckeri AB, 1935.

Fyrtioårsberättelse öfver Åmals Baptist-församlings verksamhet. Dalsland, Sweden: Åmal Tryckeri, 1919.

Göteborgs distriktloge af I.O.G.T. : ett tioårsminne och ett tjugoårsjubileum : 1879-1889-1899. Göteborg, Sweden: Wald Zachrissons Boktryckeri, 1879, 1889, 1899.

Hultgren, Carl. *Emanuels-församlingen i Göteborg, 1868–1918.* Göteborg, Sweden: Wald Zachrissons Boktryckeri, 1918.

International Order of Odd Fellows, Gustaf II Adolf, 1895–1920. Göteborg, Sweden: Oscar Usacssibs Boktryckeri, 1920.

Johanson, Werner. *Nykterhetsrörelsen i Halland : några anteckningar ur dess historia.* Halmstad, Sweden: Nykterhetsfolkets länsarkiv, 1983.

Kort historik öfver Göteborg avgiven till kyrkans 50 års jubileum. Göteborg, Sweden: Henrik Struves Boktryckeri, 1931.

Kort historik samt program vid jubileumsfestligheterna. IOGT-NTO, Leon Gambetta Varberg, 1883–1983.

Logen N:r 452 Göteborg av Vasa Orden av Amerika. *Medlemsmatrickel.* January 1933.

Logen Skåne N:r 570, Vasaorden av Amerika. *Minnes-skrift.*

Mannström, Oscar. *Den wieselgrenska nykterhertsrörelsen.* Stockholm, Sweden: Victor Pettersons Bokindustriaktiebolag, 1936.

Metodist Episkopal Kyrkan i Göteborg. Göteborg, Sweden: Bröderna Weiss Boktryckeri, 1923.

Petersson, Oskar. *Godtemplarordens i Sverige historia.* Stockholm: Svenska nykterhetsförlaget, 1903.

Templaordens. *30 år: mines-skrift.* 1914.

Vasa Order of America. *Golden Jubilee.* 1896–1946.

Vasa Orden av Amerika Logen "Göteborg." Manuscript Collection. Stadsarkivet, Göteborg, Sweden.

INDEX

A

Abounding in Thanksgiving, 169n31
Abrahamson, L. G., 132
adaptation, 2–3, 7
Addams, Jane, 180n36
ADS (American Daughters of Sweden), 147, 149–50
African Americans, 155, 156
"Age Distribution in the Covenant" (Kullberg), 172n90
alcohol, 99, 105–6, 130, 148, 174n32
"Almost a Century's Work" (Limberg), 183n92
Alpha No. 50, 115
Alternative Culture, The (Lidtke), 172n1
American Association for the Advancement of Science, 132
American Bible Society, 81
American Daughters of Sweden (ADS), 147, 149–50
American Union of Swedish Singers (AUSS), 96, 125, 128, 129
Andersdotter, Kajsa, 17
Andersen, Paul, 57
Anderson, Charles, 59
Anderson, Charlotta, 17, 162n27
Anderson, Painter, 67
Anderson, Philip J.
  "Covenant and the American Challenge, The," 172n90; "David Nyvall and Swedish-American Education," 168n23; discussed, 155; *Swedish-American Life in Chicago,* 3–4
Andersonville, 29
Andersson, Brita Lena, 17, 161–62n25
Andersson, E. Einar, 149
Andersson, Emma Christina, 17, 161n25
Andersson, Johannes, 176n65
Andersson, Karl August, 161n23
Andersson, Lars, 17
Andersson, Peter, 16

Anti-Saloon League, 81
"Appeal to the Swedes in Chicago," 142
Arden, G. Everett
  Augustana Heritage, 167n19; *School of the Prophets, The,* 178n3
Armour Square, 27
Arvid (Herman Olson's relative), 42
Association for the Preservation of Swedish Culture in Foreign Lands, 183n92
Association of English Churches, 75–76
Atterbom, P. D. A.
  Lycksalighetens Ö, 120
Augsburg Confession, 57, 58, 61, 167n19
Augustana, 137
Augustana Children's Home, 170n57
Augustana College, 147, 150
Augustana Heritage (Arden), 167n19
Augustana Hospital, 79, 170n57
Augustana Lutheran Church, 55, 57, 58, 60–62, 78
Augustana Lutheran Church in America, The (O. Olson), 167n19
Augustana Lutheran Mission Board, 63
Augustana Lutheran Synod, 57, 59, 75, 167n19, 171n89
Augustana Ministerium, The (Bergendoff), 168n26
Augustana Synod, 58, 61, 81, 82
AUSS (American Union of Swedish Singers), 96, 125, 128, 129
Austin Covenant Church, 16, 17, 161n21, 162n26, 176n65
Austin Messiah Lutheran Church, 176n65
Axel Gustafson's Men's Store, 38

B

Babchuk, Nicholas
  "Instrumental and Expressive Voluntary Associations," 172n6

"Ethnic Preservation and Americanization,"
181n62; "Othelia Mörk Myhrman,"
179n26; "Teaching Swedish in the
Public Schools," 182n69; "We Hope
to Be Able to Do Some Good,"
170n67, 177n89
Gustafson, Hanna, 43
Gustafsson, Anders, 15, 40–41, 43–44, 48
Gustavus Adolphus (king), 38

H

Hagström, John, 65
Hale, Frederick A.
    *Trans-Atlantic Conservative Protestantism
    in the Evangelical Free and Mission
    Covenant Traditions*, 168n24
Hallberg, Simon, 107, 175n58, 175n59
Handlin, Oscar
    discussed, 4, 53; *Race and Nationality in
    American Life*, 178n10; *Uprooted,
    The*, 160n15
Hanson, Hart, 145
Hanson, Otto, 115
Harmoni Singing Club, 129
Hasselquist, Ture Nilsson, 57
health, 27, 43–44
Hedstroms and the Bethel Ship Saga, The
    (Whyman), 167n15
Hedtrom, Olof, 58
Heidenstam, Verner von, 121
hembygdsföreningar, 148
Hemlandet, det Gamla och det Nya, 40, 123
Hemwall brothers, 108
"Henry Bengston and Socialism" (Westerberg),
    183n90
Henschen, Henry, 141, 142, 145
Herrick, Mary J.
    Chicago Schools, The, 181n63
Hessling, E. Knut, 100
Higham, John, 147
Hill, Joe, 130, 179–80n36
Hillström, Josef, 179–80n36
History of Swedes in Illinois, The (Engberg/E.
    W. Olson/Schön), 133
*History of the Swedish Evangelical Lutheran
    Bethany Church of South Chicago,
    Illinois, A*, 170n57
Hjorthén, Adam
    Border-Crossing Commemorations, 178n11
Hoffsten, C. E., 141

Högfeldt, Otto, 65
Holli, Melvin G.
    Ethnic Chicago, 184n4
Holmstrom, Ludvig, 135
Home for the Aged, 109, 126
Home of Mercy, 79
homes of refuge, 79
Hulten, Axel
    "Swedish-American Participation in 'A Cen-
    tury of Progress,'" 174n31, 175n60

I

Iduna, 25
Iduna Singing Club, 129
Illinois and Michigan Canal, 18, 37
Immanuel Lutheran Church
    discussed, 28, 57, 63, 169n31; and Sunday
    school, 73; and Tract Society, 77
Immigrant Missions, 78–79
"Immigrants and Their Gods, The" (Dolan),
    167n8
Independent Order Ladies of Svithiod, 115–16
Independent Order Ladies of Vikings, 109, 115,
    116
Independent Order of Good Templars, 89
Independent Order of Svithiod
    benefits of, 107; bylaws of, 110–11, 115; char-
    ter of, 175n58, 175n59; discussed,
    100, 154, 176n71; founding of, 104;
    and Independent Order Ladies of
    Svithiod, 116; membership of, 93,
    104–5, 118; name of, 175n58; rituals
    of, 106; and Sheldon, 133; and Sick
    Committee, 107
"Independent Order of Svithiod, The" (T. John-
    son), 175n60, 176n63, 176n75
Independent Order of Vikings
    charter of, 109; discussed, 100, 117, 154;
    founding of, 104; and Home for the
    Aged, 109; and *Runristningar*, 126;
    and shooting, 126; and Viking Tem-
    ple, 113; and women, 116
"Industrialization, Class, and Competing Cultur-
    al Systems" (Oestreicher), 172n4,
    172n7
Industrial Revolution, 90
Ingeborg Ladies of Drake, 114
institutional completeness, 79, 99, 106, 171n77
"Institutional Completeness" (Breton), 166n44
"Instrumental and Expressive Voluntary Associ-